DUQUESNE STUDIES

Philosophical Series

18

SOCIAL PHILOSOPHY

DUQUESNE STUDIES

Philosophical Series

18

SOCIAL PHILOSOPHY

by

MARTIN G. PLATTEL, PH.D.

DUQUESNE UNIVERSITY PRESS, Pittsburgh, Pa.

Editions E. Nauwelaerts, Louvain

1965

DUQUESNE STUDIES

PHILOSOPHICAL SERIES

Andrew G. van Melsen, D.Sc., D.Ed., and Henry J. Koren, C.S. Sp. S.T.D., editors

Volume One—*Andrew G. van Melsen*, FROM ATOMOS TO ATOM. Pp. XII and 240. Price: paper $3.50. Published also in Dutch, German, Spanish and Italian editions.

Volume Two—*Andrew G. van Melsen*, THE PHILOSOPHY OF NATURE. Pp. XII and 265. Third edition, fourth impression. Price: paper $3.75, cloth $4.50. Published also in Italian, Dutch and Polish editions.

Volume Three—*P. Henry van Laer*, PHILOSOPHICO-SCIENTIFIC PROBLEMS. Out of print.

Volume Four—*Cajetan's*, THE ANALOGY OF NAMES and THE CONCEPT OF BEING. Pp. X and 93. Second Edition. Price: $2.25, cloth.

Volume Five—*Louis de Raeymaeker and others*, TRUTH AND FREEDOM. Pp. VII and 132. Second impression. Price: $3.00 cloth. Published also in French.

Volume Six—*P. Henry van Laer*, THE PHILOSOPHY OF SCIENCE. Part One: Science in General. Pp. XVII and 164. Second edition. Price: cloth $3.75.

Volume Seven—*Stephen Strasser*, THE SOUL, IN METAPHYSICAL AND EMPIRICAL PSYCHOLOGY. Pp. X and 275. Second impression. Price: cloth $6.00. Published also in German, Dutch and French.

This book is translated from SOCIALE WIJSBEGEERTE, I and II, by Martin G. Plattel, Ph.D., published by Het Spectrum, N.V., Utrecht, The Netherlands, Copyright 1959, and 1964.

Library of Congress Catalog Card Number: 65-10054

Volume Eight—*Albert Dondeyne*, CONTEMPORARY EUROPEAN THOUGHT AND CHRISTIAN FAITH. Pp. XI and 211. Second impression. Price: paper $5.00, cloth $5.75. Published also in French.

Volume Nine—*Maxwell J. Charlesworth*, PHILOSOPHY AND LINGUISTIC ANALYSIS. Pp XIII and 234. Second impression. Price: paper $4.75, cloth $5.50.

Volume Ten—*Remy C. Kwant*, PHILOSOPHY OF LABOR. Pp. XI and 163. Price: paper $4.50, cloth $5.25. Italian edition in preparation.

Volume Eleven—*Remy C. Kwant*, ENCOUNTER. Pp. VIII and 85. Price: cloth $3.25. Published also in Dutch.

Volume Twelve—*William A. Luijpen*, EXISTENTIAL PHENOMENOLOGY. Pp. XIII and 355. Fourth impression. Price: cloth $6.25. Published also in Dutch.

Volume Thirteen—*Andrew G. van Melsen*, SCIENCE AND TECHNOLOGY. Pp. X and 373. Price: paper $6.20, cloth $6.95. Published also in Dutch and German.

Volume Fourteen—*P. Henry van Laer*, PHILOSOPHY OF SCIENCE. PART TWO: A STUDY OF THE DIVISION AND NATURE OF VARIOUS GROUPS OF SCIENCES. Pp. XIII and 342. Price: paper $5.75, cloth, $6.50.

Volume Fifteen—*Remy C. Kwant*, THE PHENOMENOLOGICAL PHILOSOPHY OF MERLEAU-PONTY. Pp. IX and 257. Price: paper $4.50, cloth $5.25.

Volume Sixteen—*John A. Peters*, METAPHYSICS: A SYSTEMATIC SURVEY. Pp. XVIII and 529. Price: paper $9.00, cloth $9.75.

Volume Seventeen—*William A. Luijpen*, PHENOMENOLOGY AND ATHEISM. Pp. XIV and 342. Price: paper $5.75, cloth $6.50.

Volume Eighteen—*Martin G. Plattel*, SOCIAL PHILOSOPHY. Pp. XI and 346. Price: paper $7.20, cloth $7.95.

IN PREPARATION:
A. G. van Melsen, EVOLUTION AND PHILOSOPHY.

Part One of this book differs in some respects from the original Dutch edition published in 1960, notably in that it is less polemic.   Part Two, which was translated directly from the author's manuscript, has been adapted in a few places to correspond better to the situation prevailing in the United States.   A section about the natural law has been added to it. The translation of both parts was made by the undersigned and submitted to the author for his approval.

Duquesne University, February 22, 1965

Henry J. Koren, C.S.Sp.

TABLE OF CONTENTS

———

INTRODUCTION

The Changed Cultural Picture. By means of technology man has given himself a new power over nature. He now creates his own artificial world. In his daily life he no longer adapts himself to the regularity of nature. Contemporary man experiences the world which he himself has constructed as an orderly whole and untouched nature as a disordered chaos. In former times life ran its course within the confines of a closed sphere capable of being comprehended by man. Attachment to the soil and to the milieu of his birth and youth contributed to give him a great sense of belonging and security. As soon, however, as technology began to develop, the limitlessness of space and time invaded his closed world. Man began to outgrow the world of nature, to view it as something to be controlled and dominated, to plan the world.

In our contemporary society everyone is "going somewhere," everything is purposive and functional. The artificially constructed world of man demands that each of us remain mobile. In the technological order man has become homeless. He has demolished his old familiar milieu and still searches for a new abode in which he can dwell securely.

Whatever one may think about the dark shadows of technological power, it remains undeniably true that the modern technological order exhibits a socializing character. The new structures, resulting from man's own creative productivity, confront him with the fact that everyone needs everyone else. True, the concentration which takes place in the demographic, economic and technological realms is brought about by a kind of physical compulsion and still lacks somewhat what we may call a "soul." Nevertheless, it gives rise to a greater sense of human solidarity. Mutal respect for our fellow-men increases because man begins to realize that in his working role each one contributes an equally indispensable factor. In the modern world life becomes more and more functional and, as a consequence, the level on which man works at his function points beyond itself to the more profound dimensions of human co-existence as the personal encounter of other subjects in mutual respect and love. The home of contemporary man does not lie primarily in a localized milieu but in his fellow-man. Man becomes a person only when he feels that his fellow-man affirms him as such. It is here that lies the mysterious characteristic of man which we may indicate as his co-existence. He is a human being among fellow human beings.

Contemporary Philosophy and the Changed Cultural View. The philosophy of our time reflects the modified picture of culture. In the Aristotelian-Thomistic tradition the question about man arises against the background of the cosmos. Its anthropological inquiry in a sense reaches its apex in endeavoring to determine the place of man alongside that of the other things in the world. Most scholastic textbooks clearly reveal that they are inspired by this idea. After speaking about the philosophy of nature, i.e., lifeless material beings, they proceed to the philosophy of vegetative and animal life, and then only consider the rational life of man. Such a sequence views man as a particular species alongside the other species of life against the background of the world as the hierarchical totality of all things. It is hardly possible any longer to maintain such a classification.

Contemporary philosophy asks about man in an existential fashion. It searches for the meaning which man can give to the world of his own planning. The anthropological vision is no longer the one which seeks to determine the status of man as part of the cosmos. In its stead, the world is now viewed from man as its organizer and planner. Today's philosopher is confronted with the problem that man's powerlessness increases in direct ratio to the growth of his power over nature and that every attempt to overcome this powerlessness serves only to increase it even more. The entire world has become man's increase of selfhood and at the same time his loss of selfhood. Gradually the idea is gaining ground that these two aspects, the increase and the loss of selfhood, cannot be meaningfully integrated within the artificial structure of the world but only within the intersubjective bond of man with his fellow-men. On the level of this "fellowship" aspect, the person really becomes himself by losing himself. Thus it is not without reason that this co-existential aspect constitutes the central theme of contemporary philosophy.

Scope of this Book. The chapters forming this work have gradually matured and developed in the course of the lectures which we have given during a number of years to the students of the Higher Institute of Economics at Tilburg, Netherlands. For this reason it was difficult to determine exactly in all instances which authors exercised influence upon the writer until the work reached its final form. Quotations, therefore, have been kept at a minimum. On the other hand, however, the bibliography at the end of the book mentions the authors whose works we have gratefully used. This list is not meant as an exhaustive enumeration of all studies devoted to the subject matter, but contains only the books and articles which we have consulted.

This book endeavors to expand and develop the traditional social philosophy of solidarism in the light of the data supplied by contemporary philosophical thought. The first part considers the co-existential aspect of man, to which classical solidarism does not do justice. The second part studies a number of social questions, such as right, labor, property and state.

We may terminate this brief introduction by expressing the wish that social philosophy may gradually be removed from its marginal position in the study of philosophy. Hitherto it has usually been assigned a precarious place as a relatively unimportant discipline on the boundary of philosophical thought. Yet neither theology nor moral philosophy will be able to reach full development if they are pursued without a correct appreciation of man's intersubjectivity. It is in the hope of promoting the understanding of this intersubjectivity that this book has been written.

PART ONE

EXISTENCE IS CO-EXISTENCE

CHAPTER ONE

THE PHILOSOPHICAL ATTITUDE

1. *Preliminary Remarks*

The value of philosophy does not reveal itself to anyone before he is an authentic philosopher. For this reason it remains difficult to start by clarifying the philosophical attitude of mind, for the very question, What is philosophy? is a philosophical question *par excellence*. On the other hand, it is possible to meet this difficulty. For, the human being who seriously inquires about philosophy, by this very fact, is actively engaged in the pursuit of philosophy.

Anyone who seeks to understand the meaning of life is on the road to being a philosopher because he is on the road to being man. Any profound human experience is always based upon a philosophical view. Strictly speaking, then, the authentic philosophical attitude consists in nothing else but living thought and thoughtful living. Philosophical reflection is concerned with the meaning, the orientation of life; it directs its attention to the horizon of human existence within which man's everyday experiences occur.

This spontaneous and living philosophy is capable of being rendered more profound by means of more deliberate and systematic reflection. It is for this reason that philosophy as a science endeavors to place the background of life more explicitly and systematically in the foreground. Its goal is to refresh the meaning of life, faded by the routine of daily living, and to make it shine with greater clarity.

Nevertheless, the pursuit of philosophy remains a hazardous undertaking. Any attempt to philosophize is both meaningful and foolish—meaningful because it reaches its goal to some extent, but also foolish because the closer it comes to reaching the goal, the more this goal recedes. In spite of, or rather because of, this meaningful contradiction, philosophy stays alive. What the philosopher does is an attempt to throw light upon the very light of life; he tries to make the ever-receding background into a foreground. In doing so, he feels foolish because he is forever trying to catch up with his intuitional insight. At the same time, however, the realization of being foolish is the highest philosophical wisdom, for it is precisely the light itself which makes the philosopher aware of the fact that he falls short. His realization that the background is so profound places emphasis upon the deficiency of his philosophy. Briefly expressed, the lack of philosophical knowledge grows in direct ratio to this knowledge itself. Small wonder, therefore, if in the eyes of the positive scientist philosophy appears to be a strange pursuit.

The situation is quite different for the positive sciences, which from now on we will simply refer to as the sciences or science. Unlike philosophy, they are capable of predetermining their object fairly accurately and are able to investigate the method through which the object is to be studied. Strictly speaking, philosophy does not even have an object which is situated at a distance from the subject, as is the case in science, for the philosopher questions the whole of reality, which includes also himself as the questioner. While science considers certain profiles of reality as its object, philosophical thinking endeavors to penetrate into the very horizon of these profiles.

Philosophical insight, even into what philosophy is, has to reveal itself with a certain immediacy in the philosophical endeavor itself. However, for a first acquaintance it may be most convenient to place philosophy in opposition to science. Although such an approach is more mediate, it is better adapted to the natural progress of human knowledge. For in our everyday experience of knowledge we search for the specific character of a thing by comparing it with previously known things which it resembles somewhat and from which it also differs. Nevertheless, this first mediate acquaintance with philosophy will subsequently have to be more and more purified. For this approach presupposes that science is better known that philosophy, while we may legitimately ask whether it is not merely apparently true that we are better acquainted with science than with philosophy. It is, indeed, undeniable that philosophical views exercise a very great influence upon man's conception of science. The so-called "natural" progress and development of knowledge is not without artificial aspects. For this reason it may appear contradictory

to attempt to clarify philosophy by way of science. Nevertheless, philosophy stays alive in spite of, or rather because of,
this meaningful contradiction.

2. *Philosophy Versus Science*

Unlike Science, Philosophy Does Not Seek to Control.
Positive science is pursued in an atmosphere of knowing for
the sake of control. The growth of this type of knowledge
confers upon man an ever-increasing power over the reality
which he investigates. Exact research aims at understanding
the object to make it manipulable. In science truth is to a
certain extent, as it were, manufactured. Strictly speaking,
the criterion of truth here is nothing else but the efficacy of
man's grip on the object. Even the human sciences find their
justification only in the fact that human behavior reveals a
thing-like aspect and therefore has a technical-hygienic
side.

The philosophical attitude, on the other hand, may not
seek to dominate and control, but has to listen in a spirit of
love. Man's cognitive efforts here do not seek power over
reality but rather demand that he actively surrender to reality. Scientific insight is based upon power, while philosophical
insight has its basis in love. The less I attempt to make
reality manipulable, the more irresistibly philosophical insight
imposes itself. Philosophy transcends the categories of the
serviceable and the useful. The sciences, on the other hand,
derive their value from the fact that they are so useful and
can render so many services. Philosophy, however, is not
useful for anything and precisely for this reason possesses so
much value. The value of science flows from its usefulness,
but the "usefulness" of philosophy arises from its value.

Unlike Science, Philosophy is Not "Objective." Scientific
knowledge is "objective." It considers things from a distance
as objects. Material things and living beings, including even
man himself in all the manifestations of his life, fall under the
scientific approach because they possess the character of objects, although there are, of course, large gradual differences
between the various levels.

Philosophy, on the other hand, transcends the distance
between subject and object, between questioner and ques-

tioned reality. It is pursued within the interconnectedness of man and world. Only within this horizon is it possible to distinguish between the subject and the object of knowledge. A philosophical problem is not considered from without but from within. The philosophical approach bears the marks of a reflection. It is not so much a question of discovering a truth than of clarifying and realizing truth.

Unlike Science, Philosophy is Not Fragmentary. In science the way of viewing reality remains fragmentary and abstract from both the extensive and the intensive viewpoints. Extensively, because science always takes as the object of its investigation only a part of reality, a certain limited complexus of aspects. In other words, it has a material object. Intensively, because science always considers the material object from a certain viewpoint, its formal object, and abstracts from the other aspects, especially from the horizon against which this object is delineated only as a certain profile. Because of this selective approach the pursuer of science needs only a limited type of study and limited functions. He is a specialist. He endeavors to become more and more specialized and even wants to substitute algebraic numbers for the sharply-defined concepts of his science. He attempts to make the necessary human observations even more accurate and refined by means of instruments and ingenious techniques.

Philosophy, on the other hand, does not proceed in a fragmentary fashion. It seeks to fathom the meaning of reality in all its breadth and depth. It transcends, strictly speaking, the distinction between material and formal objects. This transcendence implies at the same time that the questioning subject may not assume an abstractively selective attitude. The entire wealth of human experiences in all realms, the esthetic, the technical, the ethical, the religious, etc., must be brought to bear upon the philosophical inquiry into the meaning of reality. For this reason philosophical thought demands that the philosopher be a harmoniously developed person who authentically experiences his being-in-the-world.

Science is Abstract, Philosophy is Intuitive. To the specialist in an exact science the philosopher may sometimes appear to pursue his task in the seclusion of his study and to be out of touch with reality. This impression is created by the fact that the philosopher does not need any laboratory, instruments or measuring techniques. However, the philosopher wants to penetrate into authentic and original existence and therefore may not neglect any human experience. Thus, as compared with the philosopher, it is precisely the scientist who should be considered to pursue his task in seclusion and out of touch with reality. Because of his interest in all human experience, the attitude of the philosopher is not one of abstractive selection but of integral intuition.

Philosophy is reflective and wants to let that which is given in reality speak in all its purity. It endeavors to set aside all apriorisms arising from milieu, customary patterns of thinking and other similar sources. The technical term indicating this process of purification is "phenomenological reduction," an expression introduced by Husserl. Science, on the other hand, is much more constructive and this is one of the reasons why science starts from presuppositions. The view of the object investigated by it is determined by the previously established method. The subject himself helps to make and construct the truth of science. In philosophy the situation is different—truth unveils itself to man as a gift because he surrenders disinterestedly to it.

Science is Discursive, Philosophy Explicitates. Only positive science is a science of discovery in the strict sense. It proceeds from the known to the unknown. Philosophy, on the other hand, is far more a question of making one explicitly aware of what is implicitly contained in everyday experience. Philosophy does not strictly reason from the known to the unknown, for the known is also still unknown, and the unknown is also already known somewhat. The negativity of the unknown is part of the foundation on which rests the positivity of the known, and vice versa. At the end of a philosophical inquiry one undergoes a double experience: that which seemed to be unknown was really already known but is now better realized; and, on the other hand, what first was known, now, after philosophical reflection, appears to be less known and more mysterious.

Problem and Mystery. To distinguish positive and philosophical knowledge, Gabriel Marcel uses in this connection the terms "problem" and "mystery." A problem presents itself in principle as soluble if one can dispose of sufficient data and knows the correct method. While the solution of a problem may evoke new questions, at least part of the problem is solved. Philosophy, on the other hand, deals in mysteries which, in principle, cannot be solved. Nevertheless, despite the powerlessness of any effort to find an explanation, philosophical thinking remains meaningful, because mysterious reality itself invites man to penetrate ever more profoundly into it and to clarify the mystery.

Sometimes this situation is expressed by the image of a light shining in the darkness. As a light, philosophy shines through the darkness of the mystery. The stronger is the light thrown by philosophy, the greater the encircling darkness and the more striking also the contrast of darkness and light. This comparison is somewhat faulty, in the sense that the light of philosophical reflection itself must be considered to be a reflex cast by the glowing darkness of the mystery. The highest knowing on this level is really a profound not-knowing, and the highest realization of not-knowing is really a profound form of knowing. Philosophy stays alive in spite of, or rather because of, this meaningful contradiction.

3. *The Contradictory Character of Philosophical Thought*

After this first philosophical orientation it is necessary to proceed with greater clarity in formulating the inner contradiction which we always encounter in our philosophical thinking. The sciences make use of genuine concepts by means of which they grasp the objects. For them the concept is a "cognitive means," through which objective material reality is seized. The more artificial and the sharper defined the concepts are with respect to the objects that are to be seized in a scheme of concepts, the higher will be the degree of scientific understanding. The scientist makes use of concepts which he determines as sharply as possible in a univocal fashion. Scientific understanding arises, on the one hand, through the concept as a cognitive *means* and, on the other, it finds its adequate expression in the concept as a *cognitive* means.

Philosophical Insight and Conceptual Expression. Philosophy proceeds, strictly speaking, in the opposite way. In philosophical intuition there is question of immediate insight. Truth here appears evident to itself. There is a certain identity of the knower and the known, so that no distance has to be bridged through concepts as cognitive means. The wording of the insight flows, as it were, spontaneously from the abundance of the intuitive knowledge of the totality.

Philosophy, however, is unable wholly to attain this ideal of immediate spiritual knowledge of the totality, for the human spirit is an embodied spirit. It is here that the contradictory aspect of the philosophical undertaking and its hazardous nature reveal themselves most strikingly. Philosophical insight, as pure immediate intellectuality, has to pass through mediate conceptual reflection. Philosophy cannot escape from making use of scientific concepts to become more aware of what implicitly is known immediately and to appropriate it. This necessity is the reason why above we offered a first clarification of philosophy by means of science. Man's spontaneous supra-conceptual intuition can be given shape only by means of artificial concepts. Philosophy's surrender in respectful listening to reality has to be interpreted through the mastering knowledge of science. Philosophy's "surrender" can be attained only by means of science's "control." To know itself, the subject has to reduce itself to an object.

Univocity and Analogy. Does the conceptual explicitation of that which is seen in immediate intuition enrich or impoverish the intuition? The reply is that this conceptual embodiment of pure intellectuality is not a question of either-or but of both-and. The implicit intuition becomes conscious human knowledge in its explicit expression. In this sense there is question here of an enrichment, for the philosophical insight is alive thanks to the concept. On the other hand, the conceptual expression always remains imperfect. It vainly tries, as it were, to catch up with the immediate insight. The concept reveals itself here as an inadequate expression and wording of an anterior insight. In this respect the conceptual "making of truth" shows itself as deficient. The philosophical insight in this sense lives in spite of the concept, so that we may justly speak of an impoverishment.

A metaphor may be used to express this inner contradiction of the philosophical approach. In asking about the meaning of reality, the philosopher endeavors to throw light upon light itself and thus at the same time obscures the light. He wants to reflect upon the light-giving perspective in which profiles appear, but in doing this he narrows at the same time the openness of the horizon into the closedness of a profile. There is no way for the philosopher to escape from accepting this inner contradiction. Such an acceptance, however, does not mean that he has passively to undergo the contradiction, but means a constant effort to overcome it, even though he will never completely succeed.

It remains difficult to express spiritual reality through univocal concepts borrowed from the material world. All too easily such concepts will obscure what they intend to clarify. When the philosopher endeavors to express his insight in univocal concepts, he has to correct his rendition through a different and even an opposite concept at the moment when he mentally appropriates the insight in its totality. In the eyes of a specialist in the sciences such a procedure gives the impression of being a meaningless juggling of conceptual contents. Nevertheless, if the philosopher would attempt to express the intuitive insight wholly in a single concept, i.e., if he wanted to give the insight an abstractly general univocal function, he would betray his very vocation as a philosopher. His abstractive procedure would cut the concept off from its feeding ground in intuition or, as it is sometimes called, "lived experience" (*expérience vécue*). For this reason the philosopher must relax his suffocating conceptual grasp and correct it by means of an opposite conceptual rendition. We have seen an example of this philosophical technique above where we indicated that the conceptual expression of the intuitive insight is an enrichment as well as an impoverishment. By constantly purifying concepts which evoke one another, the philosopher endeavors to make his insight more profound. He attempts to resist the temptation presented by the apparent clarity of conceptual univocity. True, he is forced to make use of this clarity, but he constantly endeavors to break through the univocity and change it in an analogous sense.

4. *Philosophy as Unscientific Science*

Conceptual and Non-Conceptual Knowing. The understanding attained in the various sciences has an abstract character. The plurality of the individual data is reduced to the unity of the univocal concept through abstraction from the individual characteristics. Philosophy, on the other hand, endeavors to find the original ground of unity whose unfolding constitutes the plurality of data. Unlike the scientist, the philosopher does not view the world as a unity in plurality but as a plurality which ultimately arises from a unity. Scientific thought attempts to arrive at hypothetical general laws: if *A* happens *B* happens. Science reasons, and scientific understanding is nourished by reasoning processes.

Philosophy wants to see through reality vertically rather than consider it horizontally. It uses the penetrating intellect rather than the reasoning power. While, in attempting to see through concrete reality, philosophy has to make use of the abstract universality of concepts, it uses these concepts to proceed ultimately in a meta-conceptual fashion.

Systematic Versus Non-Systematic Knowledge. Science aims at theories and systems. According as scientific understanding grows in some limited realm, science arranges the laws governing this realm in a logically connected whole. The scientist is successful if he manages to formulate a good theory. Philosophy, on the other hand, views the system as both an enrichment and an impoverishment. It cannot do without some measure of systematic approach and expression. Yet the philosopher makes use of a system to transcend it and thereby be non-systematic.

Methodic Versus Non-Methodic Approach. The success of exact thinking depends upon the correct methodic approach. Philosophy, however, makes use of a method to be ultimately unmethodic. Phenomenological philosophy uses the phenomenological method of reduction. The human sciences, such as psychology and sociology, also have recourse to the phenomenological method. Yet it remains true that the phenomenology of these sciences still is a rational, albeit refined, form of controlling knowledge. A certain apriorism remains inherent in this phenomenology. Phenomenological

philosophy, on the other hand, makes use of the phenomenological reduction in order to transcend it as much as possible.
Differently expressed, this philosophy attempts to be meta-
phenomenological.

Scientific and Philosophical Working Hypothesis. Scientific research makes use of working hypotheses. Suspecting
that the investigated connection is of this or that kind, the
scientist is guided in his work by a hypothesis to see whether
or not the facts agree with it. The working hypothesis is
more or less aprioristic because there is not yet any fully
proved understanding. Philosophical reflection also has recourse to working hypotheses. Here, however, the imagination does not rely on a supplementary surmise concerning
something which is not yet fully known, as is the case in
science. We may even say that in philosophy the situation is
diametrically the opposite. Through intuition, insight is implicitly present and, as a philosopher, I am on the way to
appropriate this insight in a conceptual fashion. The working
hypothesis here is based upon the imaginative power of intuitive insight. It does not flow from a lack of knowledge, but
from a surplus of knowledge which has not yet been fully
assimilated. Ultimately, then, for the philosopher the hypothesis is the thesis.

From the preceding considerations it is evident that the
scientific structure of philosophical knowledge differs essentially from that of the special sciences. Everyone is naturally a
philosopher insofar as he reflects upon life and asks about the
meaning of his deeds. Man becomes a philosopher, in the
narrow professional sense of the term, when he inquires about
meaning in a more explicitly systematic fashion, so that his
inquiry becomes scientific in the broad, classical sense. This
professional philosophical knowledge, however, is valuable only
if, on the one hand, it arises from lived experience and, on the
other, renders this lived experience more profound. A philosophical treatise has to be lived, while a scientific treatise must
be handled. There is a very intimate connection between
philosophy and wisdom of life.

5. *The Relationship Between Conceptual
Knowledge and Intuitive Ideas*

The repeatedly made distinction between concept and intuition needs to be explained more fully here.

Univocal Concepts and Analogous Ideas. The distinguishing characteristic of intuitive knowledge is the fact that reality, in contrast with every mediate (conceptual) understanding, is immediately evident to itself. There is a certain identity of the knower and the known. In intuition man attains reality in its concrete individuality. The concept, on the other hand, attains its object only in an abstract, logically universal respect. Man's intuitive knowing, however, is confused and implicit, while his categorical conceiving possesses an explicit, circumscribed clarity. The types of knowledge corresponding to these two modes of knowing are called idea-knowledge and conceptual-knowledge.

Univocal concepts have a logical universality, arising from the fact that they abstract from individual and specific differences. The comprehension of such concepts is in inverse ratio to their extension. Univocal concepts can be arranged in an orderly fashion according to predicaments or categories. Alongside these concepts there are analogous ideas, which are transcendentally universal. Such concepts are all-embracing not only in extension but also in comprehension. Their universality is concrete rather than abstract. The ideas actually, albeit only confusedly, include the distinct particular modes of being.

Lest the analytic distinction of ideas and concepts cause confusion, it is necessary to indicate at once in a synthetic fashion how these two forms of knowledge are related to each other. The implicit idea-knowledge and the explicit conceptual knowledge are merely two aspects of one and the same cognitive reality. Both aspects are always present. Accordingly, it is merely a matter of emphasis if science is said to proceed conceptually and philosophy intuitively. Idea-knowledge becomes human knowledge only when it is appropriated in concepts. Reversely, the abstract concept has cognitive value only insofar as it expresses intuitive knowledge. For by means of intuitive knowledge the abstract concept has contact with reality, so that it obtains cognitive value. The concept tends to an ever-greater awareness of the intuitive idea.

The abstract expression, then, has value as a symbol. It is proper to a symbol to surrender its meaning while veiling it and to veil its meaning while surrendering it. In its explicit rendition of idea-knowledge, the concept veils the fullness of the idea because its abstract character prevents the appropriation of the idea from being perfect. On the other hand, the concept reveals the richness of the idea to some extent because it tends to seize the idea's fullness, albeit only abstractly.

The Bi-Unity of Intuitive and Conceptual Knowledge. Accordingly, in intuitive and conceptual knowledge there is question of a distinction made within the unity, imperfect though it be, of man's cognitive activity. Even here in this purely introductory consideration we may not lose sight of the fact that we can only inadequately express human knowing itself. Conceptual thought conceives the relationship between the two cognitive aspects as a relation between reconciled opposites. In reality we are dealing here with an oppositional bi-unity. The distinction between the two cognitive aspects lies in the imperfection and the resultant opposition present within the identity of human knowing. This distinction is real, but not in the univocal meaning attached to this term in the conceptual sphere. The conceptual sphere will represent the situation as referring to really distinct things. The difference in question, however, is real in an analogous sense. A more univocal reflection will place intuitive and conceptual knowledge in opposition as two positive magnitudes which are fundamentally one, although only imperfectly so.

Man can arrive at an "idea" of the bi-unity in question only from the starting point of integral cognitive experience itself. The analogous consideration which is based upon this philosophical insight views man's intuitive knowledge as an imperfect intuition. In this way conceptual knowledge does not become a positive element but marks intentionality as a deficient form of intuitive knowledge. Intuition receives its limitation in the concept and, on the other hand, the concept obtains its perfection from the intuition.

Thus we see that the very foundation of philosophy's paradoxical approach has to be expressed in a paradox. A non-conceptual difference is capable of being clarified only in a conceptual fashion. Human intuition can be clarified only by means of the abstract concept, and the abstract concept only through the intuitive idea.

6. *The Various Philosophical Forms of Knowledge*

Intermediaries Between Analogous Ideas and Univocal Concepts. The relationship between ideas and categorical understanding indicates that all kinds of mixed forms may occur in between all-embracing ideas and strongly univocal concepts. The univocity which leaves behind the differences manifests itself most clearly in concepts about material things and living bodies, although even here there is already a certain gradation. These material things and living bodies reveal few individual characteristics in the qualitative sense. Specific traits dominate, so that such beings are primarily individuals of a species. They resemble one another like "two drops of water," and differ only through quantitative features. Higher individuals, however, such as men, differ from one another by their individual forms themselves. For instance, one may say that the dog is faithful and that the cat cannot be trusted, but it is not possible to state that man is faithful or cannot be trusted. The common specific element is not decisive here. Of course, man has specific qualities which he possesses in common with all human beings, but these qualities remain much more in the background. Man has the typical ambiguity of spirit-and-matter. On the one hand, because of his bodily being, he is an individual of the human species, but on the other, because he is a spirit, he is his own species, i.e., he is a wholly original realization, not of the concept of man, but of the all-embracing idea of man.

Analogous Overtone of Concepts Concerning Man. In this way the concepts which refer to human reality acquire a strongly analogous overtone. They become ideal concepts, which imply a kind of infinity of the moral ideal and are embodied in constantly different ways in persons and society. Examples of such concepts are person, society, love and freedom. From the viewpoint of the intuitively known, man knows many of these realities, but he has little knowledge of them insofar as clear conceptual knowledge is concerned. Everyone, for example, knows what freedom is, but as soon as one has to explain it, he no longer knows it. If an attempt is made to express conceptually such realities as love, spirit and freedom, the resulting concepts are very poor in content. Intuitive clarity is in inverse ratio to its conceptual counterpart.

Concepts which express the spiritual aspects of man are much more analogous than those which express at the same time a material-bodily aspect. Such concepts lend themselves less to univocal categorical conceptualization. Examples of concepts expressing both aspects of man are "to work" and "to possess." They are more univocal than concepts expressing only spiritual aspects. Nevertheless, as expressions of human activities, these concepts are still more analogous than univocal.

Concepts Expressing Man's Spiritual Reality. There are concepts which express spiritual realities without including any imperfection in themselves. We may think here, e.g., of such concepts or rather ideas as knowing, loving, and contemplating. In the analogous mode of consideration proper to philosophy, man's knowing and loving are conceived as graded perfections and approximating participations of absolute knowledge and absolute love. With respect to such ideas which do not include any imperfection, the primary analogate lies in the fullness of the perfection, insofar as the intuitively known quality is concerned. Insofar, however, as the expressed content of the concept is viewed, the primary analogate lies in the created condition of this perfection. The implicit real intuition opens here a perspective upon the fullness of the perfection touched by the spirit. Such ideal concepts as knowing and loving greatly transcend the improper logical analogy of attribution. We face here a proper metaphysical analogy, although from the viewpoint of expression the stage of logical analogy of attribution is not fully overcome.

Concepts Expressing Man's Spiritual-Material Aspects. As we have mentioned above, concepts such as to work and to possess, whose content includes also man's bodily structure, offer more scope for a univocal approach. They remain markedly in the stage of improper logical analogy, which is reducible to univocation. The primary analogate of such an analogy of improper proportion or attribution lies in those forms in which the imperfection of the material structure manifests itself most strikingly. To possess, for example, is predicated primarily of a material object, and to work applies primarily to manual labor. This analogy of attribution passes from the lower to the more perfect by means of the conceptual addition of greater perfection. In this way intellectual work becomes a higher form of labor, and having a friend is characterized as a higher form of possession. Since, then, activities of this type are human and possess a spiritual value, they are already permeated with the properly analogous idea of value. For this reason one may even say that God works and possesses.

7. *Conclusion*

The Dialectics of Philosophical Reflection. Philosophy wants to reflect upon life. In our everyday dealings with men and things we all too frequently neglect the profound meaning of life. It is as a philosopher, therefore, that I must endeavor to grasp this meaning. Phenomenological philosophy speaks in this connection about a "lived experience" which is not yet reflected upon (*irréfléchie*) and which the philosopher wants to bring more in the center of our consciousness. Because of its inner paradox, however, philosophical reflection has to proceed dialectically in its explicitation of this lived experience. It has to appeal to conceptual univocity, i.e., it must attempt to clarify spiritual being by means of the logical apparent clarity of material reality. We may call this the upward or ascending approach. On the other hand, philosophical reflection must precisely try to overcome this univocity through analogous knowledge. Starting from concrete integral being-man, the philosopher must try to take these concepts in an analogous sense. Lived experience has to nourish man's reflective expression of life. Here we meet the downward or descending approach. This downward approach clearly manifests the purely apparent clarity of conceptual knowledge. The concept aims at things in the lowly function of their material-quantitative determination. The more, however, a being is determined in this fashion, the less it participates in the value of being. In the analogous approach, which starts from known spiritual reality, lower beings are understood as deficient and imperfect forms of reality. The reflection of philosophy will have to make dialectic use of both the univocal upward approach and the downward analogous approach. However, this twofold approach is ultimately one.

Circular Progress of Thought. The progress of philosophical thinking resembles a circular form of reasoning. Its analogous consideration is clarified by its univocal counterpart, and the univocal consideration is corrected by means of the analogy. The philosopher will accept this circular type of thought process as meaningful. In a scientific thought process, which proceeds through reasoning and syllogisms from one judgment to another, such a procedure would be a vicious circle. The philosophical circular movement of explicitation, however, runs its course within spiritual reality, which is evident to itself with a certain degree of immediacy.

In the following chapter we will apply the preceding data to the philosophical approach of social reality. It will become evident there that in philosophy we do not really demonstrate anything but are capable only of pointing out what is.

CHAPTER TWO

THE INESCAPABLE EXPERIENCE
OF BEING-A-PERSON AS CO-EXISTENCE

1. *The Rationalistic "Theory" of Society Versus the
Personalistic "Idea" of Community*

Everyday experience seems to suggest that man first exists in himself and then, for the sake of his development, enters into all kinds of social contact with others. In his active occupations he experiences himself as placed opposite other human beings, with whom he now enters into contact. This superficial contact gives rise to the impression that we first feel ourselves alone in the world and then appeal to other persons because of our need. It seems that man has first to acquire consciousness of an "I" and that subsequently this consciousness makes it possible for him to know other human beings. According to this experience, the "I" sees itself placed before an external world of persons and objects and then attempts to bridge the distance to this external world through social contact. Being-social seems to be merely an addition— albeit an important one—to being-a-person.

Such a view of social reality has a very pronounced solipsistic content. It is the social theory of a rather primitive realism which is wholly encompassed by the realm of the senses. However, such a sensistic attitude, which is promoted by the successful rationalism of the positive sciences, does not go beyond the first-known impressions derived from man's bodily behavior. It does not transcend the material world, in which human beings appear opposed in spatial distance from one another and in their relationship with objects. Such an attitude is typical of the depersonalized (*das 'Man'*) approach, which does not go beyond the externality of the world. But the authentic man transcends this limitation. So far as he is concerned, his being-a-person unveils itself in his being-together-with-his-fellow-men. He conceives his relationship to the other as co-constituent of the person. It is only within co-existence that man arrives at existence. His self-consciousness manifests itself as an open co-consciousness. The separate "I" is not the original "I," and man as an isolated being is simply inconceivable. Self-isolation, hatred, envy and all other manifestations of antisocial and asocial behavior remain a kind of social relationship, albeit in a degraded form. Even as a bodily being, man is essentially in-the-world. Only within this fundamental unity of man with his fellow-men and the world is it possible to distinguish a kind of external world.

Such a strongly solipsistic theory of sociality, which views interhuman contact as a reciprocal supplement and aid to the previously existing "I," is defended by, e.g., classical solidarism. This solidarism is based on the works of H. Pesch and defended, with some variations, by Welty, von Nell-Breuning, and others. The opposite view may be called the personalistic conception of community.

We will oppose the two views in this chapter and see that the issue is ultimately a struggle between "rationalistic" and "phenomenological" philosophy. The point at stake is a choice between a univocally rational conceptual philosophy, leading to a rationalistic "theory" of society, and an analogous philosophical approach, terminating in a personalistic "idea" of community. In the following pages we will make frequent and grateful use of Maxime Chastaing's excellent book, *L'existence d'autrui.*

2. *Methodic Doubt of the Other's Existence*

A scientific attitude seems to demand that one does not accept the personalistic view without convincing demonstration. Such a position would appear to be eminently reasonable because rationalism definitely makes an effort to demonstrate its social view by means of the classical argument that man is characterized by his need of assistance. Accordingly, it is important to start only from what is not subject to doubt. Thus, as Chastaing says, we should start by doubting everything to arrive ultimately at that which cannot be doubted. Such an attitude would seem to be strictly scientific.

One may start by saying that my own self-consciousness cannot be denied or doubted, for in my very doubt of my self-consciousness it is evident that I am conscious of my doubt.

My own self-awareness, therefore, reveals itself as an irreducible and original starting point. But, if my consciousness is a co-consciousness of others, does the doubt or denial of the other's existence likewise imply the affirmation of this existence? Is co-existence also such a prepredicative primordial experience that cannot be doubted? It would not appear to be so. The other's existence is clearly very easy to doubt and very difficult to prove.

True, my fellow-man says that he knows and likes me, but does he really do so? Of course, he claims that he does, but does he really say what he thinks and means? I am unable to verify it because I have no immediate access to his immanent activities. If the label on a grocery bag tells me that the bag contains peanuts, I can easily verify the claim by tasting the content, but such a procedure is useless to verify the thoughts of a fellow-man. Any external behavior may conceal a hidden inner meaning. Who can guarantee, for instance, that his smile does not hide his enmity? Accordingly, it would seem that I can never be certain of someone's inner intention.

This conclusion leads me to even greater doubt about my fellow-man. If I am unable to discover with certainty what is hidden behind this smile, I feel tempted to ask, Does this exterior conceal anything at all? True, I address the other, ask him questions, give him signs of my love, and the other replies to my invitations; but are not these replies wholly responses to my questioning attitude? Is it not possible that, as behaviorism explains, his replies are refined reactions to the stimuli originating in me? Are not his expressions simply refined body phenomena that do not conceal anything spiritual? It is not possible for me to demonstrate the opposite in a scientific way.

I may make a last attempt to save my conviction of the other's existence and propose a formal syllogism. The major premise is: I perceive in the other expressive movements similar to those in myself. And the minor: I experience my own expressive movements in a self-conscious way. Thus the conclusion would follow that the other also is conscious of himself. The difficulty, however, is to deliver the proof of the syllogism's major premise. How do I know that the other's expressive motions are similar to mine and therefore accompanied by self-consciousness? Moreover, similarity to something always implies also a difference. Could the difference in question not be precisely that my expressive motions are self-conscious while those of the other, despite their similarity, are merely refined mimicking behavioristic reactions?

Accordingly, it would appear that scientifically one is justified in accepting only one's own existence and that the other's existence is, to express it quite strongly, merely an object of belief based upon more or less reasonable grounds. It is not possible to demonstrate the other's existence in a critical scientific fashion. Thus solipsism seems to be the only possible scientific attitude. I have no "certainty" whatsoever about my fellow-man. I even have to keep in mind the possibility that sooner or later I may discover that the other is merely a projection of myself.

One who wants a strictly scientific proof, therefore, seems to be right in his idea that the personalistic view of community cannot be provided with a critical basis, but he will note at the same time that the more rationalistic view of sociality likewise is built on quicksand. The only scientifically justified position seems to be that of absolute solipsism.

3. *Methodic Doubt as an Incorrect Rationalistic Starting Point*

Do the preceding considerations have to lead to the conclusion that no convincing proof can be given in favor of the personalistic view of sociality? A distinction must be made here in the sense that no certain proof can be offered in the way exact, sense-verifiable, positive science demonstrates its assertions, although a certain proof can be proposed from the standpoint of a suprarational, integrally human attitude. This meta-scientific attitude regarding the knowledge of spiritual realities has, as we will see more in detail, the almost paradoxical feature of providing a higher degree of certainty the less one looks for scientific demonstrability. There is nothing shameful about the fact that the personalistic view of community is unable to establish man's co-existence by means of a scientific, i.e., positivistic, demonstration. On the contrary, one could point out that we should be ashamed of having attempted to offer such a proof. The burden of proof lies on the other side. I do not have to demonstrate that my fellow-man exists, but an explanation should be offered of why co-existing man, through doubting his fellow-man, is induced to demonstrate the other's existence.

Anyone who attempts to demonstrate the existence of his fellow-men in a scientific way is the victim of a kind of sensism. This rather positivistic attitude arises from the "fallen state" (*Verfallen*) of man's existence, a state which reduces all "being" to the level of things (*Vorhandenes*) and to an "objective" magnitude, i.e., to an object which the man of science can handle. Quite correctly Heidegger points out that, in making such an attempt, man is fully submerged in inauthenticity, in inauthentic being.

The attitude of doubt allegedly arose from a critical absence of prejudice. One wanted only to accept that which revealed itself as undoubtedly true to the intellect. But, we may ask, is this attitude really as unprejudiced as it pretends to be. True, Descartes wants us to reject everything which is not quite certain, but alongside him we may place Blaise Pascal who asks us to retain everything until we are certain that it is false.

It is a sign of great arrogance to accept only that which reveals itself as certain to my limited and poor human intelligence. It means that through his intellect man wants to raise himself above the totality of reality. He declares himself the "god" of being. Hegel also assumed such an attitude. For this reason idealism is fundamentally a form of materialism because in this system man's "working" mind makes reality just as, in the philosophy of Marx, the "thinking" hand produces reality.

Sharply formulated, the faulty fundamental attitude can be expressed as follows: the proposition "all mathematical judgments are clear" is simply transformed into the proposition "all clear judgments are mathematical judgments."

The demand that personalism offer a proof is inspired by the idea that positive mathematical certainty can be reached in the realm of spiritual personal co-existence. The solidarist, for example, is capable of scientifically proving his social view because he restricts man's sociality to physical, biological and psychical needs. This social dependence of man lies indeed on the sensitively perceptible level and consequently is subject to verifiable demonstration. The personalist, however, does not view co-existence from without as an object but looks at social reality from within. He goes deeper than the solidarist and penetrates into the very mystery of spiritual intersubjectivity. If personalism were able to demonstrate its view, it would effectively prove the falsity of its position.

4. *The Rationalistic Theory of Society Starts from an Aprioristic Standpoint*

By attempting to present a rational proof of man's social being, I actually closed my mind to spiritual reality as soon as I began my attempt. My attitude could be compared with that of a man who tries to find something red by means of spectacles that are impervious to red light. For the question was, Is there another "I" "outside" me? But whatever I met outside myself was not a spiritual subject but at most a material and extended substance. In other words, my attempt looked for a *thing* and not for a human being. Such a cognitive attitude cannot go beyond the bodily being of man.

The question whether any human being exists "outside" me refers to my own consciousness as the "inside." In this way my own consciousness, which allegedly is undeniably present, is likewise reduced to something objective and thing-like in contrast with the external world. By the very fact that I look for my fellow-man outside myself, the other disappears *a priori* from my field of vision. All that remains is my own interiority, but it, too, is no longer a properly spiritual interiority. I have become estranged from myself and, paradoxical as it may seem, I am really "outside" myself.

When I speak of my fellow-man as "outside" and of myself as "inside" and neglect, as the rationalist does, the analogous character of these expressions, I am in fact speaking of the physical world, in which there is no room for either the other subject or for myself. Such a world is a world-without-spirit. In it, the entire being of man is scattered in things; his entire wealth is levelled to a working and caring concern with things. There is no place in it for the gaze of love, and the integrally human attitude is shrivelled down to a rational and nihilistic attitude of life.

By means of the Cartesian attitude I wanted to isolate and appropriate certainty as my possession. When I attempt to appropriate the certainty of spiritual-being in an attitude of "having," "being" escapes from my field of vision. All that remains is a shadow, for "being" cannot be reduced to "having." By attempting to present a scientific demonstration for the personalistic viewpoint, I *a priori* accept the rationalistic standpoint. This standpoint is an unjustified and inacceptable form of scientism. The great task of personalistic thought is not to discover such a demonstration but to overcome the rationalistic temptation which reduces all being to the level of things and seeks the highest form of certainty in a scientific demonstration. In other words, fundamentally speaking, it is a question of choice between, on the one hand, a "rational psychology," which is the basis of, e.g., solidarism, and on the other, a "phenomenological anthropology," on which personalism is founded.

5. *There is a Suprarational or Metarational Certainty*

Everyone agrees that the cognitive attitude and methods have to be adapted to the reality-to-be-known. Scientific thinking devises methods by means of which man acquires a grip on the reality which he studies. The concept is here really a cognitive means giving us a grip on the objects. Thus scientific understanding is acquired at least in part by means of the conceptual construct. Our rational certainty is the result of a demonstration.

Certainty of Spiritual Reality. When the human mind wants to explore the realm of the spirit, it has to abandon its dominating attitude. It does not face here as a subject an "object"-like subservient reality. Knowledge of the spiritual as a reality transcending me demands that I assume an attitude of willingness to listen to, and confirm what is unveiled to me. In this way I do not make reality intelligible from the standpoint of myself, but the spiritual reality, in which I as a person actively participate, reveals itself through me. Understanding does not show itself here as resulting from the concept, but is already present and the concept is merely a subsequent explicitating and inadequate expression of this understanding. Certainty remains here the light that illuminates my conceptual understanding, while in science my conceptual understanding is the light illuminating the object.

Because spiritual reality, as it were, envelops me and is more immanent to me than I am to myself, it is not possible for me to appropriate this form of certainty through a demonstration. While in scientific knowledge certainty is based upon demonstration, in spiritual, metascientific knowledge the proof is founded on certainty. Through the integrally human attitude I stand in the light of this certainty, and every conceptual explicitation is permeated with this light and becomes a proof in the sense that it is a sign and a manifestation of this suprarational certainty. Let us illustrate the matter by means of an example and consider the case of being certain of someone's trustworthiness. If through an integrally human attitude I know the other as trustworthy in intersubjectivity, I would destroy the certainty of his trustworthiness by wanting to verify and test it. Moreover, in this sphere of intersubjectivity I feel no need to verify the point, for I am quite certain of it. In this way I evaluate all signs of trustworthiness not as proofs for an as yet undemonstrated certainty but as manifestations of an existing trustworthiness.

If, on the other hand, I want to discover and base the other's trustworthiness merely upon proofs, I will never be able to go beyond a certainty that in his socio-economic relations and his functional contacts he will probably show himself trustworthy. On "rational" grounds I am certain of his reliability. This socio-economic and functional reliability, moreover, is not yet the certainty of being able to trust someone in all the conditions of life. Yet it is of this trust that I possess a suprarational certainty in my mutual intersubjective surrender to my fellow-man. This form of certainty on the spiritual level is not verifiable; besides, I have no desire at all to seek any verification. I have become the other in his spiritual intimacy and in this way I know him. On the other hand, I am not yet totally the other, so that my knowing is also a believing. Moreover, it is only by believing that I arrive at this knowing. I know the other believingly, and I believe the other knowingly. From the very start my knowing is a believing, and my believing is a knowing.

Believing and Knowing. The exaggerated scientific and rationalistic kind of knowledge prevailing in our time leads man easily to conceive believing as a diminished form of knowledge. In the realm of rational knowledge faith and science are indeed contraries: what man knows here, he no longer believes, and what he believes he does not yet know. On this level it is really true that faith is a diminished form of knowledge. But in knowing the spiritual, in intersubjective knowledge, believing and knowing are not inversely proportioned to each other. Faith is no substitute here for knowledge, and knowledge does not replace belief. In this realm my believing is a knowing of the other, and my knowing is a believing in the other. Anyone who, with respect to knowledge of spiritual reality, raises the question of "either faith or knowledge" would be guilty of exaggerated rationalism.

Certainty on the Spiritual Level. Scientific evidence, which at first seems to be most certain, appears now not to be the summit of certainty. For, "to be certain," a scientific idea or theory is always tested through experiments, while certainty on the spiritual level is self-revelatory. On this level the evidence is its own guarantee. Being certain here means that I do not even consider the possibility of testing or experimenting. The certainty itself is here the light that illuminates my intellect, while in science the object is illuminated by my intellect (which can so easily show the object in the wrong light).

All scientific knowledge has a provisional character, i.e., it is possible that by means of a more refined perception and a more subtle understanding man will reach a more perfect grasp of reality. For this reason scientific theory is always subject to revision and has a hypothetical character. Spiritual, metarational knowledge, on the other hand, is not provisional but has an element of absoluteness. This absolute element is, of course, capable of growth because, through my integrally human consent to spiritual reality, I increasingly participate in this reality and place myself more fully in the light of its evidence.

6. *Suprarational Knowledge Demands a Correct Attitude of Life*

The difficulty against the acceptance of the personalistic idea of society does not lie primarily in the realm of demonstration but rather in that of the attitude of life. The choice between the rationalistic view and the personalistic standpoint cannot be solved by means of a scientific approach alone. What is needed, too, is that I overcome the attitude of unbelief and distrust by which I close my mind to this lofty truth. For knowledge of spiritual reality, of spiritual beings, implies a free act of self-revelation on the part of that which is known. For this reason I must humbly believe in this free self-revelation of spiritual beings and trustingly hope that they will reveal themselves.

The rationalist has to watch that he does not let himself be blinded by the apparent clarity of logical-conceptual understanding, for the metalogical level of spiritual beings, the sphere of the mystery, also possesses value as reality. Logical clarity and logical evidence do not suffice in this sphere. The verification of personal intersubjectivity is always defective and will have to be so of necessity because with respect to the mysterious realm of spiritual realities we are unable to do more than stammer like a little child. But if we open ourselves to the other's subjectivity, if we assume the attitude of creative surrender to him, spiritual reality will unveil itself in an ever-increasing way.

In a rationalistic philosophy one may speak of a "theory" or "doctrine" of society, but in the personalistic conception there is question rather of a vision, an ideal picture. I merely have an "idea" of intersubjectivity, of the personal community.

7. *Solidarism Needs to Be Complemented*

The solidaristic theory views communication with the other too much as a remedy of one's own insufficiency. It is true, of course, that man as a bodily being interacts in a physico-biological way with his spatio-temporal environment. The co-existence, however, of which personalism speaks, lies not merely in the sphere of complementing an insufficiency but primarily in the personal encounter that enriches the communing subjects. As compared with man's physical dependence on the other, this co-existence is much more characterized by independence. However, this more spiritual independence implies precisely a reference to the other. Through his one-sided, objectifying and conceptual way of looking at man, the solidarist is led to neglect the level of spiritual community, the level of love.

Accordingly, it is a typically solidaristic question to ask whether it could not happen that only one man would exist, and to press this question as an argument against the idea that being-man is a being-together, co-existence. The question is raised in the realm of the imaginable, but in raising it one remains wholly within the confines of physical contact with the environment. The question, moreover, is also typically rationalistic, for it proceeds from a mentally conceived possibility and does not allow reality to speak and reveal itself.

The only possible reply to such a question is that such a man growing up all alone in the world would still be a person because he would retain his spiritual reference to the other, even though this being-toward-the-other would be able to develop only very poorly because of the other's physical absence. As a kind of sign in favor of this assertion we may point out that people who are forced into a solitary condition begin to talk with the things around them, so that they live even with material objects as if they were living beings.

We may add that the encounter of "I" and "you" does not have to be physical. It is even possible that, to serve the other, one will withdraw from the world into a kind of solitude, not in order to escape from the other but precisely to manifest one's spiritual community in a more profound way. This love also, which does not receive any response of love from an individual fellow-man, knows its reciprocity from absolute Love.

Accordingly, we must change the one-sided attitude of the solipsistic and closed Cartesian *cogito* into an open and communicating *cogito*.

8. *Doubt About the Existence of Fellow-Men is Self-Contradictory*

Every effort to make the other's existence acceptable presupposes that the other is unconcealed and present to us.

The thesis of intersubjectivity cannot be proved in the strict sense because it cannot be deduced from a prior and more fundamental insight. Its truth can merely be pointed out by showing that every assertion regarding the other presupposes that the other is present.

The facts that selfhood is communication and that self-consciousness is reciprocal co-consciousness manifest themselves especially in this that doubt about the other is self-contradictory. Even as in the act of denying my existence I must of necessity affirm this existence, so also I affirm the other's presence in the very denial of his existence. We have made an effort to doubt the other's existence, but both doubt and denial of our fellow-man are possible only by virtue of the other's existence. Our attempt to demonstrate the other's existence by first doubting it resembled the attitude of a near-sighted man looking for his spectacles, unaware of the fact that they are on his nose and that he is capable of looking for them only by virtue of these spectacles.

I could think, for example, that the other is merely appearance or a projection of my own self. But the very fact of thinking that the other is merely an imaginary projection shows that I must have gone already beyond the realm of the imaginary to realize that the other is purely imagination. I must have known my fellow-man as real or possibly real; otherwise I would not be able to call him mere imagination. If I had never known him as real, the idea of doubting his reality simply would not arise in my mind. Even my knowledge of the other as possibly real presupposes that I have had experience of my fellow-man's reality.

One would object perhaps that I have experienced the other's real existence, but that later I was forced to revise my view about him on the basis of new experiences. This objection raises the question of how the evidence of the other's existence can now be disputed. Such a revision could only be based upon the other. The procedure would be more or less as follows. I see a human being animated as I am. Someone else explains to me that man is purely a robot. Evidently, there is no escape here from the fact that I needed this "someone else" to revise my former certainty of the other's existence.

There remains a last, purely theoretical, possibility. I could say that my present actual experiences have to be doubted on the basis of former experiences, although it is difficult to see to what previous experiences this assertion could possibly refer. The possibility, then, is rather theoretical. Yet even this effort to doubt or deny the other's existence I can make only because of you. What I am really doing is this—with the aid of you I reconstruct my previous experiences and then use these reconstructed experiences, which bear your imprint, to reject you. In Chastaing's words, such a procedure may be compared with that of an old man who sees a boy, is thereby reminded of his own youth, and then says that this boy does not exist but that he himself is this boy.

No matter how subtly I try to doubt and deny my fellow-man, the other constantly reveals himself as present in my very act of denial. Because the act of denying my co-existence is an effort to place myself prior to my own existence, the attempt is obviously doomed to failure. In every endeavor to deny the other, my fellow-man reveals himself as a prepredicative and inescapable fundamental experience.

9. *Conclusion*

The important conclusion following from these considerations is that social philosophy should not be conceived as the formulation of assertions to be proved in a so-called objective way, i.e., by first suspending the judgment as to whether or not these assertions are true. Such an attitude really lacks objectivity, in the sense that it is not open-minded with respect to truth. By assuming this attitude, I place myself above truth and I "make" truth. Of course, in the realm of positive science the attitude is justified, for in this sphere truth consists in efficient usefulness, so that I may assume the relationship of master to servant with respect to the object considered. In the realm of philosophy, however, I must allow reality to speak for itself. The attitude here is that of subject to subject, and my philosophical explanation cannot go beyond an explicitating description which fall short of a reality that forever transcends me.

In knowing spiritual beings, the principal point is that I should beware of the attitude of bad faith and distrust lest I allow my own critical viewpoint to act as norm of my truth. Such a rationalistic attitude takes an extreme position from which it is irresistibly driven to the opposite extreme. One who claims that he can make reality wholly intelligible from within himself puts himself on the level of God. On the other hand, however, by identifying himself fully with this rational way of thinking and forgetting that this approach is only one of many possible ways, one that is applicable only to the corporal world, such a man sacrifices his own essence and lapses into materialism. Consequently, he will see his fellow-man likewise only in this materialistic light and reduce him to a material and thing-like reality.

In my attempt to offer a scientific demonstration of the other's existence, I tried, on the one hand, to assume the attitude of a god but, on the other, I acted as if I were merely a form in which matter appears. According to Chastaing, whose train of thought has often inspired us here, the rationalist does wrong to God, to his fellow-man, and to himself. The only possible escape from the narrow circle of scientific reasoning lies in simply listening to truth. This means that my cognitive attitude must be inspired by love and include at the same time faith and hope. It is not possible to clarify philosophical insight to anyone who lacks this correct attitude of life. To quote Husserl, "One cannot come to an agreement with someone who does not want to, and is unable to see."

Because of this personal and ethically inspired character of my cognitive activity, the philosophical insight is never complete but is always capable of growth. This incompleteness does not mean a denial of the absolute character proper to truth, but implies that man's perspective always remains open to greater depth and correction. The correct philosophical attitude demands a great openness and a willingness to engage in dialog. For my love is here a source of real knowledge, because the other's intimacy reveals itself to me only in a loving encounter.

CHAPTER THREE
PERSON AND COMMUNITY

1. *Preliminary Remarks*

In discussing the character of philosophy we sought our starting point by preference in the natural or everyday development of human knowledge by comparing philosophy first with science and especially with exact science. In the present chapter we will proceed in a similar fashion by endeavoring to clarify being-man through a comparison with material being. This approach is the more mediate, univocal, upward approach, in which use is made of the greater explicit, albeit only apparent, clarity of conceptual knowledge. The emphasis will fall here upon comparative understanding, but in the background the immediate analogous consideration of human reality will make its presence felt. For the two approaches permeate each other as two aspects of man's one imperfect cognitive activity. In the next chapter, on the other hand, our considerations will be more closely connected with the intuitive analogous approach, but there also it will not be possible to do without the clarity proper to concepts.

The univocal categorical method implies that especially man's spiritual being is compared with brute material reality, because it is between these two that the comparative difference manifests itself most characteristically. In this logical clarification the starting point lies in the everyday experience of the material world and not in philosophical experience. We meet here again the paradox of philosophy, which somehow has to start from univocal non-philosophical clarity if it is ever to attain to analogous philosophical insight.

2. *The Person is an Open Self*

The Being of Things and of Man. Material being is, on the one hand, exteriority, directedness to the outside, non-selfhood, self-estrangement, constant change, and being simply different; on the other hand, however, the thing is somewhat itself because it manages to exclude the outer world or to subject it to itself. Man, as a spiritual being, on the one hand,

37

is with himself; he is essentially selfhood, immanent to himself. In contrast with material things man is the free origin
of his own being, he is a person. In his autonomous freedom
man has something ultimate and unique. On the other hand,
man's spiritual being in his selfhood is precisely directed to
the other beings. In this spiritual directedness to the other,
whether things or persons, man is not exteriorized and estranged from himself but immanent and eminently himself.
The more the spirit goes out of itself, the more it affirms itself. Its going-out does not bear the marks of constant change
but of permanently being more itself. In the material world
directedness to the other leads to estrangement and absence
from the self, but in the spiritual order it means greater
freedom and more profound interiority.

In the realm of matter interiority is opposed to exteriority, but in the spiritual world interiority and exteriority appear
to include each other. Selfhood and closedness are identical
properties with respect to material things, but in the realm of
the spirit selfhood is identical with openness. Man is a closed
openness or an open closedness, an interior exteriority or an
exterior interiority.

Analogous Character of Subsistence. These paradoxical
terms themselves indicate that the concepts in question must
not be understood univocally but in an analogous sense in
reference to spiritual reality. The univocal consideration has
to be corrected at once and rendered more profound through
the intuitive analogous view. Self-possession or subsistence is
such an analogous reality of which man has an analogously
universal idea. Man as a person, then, is more fully subsistent than material things and living bodies, which subsist only
in a diminished degree. The clarity of the univocal *concept*
of subsistence, derived from the material world, has to be
unmasked as a merely apparent clarity from the viewpoint of
the analogous *idea* of subsistence. The subsistence which
man known intuitively first is that of his own self-being. The
primary analogate lies in the ontological perfection of subsistence, and it is only from the viewpoint of the conceptually
expressed knowledge that there can be question of a priority
to be attributed to material reality. Accordingly, infrahuman

things are said to subsist primarily because we understand the selfhood, the self-being of man, and not vice versa. The closedness and circumscribed character which mark the individual subsistent beings of the material world arise, therefore, more from the imperfection of their ontological individuality than from this individuality itself. They have to maintain themselves as individuals by excluding the other because of the fact that a material thing, strictly speaking, is not yet itself. The more a being is itself, the more profound its communication is with the other beings.

3. *The Person Becomes Himself Through Disinterested Deeds*

To Be a Person is to Have the Task of Self-Possession. Men as well as material things are finite beings. This finite character means that their self-possession, their identity is still in an imperfect condition. The active exercise of their self-possession is marked by a "to be not yet," by a dynamic coming to be and a tension toward higher self-affirmation. The finite being is constantly becoming more itself. Expressed in scholastic terminology, the subsistent being or substance, as "first act," can simply be itself only in the process of coming to be, as "second act," which is not adequately distinct from the first act. The higher the form of self-possession is, the greater also the thirst for deeper draughts of being. So far as man is concerned, this means that he is a person in potentiality rather than enjoying the actualized state of being a person. By means of a free project man has to try to become more and more a person. The statement that man "is" a person does not refer to an established condition but is a mandate, a task to be performed—that of self-posession.

If it is man's task to make himself a person through his deeds, our consideration of the person will have to pay attention to the specific features of human activity. Because this chapter is devoted primarily to the comparative logical approach, we will have to compare especially man's spiritual activity with the activity of matter.

Spiritual Deeds and Material Activity. There is a very sharp difference between the spiritual deeds of man and the material activity of the world of nature. The picture offered by the physical world is one of repulse and conquest. To maintain itself, a material thing has to exclude the other. To become greater, it has to overcome the other. Its activity consists, on the one hand, in repelling the other and, on the other, in conquest of the other. Living things, plants and animals, likewise, are able to perfect themselves only by overpowering the other and reducing it to nourishment. The animal experiences its surroundings only in reference to itself as either danger or prey. When in the world of animals there is question of a certain openness to the other, as is the case, for instance, between male and female, this openness is achieved at the expense of the individuals—they are subservient to the species. Two chemical substances may repel each other and in this way manage to retain their "selfhood," one of them may succeed in absorbing the other, or both may lose their selfhood and become a new kind of substance.

As a spiritual being, man transcends this world of contrariety. He does not enrich himself at the expense of the other, but becomes more himself by freely giving away his own perfection. When a material thing cedes something to another, it incurs a loss for itself; but in the sphere of the spirit, giving-away means self-enrichment. If in the physical world a thing's coming to be is typically a drawing something to itself, in the world of the spirit the activity of coming to be reveals much more the opposite characteristic. In his activity as a person man does not make his milieu subservient to himself, but by means of his attitude of loving surrender he allows his milieu to be itself. The person enters into communication with the world without thereby becoming the other as other. Precisely the opposite is typical of the material world. The thing becomes the other as other, suffering a loss in selfhood. It becomes much more the other than itself. The spirit, however, which transcends the sphere of material opposition, does not come to be the other as the other through estrangement, but becomes "one" with the other in a communicative enrichment of itself and of the other.

In the order of being-a-person, to-be-for-the-other assumes an entirely different form than it has with respect to material beings. That which in the material world is for the other has to make room for the other and be sacrificed to it.

The individual animal is there for the species and it perishes in this orientation to the other. But that which is for the other in the spiritual sphere becomes more itself through its direction to the other. Disinterestedness, unselfishness, and liberality, for instance, do not disfigure human activity but greatly enhance it.

The Characteristic of Disinterestedness in Man's Activities. It is not difficult to discover these qualifications in the various forms of human activity. Unselfish liberality leaves traces even in man's utilitarian actions. The most simple utensils, for example, cups and saucers, are elegantly formed. Man embellishes such objects with adornments, devoid of meaning in the order of use, to give expression to his disinterested liberality. He executes his technical activity with an esthetic expression.

In the realm of art it is even more evident that man meets his world not merely for the sake of usefulness and serviceability. Art means the expression, the communication of inner wealth. In his esthetic enjoyment man is open to the beautiful in a disinterested fashion and transcends the utilitarian world of technical and economical labor. Artistic creativity and esthetic enjoyment are really useless, in the sense that they are not pursued for the sake of something else to which they are subservient. Esthetic enjoyment, however, does not yet reveal disinterested surrender in all its depth. The subjective state of enjoyment remains a partial phase of the experience of beauty, so that the esthetic enjoyment can easily degenerate into a kind of estheticism—namely, if man is fully absorbed by his subjective state of sensitive enjoyment. Pure artistic activity and delight, on the other hand, point beyond themselves toward the genuinely spiritual activities of knowing and loving truth and goodness.

In the act of knowing, man endeavors to penetrate into the value of being possessed by the object itself. He is aware that his act of knowing must take place in a disinterested sphere if it is to attain truth. Here, too, however, there are degrees of disinterestedness. Science, for example, seeks knowledge for the sake of knowledge, but at the same time it is true that scientific theories are formed with the intention of making the object known serviceable for man. But the more the act of knowing is permeated with disinterested features, the more it becomes transformed into wisdom of life. Genuinely disinterested knowledge is steeped in morality.

Thus it is in ethical activity that the fundamental attitude of disinterestedness reveals itself most strikingly, for the ethical deed is *par excellence* man's most specific human activity. Purely ethical activity manifests itself as the disinterested doing of the good. A sign of this is the phenomenon of remorse, in which man bears witness against his own selfishness. Moral consciousness calls for a fundamental attitude of "being privilege to" rather than "being obliged to." So long, therefore, as a deed is done because it is prescribed and sanctioned by reward and punishment, one has not yet reached the purely ethical or moral level. The moral good is not valuable because it perfects man, but because it is good and valuable in itself it perfects man. It should be kept in mind here that we are not concerned with an abstract good or an abstract truth in the order of objects and goods, but with the concrete good and the concrete truth which find their highest embodiment in the person. In contrast, then, with the activity of the physical world, the specifically human activity reveals itself directed to self-forgetting love. The more the spirit loses itself in liberal love to a fellow-man, the more profoundly it finds itself. It is love, the social art *par excellence*, which serves most to confirm man in his value as a person.

The Analogous Nature of Coming to Be. From these considerations it follows that coming to be is not a univocal but an analogous concept and thus can be realized in a higher or in a lower fashion. In a similar way, as we have seen with respect to selfhood, the coming to be which man knows first is that of his own person. Starting from this intuitively understood idea, man next attributes this coming to be also to the material things with which he is acquainted. In direct ratio to a being's selfhood, coming to be means becoming more oneself. The material thing, which does not really have self-possession but is a part of the cosmos, always is outside itself in its coming to be. The activity which it seems to display is received by it as an outside influence, and in its activity it is estranged from itself. Strictly speaking, the material thing does not become itself, but finds itself in a constant state of estrangement and change. This situation arises, of course, from the material imperfection of its individuality. The ultimate source, however, of its changing does not lie in the urge to become constantly something different but in the tendency to become itself, a tendency which is always doomed to failure because of the imperfection of being that characterizes the material thing.

It is only in the order of man's personal being that there can be question of coming to be in the proper sense. The self comes to be here through the communicating acts of knowing and loving. In the other as in a mirror man comes to be himself. When there is a higher degree of coming to be oneself, there is always a greater measure of identity between coming to be as accidental perfection and being oneself as substantial perfection.[1]

---

[1]Scholasticism uses the categories of substance and accident to indicate the growth of selfhood. This logical distinction should not obscure the profound philosophical insight which lies behind the categorical division. It often happens that the division is clarified too much in a univocal way by means of material examples, such as that a plant can change color and leaves without ceasing to be the same plant. It is definitely wrong to represent substantial being as an inert and unmoved substratum in which all kinds of activities occur without touching the substance itself. As first act, substantial being can be itself only in the accident as its inadequately distinct second act. The categories in question must not be understood as representable in a material way. They are to be viewed philosophically in a broader analogous way. The substance is not a substratum which lies "under" the accident; in this sense it would be better to say that it is "in" the accident. However, even this expression is not quite correct, for a finite being does not have the accidental determination in perfect identity. The higher the degree of selfhood proper to a finite being, the greater also the identity achieved between substance and accident.

The accident, likewise, as "acceding" to the substance should be understood in an analogous way, for, strictly speaking, there is no question of an "acceding" addition. No enrichment or addition is possible to being. The so-called accidental determination is really much more the growth in being which is implied in the very being of the substance. Understood in this sense, the substance is much more the source of the accident, or even the accident itself, than the recipient of an additional determination. However, this expression again needs to be corrected because of the imperfect identity proper to the finite being. If the accident is conceived in a more univocal way as an "acceding" determination, then it follows that a higher being, such as a person, has constantly fewer accidents. If, on the other hand, the accident is understood in an analogous philosophical sense, than it is precisely the person who because of his wealth of being possesses the most accidents.

The distinction of substance and accidents indicates the imperfect

The immanent activities of knowing and loving, for example, are far less ephemeral than are the bodily activities of
playing and walking. Strictly speaking, such immanent activities are no longer acts possessing a transitory spatio-temporal
character, but rather permanent fundamental attitudes of the
person. The more perfect the activity of coming to be is, the
closer it approaches the permanence characterizing selfhood.

4. *The Person as Communication*

Substance and Relation. In the material world, which is
dominated by exclusion and opposition, the categories of substance (subsistence) and relation are opposites. A thing is
independent in direct ratio to the degree in which it is less
dependent upon its surroundings. In the realm of matter the
characteristics of dependence and independence are inversely
proportionate to each other. On the personal level, however,
substance and relation go together. The person's independence is in direct ratio to his relationship to other persons.
The possession of his immanence of being goes hand in hand
with his immanence to the other. He is really free and
independent insofar as he knows about his bond with other
persons. His self-affirmation grows through the affirmation
of the other. In the order of personal being, substantial and
relative being imply each other.

Here too, however, the univocal consideration which
starts from the everyday experience of matter has to be
purified. The relation which we know first in an intuitive
fashion is the human relationship. We may add once more
that, strictly speaking, every relative denomination of material
things is borrowed from man's relative being. The estrangement which characterizes the dependence of the material thing
arises again from its material imperfection. Its lasting self-
estrangement means that it constantly fails to attain genuinely communicative relationships with others. Because of their
deficient mode of being, material things clearly, in the strict
sense, are not, do not come to be, and do not have any

---

identity of the person with himself and with other beings. The more
intimate the identity of a finite being is, the more it is directed and
grows toward the fullness of being.

relations. All such terms are used only in a certain attributive sense.

In the realm of matter the relationship to the other consists in a relation of need. Being-relative here has the characteristics of a loss to the environment or of an enrichment at the expense of the surroundings. On the level of personal being, however, being-relative transcends the order of mutually impoverishing need. Although even on this level relativity still arises also from the ontological imperfection of the person's spiritual being, it exhibits the characteristics of mutual enrichment through communication.

The Relativity of the Person. Being-relative, as communication, may not be considered solely as a quality added to a human person. Communal being is not an accidental and supplementary property of man but pertains essentially to him. The entire person is social, and the entire social reality is personal. Community, therefore, may not be conceived as a subsequent unity of order among persons, or as the sum total of equals, or as a whole built of parts. Community is fundamentally nothing else but the totality of persons, and the being of community is the same as the being of the persons. There is question here of a mysterious unity of being, in which the persons participate and which each of them in his own unique way realizes totally in himself. Unity and distinction evoke each other here in identity. Every person is the same community on the level of his own spiritual selfhood. It should be emphasized, of course, that we are speaking here about man precisely insofar as he is a spiritual being, i.e., about the social character of man in his purely spiritual aspects. This social character is the highest form of communication or, better still, is communication in the strict sense, for it is intersubjectivity, community of persons, and not some diminished form, such as a work organization or an association of common interests, which receive their structural unity primarily from man's bodily being. Just as the person is not given in his actual being but is a potential being which has to form itself according to his own project, so also is the genuine community not a static datum of nature but far more a project of communication. If the statement "man is a person" contains a task to be done, then likewise, being-social does not refer so much to an actualized state of community as to a potentiality for community. There is question here of an ethical ideal of social being which man is able freely to accept and pursue, but which he is also capable of denying and rejecting.

5. *Categorical Approach to Community*

Relative Being in the Philosophy of Things. It is difficult to assign a place to communal being-relative in the Aristotelian categories, which are based upon a concept of substance that is geared to the physical world. True, Aristotelianism knows relative being, which is placed in the sphere of the second act, as the accidental perfection of the first act, i.e., of substance. However, the being-relative of which there is question here lies deeper and pertains to the level of the first act. The relationship to the other is co-constituent of the person. To be a person is identical with being-relative. The physical orientation of Aristotelian philosophy, which is echoed by certain scholastic trends, results in an overevaluation of substance at the expense of relation. In this way the concept of substance is too strongly built upon the example of immutable material things, as mountains and rocks. In such a physical world picture, which is inspired primarily by man's working and caring contact with things, plurality is given the first place because of the palpable certainty of this contact in everyday life, and unity is viewed only subsequently. A thing, and man also, must first be constituted in itself, i.e., in its limiting exclusion of the other, and only then can it form a unity of order with the other in this or that respect.

However, it is necessary to hold fast to the *meta*-physical insight into the unity of being of all things. This unity is not subsequent to their plurality but fundamental. The understanding of this philosophical truth cannot be reached by starting from man's caring contact with things, but it is possible to attain an "idea" of it by approaching it from man's integral experience of being-together. In this togetherness subjects experience themselves as distinct and nevertheless as one from within. Care is to be taken here not to hold fast too rigidly to the conceptual categories of matter and to apply them unwittingly to spiritual reality in a univocal fashion, for otherwise it becomes difficult to display the necessary openness for this philosophical mystery. When such openness is lacking, one will seek too much the clarity of a syllogistic demonstration, which can be found only in the order of objects and not in that of subjects.

Relative Being in the Philosophy of the Person. The philosophy of the person has to hold fast to the unity of substance and relation, of self-being and being-communicative. Just as the substance, as first act, realizes itself through the accessory second act, so also the communicative relation, as first act, becomes itself through the accidental relation, as second act. It is only this second accidental relation, the so-called "predicamental relation," that is the object of consideration in most philosophical treatises, notably those of Aristotelian inspiration. In the relationship of beings, however, we are dealing with a relation that is concerned with being as being in both the substantial and accidental orders. Such a relationship could suitably be indicated by the term "transcendental," i.e., applicable to all categories. Unfortunately, this terminology might cause confusion, for in Thomistic literature the term "transcendental relation" refers specifically to the relationship between the constituent principles of a concrete substance.

If the community of persons is studied one-sidedly by means of the univocal, upward approach through comparison with material categories, it is impossible to arrive at a correct understanding of community as a mode of being of persons. Such a sensistic approach would lead to one of two extremes because, in the univocal consideration, substance and relation are opposite categories. The first of these extremes is that the category of substance is given the central position, and relation that of an accessory factor. In the understanding of the person this view leads to one or the other form of solipsistic individualism, in which social being is viewed as an addition, albeit an important one, to personal being. This naturalistic philosophy of substance fails to do justice to the communicative being of the person. The second extreme attributes the primary position to the category of relation, conceived in a material fashion. Material things are now viewed as relative members of a larger unit. Attached as it is to this category of matter, this view conceives the community of persons as an organic or functional whole in which the persons are simply reduced to modalities, forms under which the community manifests itself. Such a naturalistic philosophy of function fails to do justice to the selfhood of the person. It leads to a collectivistic concept of society, in which the person is reduced to a mere subordinate part of the whole.

The mistake of such views is that the univocal categories of substance and relation are not transformed into analogous philosophical ideas by taking into consideration man's intuitive experience of the person. They neglect the downward analogous approach. In its Late Period scholasticism did not manage to break loose from the rationalistic categories of things, so that its outlook upon the metaphysical idea of being became obscured. For this reason the solidaristic theory of sociality continued to struggle laboriously with the categorical approach of social reality and exhausted itself in distinctions that seemed to be very profound but defied understanding. We will revert to this point in the following chapter.

6. *The Bodily Being of the Person*

Because we have approached man through comparison with the material world, the specific element of being-a-person has been sought primarily in the realm of the spirit. Through his spiritual being man transcends the spatio-temporal limitation and contrariety of the material world. The spirit in a way is everything. Man's knowing and loving being possesses a transcendental openness for, and an immediate identity with, the other subjects. Man, however, is an embodied person. He is essentially also material. The transcendental directedness of the spirit has always to be actuated from the standpoint of a here and now, from a determined situation in the spatio-temporal world. Man's immediate spiritual reciprocity and identity with his fellow-men, therefore, is at the same time characterized also by aspects of distance, of estrangement and opposition that are typical of the material world.

Spirit and Matter. The relationship of spirit and matter in man constitutes an age-old central problem of philosophy. Misconceptions of this relationship lead inevitably also to incorrect views about man's social being. While this is not the proper place to present a full picture of man's essential principles, we may offer the points that are important for the theme of man's being together with his fellow-men.

The conceptual objectifying approach speaks of spirit and matter. It compares the upper "layer" of being with the lower. Here especially it is of the greatest importance to keep in mind that human expressions are inadequate representations of reality. Our mode of understanding represents spirit and matter as two subsistent beings. Because of this logical distinction of spirit and body, the unity which man is, is easily conceived as a reconciliation of opposites. If this polarity of spirit and matter is assumed, the implied duality is overcome either by way of the spirit producing matter or by way of matter producing spirit. The actual result, however, is that both spirit and matter are degraded. The spirit suffers a loss in value if it is supposed to produce matter of necessity or to be a prolongation of matter. Matter loses its value as a distinct reality if it is produced by the spirit or if it itself produces the spirit. As producing the spirit, matter loses the proper character of its own reality because of its lack of relationship to the spirit. Accordingly, if one starts with the assumption of the opposition of spirit and matter, the balance swings precariously between idealism and materialism. The result is that man's social being vacillates between the extreme viewpoints of proud individualism and crude collectivism.

The Bi-Unity of Man. Philosophy may not start by presupposing the distinction of spirit and matter, for this distinction arises within the unity which human reality is. The duality in question reflects the imperfection of human identity. In philosophical thought the person reveals himself neither as pure unity nor as pure duality, but as a bi-unity. The univocal analytic vision which speaks of spirit-body needs to be corrected again by means of the analogous philosophical approach. In this way the logical clarification constitutes an

improper conceptual explicitation of a preceding intuitive experience of bi-unity. In the analogous consideration man, as
he is in reality, is not a pure spirit, but a spirit limited by his
bodily being, and on the other hand, man's bodily being receives
its value as a reality from the spirit. The human spirit is
essentially corporeal, but in such a way that, on the one hand,
it imparts itself to the body out of an abundance, while
retaining a certain independence relative to its embodied existence; but on the other hand, it remains bound up with the
body out of its own deficiency. The human body, likewise, is
both genuine matter and yet not ordinary but spiritualized
matter.

It is Thomism which provides us with the purest approach to the reality of man. In the view of this philosophy man
constitutes a unity consisting of a spiritual and a material
principle. The spiritual principle, as the form of prime matter, is called "soul." Thomism emphasizes that, although the
spirit is essentially the besouling principle of prime matter, it
is at the same time to a certain extent subsistent. Technically expressed, the human spirit is not merely a *principium quo*
but also in a way a *principium quod*. There is no adequate
distinction between spirit and body, for the body may not be
equated with prime matter. The body is prime matter insofar
as prime matter is already actuated to the level of bodily
essence through the soul as its formal principle. Nevertheless,
the imperfection of human understanding allows and even
forces us to speak of body and soul. For this reason one is
justified in using such expressions as "the spirit influences the
body" or "the body acts on the spirit." Of course, in the use
of similar expressions care should be taken not to lose sight of
the fact that conceptual knowledge tends to approach the bi-
unity of man by substantializing his constituent principles.
This substantialization, proper to the analytic approach,
needs to be corrected constantly by a return to our intuitive
experience of man.

7. *The Body and Interpersonal Contact*

The Embodied "I." The intermediary role of the body in
the contact between persons can be best clarified through Gabriel Marcel's analyses of the body. The French philosopher

asks himself the question whether I *have* my body or I *am* my body. In the proper sense of the term "having" I do not *have* my body, for the object of having reveals itself as an object that is "at a distance" from the subject. Man can dispose of it and discard it. But he is not able to dispose of his body or to renounce it without ceasing to be a man. The mysterious bond which unites me with my body is precisely the very root from which grow all my possibilities of having.

It is impossible likewise for me to say that I *am* my body. For, being a body, as such, is an estranged being-outside-itself: it cannot declare of itself that it is a body, it does not have any awareness. To identify the "I" with the body would mean that the "I" destroys itself.

To be embodied does not mean either to *have* one's body or to *be* one's body. I am unable either to distinguish myself from my body or to identify myself with it. The choice, however, between identification and distinction pertains to the world of objects. In the subject it is replaced by participation. The body participates in the spirit and, reversely, the spirit is incarnated in the body. The body constitutes a zone between *having* and *being*, in which there are all kinds of grades based upon more or less *having* or upon more or less *being*. In the coming to be of the person the body must constantly become more and more spiritualized, so that man attains to an ever-increasing unity with himself and consequently also with his fellow subjects.

Ambivalence of the Body. Because the spirit is embodied, the dialog of subjects takes place by means of man's bodily being. His body therefore possesses an ambivalent character. On the one hand, the body remains a material, biological factor, thus introducing aspects of distance, impenetrability, rivalry, etc. into the intersubjective encounter. On the other hand, because of its mysterious participation in the spirit, the body is raised from the sphere of *having* to the level of *being*, so that there is to some extent a possibility of immediate contact between subjects. Thus an element of immediacy penetrates into the indirect objective relationships with other subjects, so that there is nonetheless a contact of "spirit with spirit." This element of immediacy in the material forms of communication will increase according as a subject becomes more a person. In the coming to be of the person, the spirit, as it were, expresses itself in matter, spiritualizing it, so that the body manifests transparently the self-surrender of subject to subject. The absolute communication, however, of person to person remains for the embodied being, which man is, an ideal that is never fully reached in this life because man is unable fully to transfigure his body.

In the interpersonal contact of spirit with spirit the body's character is quasi-subjective or quasi-objective. The term "quasi-subjective" is justified insofar as the body is more considered as an instrument for acting upon and humanizing the material world. These two aspects, however, again imply each other, for self-expression to some extent is an acting on matter, and on the other hand, acting on matter itself is also a revelation of man's presence. The analogous view of philosophy sees human communication as an imperfect immediate reciprocity. In this way the mediate subject-object-subject relationship is not so much a positive element as an indication that human reciprocity is imperfect and of an intentional character.

8. *Personal Community and Functional Society*

It is the task of the positive social sciences to determine as closely as possible the various categories of human coexistence. Sciences such as sociology and social psychology have the duty to construct a typology to make it easier to understand the manifold forms of social structures. These sciences endeavor, on the one hand, to clarify the concrete forms of society by means of general basic types and, on the other, to deduce these basic types from the concrete forms. This inductive and deductive approach on the level of univocity is proper to science.

The aim, however, of social philosophy is different. It attempts to unfold the ethical ideal of being authentically a person. It places itself on the viewpoint of absolute togetherness in its perfection. Man has an implicit intuitive idea of such an absolute togetherness. But this analogous potential idea becomes actual only through his intentional approach

from actually existing and univocally conceived forms of sociality. For this reason social philosophy does not have to
present an exhaustive panorama of the various forms which
the "we" assumes. It takes its starting point in a few privileged general forms of community to explicitate the implicit
concrete-universal ideal of co-existence.

*Differences Between the Personal Community and the
Functional Society.* Personalistic philosophy sees the privileged starting point in the distinction between the personal community and the functional society, the community of being
and the society of work. The community of persons is that
type of being-together in which the spiritual aspect of love
stands in the foreground, while the work society is primarily
based upon the material and bodily structure of man. We
may point out the following differences, which logically flow
from the distinction of body and spirit. In the functional
society the interrelationship is business-like and dominated by
the work that is to be performed. I seek the other and the
other seeks me to attain together an external purpose or
object. The other person, therefore, can be replaced by a
third if the latter is capable of the same performance or able
to fulfill the function in a suitable fashion. The objective goal
to be reached is the reason why persons enter into relation
with one another in the functional society. They are unable
to reach this goal separately because of their bodily needs or
limitations and, for this reason, business-like reasons make
them constitute a collaborating unit.

In the personal community, on the other hand, the relationships are of a personal nature. I do not seek the other
out of self-interest and for this or that objective motive, but
for his own sake, because of disinterestedness without any
ulterior motives. I do not address myself to the other in a
mediate way because of a purpose to be reached, but go out
to him immediately for his own sake, seeking him for what he
himself is, so that he is irreplaceable for me.

In the functional society the relationship to the other
person has an external character, so that it is possible to
speak here of "having" or "possessing" a relation to the other.
In the personal community, on the other hand, the relation-

ship is wholly internal. It is so internal that I do not even
have this relation but *am* it. Through this orientation to the
other I am myself.

The functional society lies in the order of collaboration,
of exchange of services. The personal community, however, is
an existential community and lies in the sphere of disinterested being-together, and not in that of a solidarity of interests.
Yet this logical analytic view has to be corrected at once by
means of a synthetic consideration. The difference in question should be viewed as a distinction in an analogous sense
within the unity—imperfect though it may be—of human
communication. Personal contact remains formless unless it
be embodied in action for a purpose. Reversely, the exchange
of services and functions remains a form of personal dialog.
In the analogous consideration the functional society points
especially to the imperfect state of human togetherness. To
the extent that such a society possesses ethical value, it
participates already in the encounter of spirits. Human collaboration is a being-together of persons in their coming to be and
a coming to be of persons in their togetherness. While we are on
the way to being a community of persons, we are already a
community of persons.

9. *The Person in Reference to the Absolute Person*

*Finite Persons in Relationship to the Transcendent Per-
son.* As we have seen in the preceding considerations, the
relationship to the other revealed itself as co-constituent of
the person. Nevertheless, one person does not constitute the
other in his entire being, for such an assertion would contra-
dict the supplementary character of personal reciprocity. The
reciprocal constitution, which arises from the finiteness of
beings, demands that there be something which is supplemented and something which supplements. On the personal level
this means that there always remains the otherness of one
person with respect to another, no matter how profound their
"we" becomes, even if nothing at all in man escapes from it.
The most profound intimacy knows moments of mutual
strangeness—just as anyone is also to some extent a stranger
for himself. The reason is that the unity of intersubjectivity
always remains imperfect, even though it is capable of being

infinitely perfected. As a finite person, man does not wholly create his own self and in a similar way persons do not wholly constitute each other.

In higher forms of self-realization persons experience their own self, and consequently also their being-together, more and more as a gift which it is their task to perfect. It is precisely in his most personal attitude of being, which is at the same time a dialog *par excellence*, that man comes to his most profound recognition of an absolute, transcendent Person. Every person, as a self and as communication, refers to the Infinite as to his more profound and truer self, his more intimate and truer communication. The ultimate meaning of the person as a self-in-communication lies only in his final surrender to God. The more man becomes a person, the more profoundly and intimately he experiences this bond with the infinite Person. God is more intimate to me than I am to myself and to the other. At the same time, however, this profound immanent knowledge reveals to man that God is transcendent in the most absolute and perfect sense of the term.

Certainty of God. That there is a God can neither be strictly demonstrated nor even denied in the way positive science proceeds. As we have seen in Chapter Two, I am certain of the existence of my fellow-man through my inter-subjective surrender to him and any "proof" of the other's existence presupposes this certainty. In an analogous fashion the proof that there is a God presupposes a religious element in man. Such a proof is not so much a demonstration leading to a certain conclusion as an inadequate manifestation of a preceding religious certainty. On the other hand, as we have seen in the same chapter, I may endeavor to prove the trust-worthiness of one of my fellow-men and become certain of it on the basis of reasonable grounds. In an analogous way it may be proved likewise that there is a God.

This rational certainty, however, is overshadowed by the suprarational certainty I have of God in the religious surren-der through which I recognize God as a truly more immanent and higher Thou. Through proofs I am able to arrive only at a relative trustworthiness of a fellow-man in my dealings with him, but not at the absolute certainty that I can trust him in all circumstances of life. In a similar way, the more the demonstrations of God assume a "scientific" character, the more they lead to a rather impersonal admission of an impersonally known absolute reality.

Accordingly, man's being together with fellow-men implies an absolute attitude, receptive of being, with respect to God; but this being-relative also is marked by constant coming to be. Man's togetherness with his fellow-men has the task to realize an ever more profound union with God.

It is beyond the scope of this book to describe the roads leading to greater union with God. For our present purpose we may be satisfied with the acceptance of the absolute Thou, thanks to whom man is concreatively able to perfect his own being and that of the others. Within the framework of this book we merely want to unfold man's intersubjective experience. Nevertheless, it will constantly be evident that understanding of the human "we" is possible only through the illuminating force of the absolute Thou, of which all human understanding is a conscious participation.

10. *Conclusion*

In this chapter we have endeavored to render the philosophical insight into the person more profound by comparing personal reality with the material order. We made use of the more mediate ascending approach, clarifying the analogous view by means of the univocal consideration. Although the univocity of the categories of things was rendered less rigid, so that these categories could be analogously applied to the personal sphere, the analogy in question was mainly the logical analogy of attribution, allowing us to understand the higher by means of the lower, functioning as the "primary" analogate. This approach was chosen for methodic reasons, because of the imperfection of human knowledge. It needs to be purified. The univocal consideration in its turn has to be clarified from the standpoint of the analogous intuitive view, i.e., the logical analogy of attribution must be rendered more profound through metaphysical analogy. This procedure constitutes the meaningful circular process of philosophical reflection. In the following chapter the concrete and integral intuition of the person will have to find a transparent expression in our concepts. The descending analogous view will reveal the deficiency of the more univocal approach, which does not quite go to the essence of the person as person. Now that we are at the end of the upward approach, we realize that we are still standing at the very beginning of our attempt to understand the person. The acquired understanding is neither more nor less than "learned ignorance." Everything has to be considered again from the analogous approach. However, even at the end of the descending analogous approach new perspectives will reveal themselves inviting us to another, circular process. For such is the endless but meaningful movement to and fro of philosophical reflection.

CHAPTER FOUR

THE MYSTERY OF BEING-TOGETHER-IN-THE-WORLD

1. *Introduction*

Intersubjectivity, interpersonal community, remains a sign of contradiction for objectifying thought. The being-together of subjects has to be expressed all the time in paradoxical statements. Their distinction means their unity, and their unity is their distinction. In the intersubjective realm the unity of the community is at the same time the plurality of the persons, and the plurality of the persons is the unity of the community. The persons are equal to one another in inequality but also unequal in equality. To be oneself means to be the other, and to be the other is to be oneself. Personal freedom is a bond, and the bond is personal freedom. Personal love is attachment in detachment as well as detachment in attachment. The spiritual incommunicability of the person is precisely his communicability, and his spiritual communicability is his incommunicability.

Such paradoxical statements need not deter us from accepting intersubjectivity as a reality. Spiritual being is not an "object of knowledge," and for this reason cannot be seized immediately by an empirical syllogistic demonstration. It is by means of the integral human attitude, which demands more an ethical than a rationalistically-theoretical mentality, that one comes to the recognition of the mystery of interhuman encounter—a mystery that invites man to penetrate ever more profoundly into its wealth of meaning. Personal intuition realizes that rigid conceptual logic is not immediately applicable to the metalogical order of intersubjectivity. It is only from the standpoint of "lived" intersubjectivity that concepts may exercise their conceiving functions. In this descending approach their univocity is clarified through analogy. Of course, the approach is not wholly successful, for personal intuition needs the univocal concept also as a cognitive means. Nevertheless, it constantly endeavors to overcome the limitation proper to the concept.

In this chapter we will speak from the viewpoint of love. The more one goes to the encounter of his fellow-men, the more he will see everything through the eyes of love—more clearly even than we will express it in the following pages. The emphasis in this chapter will fall upon metaphysical analogy, in which the primary analogate is seen in spiritual perfection. The logical analogy of attribution, however, again cannot be discarded here, but the meaning of its images will remain oriented to the immediate intersubjective insight, which is constantly rendered more profound by the growing truth of love.

2. *The Transcendental "We"*

"I" and "You" are "We." From the very beginning of his existence man is in communication. Isolated man is neither the starting point nor the terminus. At most, in the abstract order one could speak of man as an isolated whole. Concretely, however, to say "man" is to say "fellow-man." Being a subject is an open dialog of the spirit. The person becomes genuinely an "I" only when he discovers the other as a "you," and together they constitute the "we." Even the monk who freely withdraws from the company of his fellow-men is an "I" only because of the absent "you." The stronger the we-relationship is, the more profound also the I-you-relation, and vice versa. The growing we-intimacy strengthens precisely the uniqueness of the persons. It is not at all a process of social levelling. On the personal level the distinction is rendered even more profound through the unity of the persons. While in the realm of matter distinction is primarily based upon being spatially alongside and outside one another, on the personal level it is growth of love for the other person which increasingly emphasizes the other's distinction and his freedom. As Madinier expresses it very succinctly, "To love is to will the other as a subject." In the interpersonal contact of the spirit the most intimate unity evokes the deepest distinction and, reversely, the deepest distinction evokes the highest unity. Intersubjectivity means the most profound unity in perfect "twoness," so that, in the words of Nédoncelle, one could speak here of a "heterogeneous identity."

When the positive social sciences speak of togetherness, they are always concerned with one or the other particular form of being-together. This situation is connected with the character of empirical thinking, which finds its object in the actually existing structure of being-together. Solidaristic thought which is too much colored by rationalism sees human togetherness as embodied primarily in "natural" groups, such as the state and the family. In this sense the personal community is not natural and real, i.e., it is not determined in a concrete material way. The intersubjective "we" is not an objective fact but escapes all efforts to objectify it. We may say in this context that it is meta-real, meta-concrete. The personal community is a transcendental "we"; it constitutes the very condition making any social objectification possible and makes every actual social structure have a social meaning. The personal "we" is not strictly an object of knowledge: it cannot be abstracted as a "thing." It is much more a kind of existential orientation within which the social phenomenon can appear as an object of inquiry.

The Primordial "We." The situation of the "we" is exactly like that of the human "I," because the "I" in its plenitude is the "we." The entire mystery of the person lies contained in the "I." The "I," however, cannot be understood in an objectifying way, it cannot be mastered as an object. True, one can make an attempt to "catch" the inalienable "I" by attempting to seize it thetically as an object. Nevertheless, it is precisely the "I" which lies behind any attempt to objectify the "I" and makes such an attempt possible. The "I" can merely be "pointed to," and only as a subject which is never an object. Thinking along the lines of things in this matter implies the risk of unwittingly conceiving the "I" as a datum of nature, as a thing, and of losing sight of its creative freedom and orientation. Accordingly, just as the person remains a self-determining and primordial "I," so also the communal "we" does not constitute a datum of "nature," but is a free ethical initiative, which can never be definitely described and outlined.

This primordial "we" gives meaning and direction to every objective "we," just as all human behavior receives its meaning from the "I" which accompanies and permeates it. The person does not know himself in an objective vision, but in his existential going forth to the other as a "you" he finds the mystery of his own being reflected in the other. Or rather, by means of their reciprocal dialog the persons discover the "we," i.e., the ideal "I" and "you." The highest form of self-knowledge arises from the most intimate knowledge of each other. Self-confidence increases through confidence in the "we" as in a more profound self. The most radical form of self-negation consists in denying the "you" of the other, in denying that I and the other are "we."

3. *The Mystery of Person and Community and*

   the Problem of Person and Society

The question whether the person is subordinate to the group or the group to the person is a meaningless problem when we approach man on a personalistic level. Such a question would amount to asking whether the "I' is subordinate to the "I." The unity of human co-existence cannot be expressed in an abstractly universal concept but only in an analogously universal idea. Each man is the original realization not of the logical concept of a species but of the philosophical idea of a species.

The Distinction of Individual and Person. It is sometimes asserted that the individual is for the sake of the group, but not so the person. In other words, a distinction is made in man between person and individual. Such a distinction, however, gives rise to much confusion. When man is called an individual, it often happens that two modes of viewing man intrude upon each other—namely the logical view and the metaphysical view. In metaphysics individuality is conceived as a transcendental property of being, so that the more a being is, the more it is individual, the more it is itself. In man, therefore, being-individual and being-person are identical. When there is question of species and individual in this sense, it is concerned with the concrete universality of the idea of the species, of which each person is a total realization with an original content.

"Individual," however, can also be viewed as a logical concept in relation to the logical category of species. In this case it is a numerical repetition of a specific concept obtained through abstraction from the differences. There is question here of the material individual, which because of the limiting principle of matter does not fully realize the specific determination. Insofar as attention is directed especially to man's material being, the logical consideration of individuals pertaining to the same species is not wholly misplaced. However, precisely in his spiritual being man is not a sample of the species but, comparatively speaking, rather his own species, i.e., he realizes being-man in an irreplaceable way.

The view which distinguishes between person and individual and declares that man as a person is above the group, endeavors to clarify the social character of man by means of the species-individual structure in the logical sense of the term. It seeks to explain man's social orientation through the participation of all human individuals in the same universal nature. In this way the individuals become limited, fragmentary realizations of this universal "human nature." In such a view, placing the accent upon the social character of man would suggest that the ideal would be the greatest possible similarity of the same uniform human nature and the obliteration of the individual distinction. In an effort to avoid such a levelling collectivism, philosophers who adhere to this view deliberately emphasize the individual participation in human nature. However, because the individual as such is limited, man's social character is reduced to a mere reciprocal need and its satisfaction, achieved by means of the diversity of specialized skills and functions.

Such a philosophy reduces man's being-together with his fellow-men to a mere problem, devoid of any mystery, which it endeavors to solve by means of laborious distinctions. Thinking abstractly on the basis of the logical species-individual structure, it bears the character of a compromise and fluctuates between the extremes of infrapersonal and anonymous uniformity and diversity. The unity and plurality of beings as persons do not receive any consideration, but in their stead man's personal and social being is viewed only on the functional level of common objective goals.

It is easy to understand why such a one-sidedness prevailed in the theory of solidarism, the philosophy which in its classical form adhered to this view. For solidarism arose in the period of rationalism and attempted to find arguments, which at the time could be judged to be solid, in favor of a more Christian position than the systems of individualism and collectivism. Our critique of solidarism, therefore, does not intend to belittle the great merits of its originators. Nevertheless, it remains true that the relation of person and group cannot be solved on the level of functional tendencies to a common purpose. In this respect the philosophy in question presents an unbalanced picture. Against individualism it emphasizes the social nature of man but, on the other hand, to avoid the trap of collectivism, it maintains that man's being is not fully encompassed by being-social.

Personalistic Approach to Person and Group. The problem of person and group on the functional level of objective purposes is transcended as a mystery when it is approached from the standpoint of intersubjectivity. From the viewpoint of intersubjective love, being a person and being social do not mean tension but just the opposite. In the dialog of subjects loving surrender dispels the fear of loss. This personalistic *idea* of community has nothing to do with collectivism, for personal being-together transcends the social character proper to the state. The state represents only a lower form of human togetherness and consequently may not lay claim to the entire person or man's entire social nature.

A philosophical view which uses the logical method in a one-sided fashion endeavors to understand man's social being by means of presupposed schemata, such as part and whole, organism, and unity of order, which are borrowed from the material world. The mistake of such a univocal procedure appears immediately from this that the part is fully subordinated to the whole and that the organ, if need be, must be sacrificed for the sake of the organism. The person, on the other hand, implies something ultimate in his freedom, so that he may never be reduced to, or sacrificed for the whole as its subordinate part. Moreover, the person is wholly the community in a way that makes it impossible to replace him. It is not from a presupposed concept of whole and parts, but from the unique personal bond, that the ideas of whole and parts must be enriched and rendered more profound in an analogous way. Starting from intersubjectivity, the concept of organism has to be changed into the idea of a mystical body.

The fact that the mysterious community of love realizes the unity of the persons does not mean that there remain no longer any *problems* of society. The philosophical "solution" of the social question does not render superfluous the task of the positive social sciences. Every human group will always have its social problems because strengthening collective unity on the functional level will leave less scope for its members, just as enlarging this scope will weaken the unity. This competing opposition of unity and scope, which has its cause in the incommunicability of matter, makes itself most strongly felt in groups characterized by external interrelationships. The more profoundly, however, being-together embodies itself in working-together, the more this opposition originating in man's bodily being changes into the heterogeneous identity of the personal community. The zealous search of the social sciences for a solution of the social problems finds its explanation in the mystery of love. On the other hand, it is precisely this mysterious love which formulates social problems as sharply as possible and which is deeply concerned with their scientific solution.

4. *The Dialog of the Subjects as Giving and Receiving*

The encounter in intersubjectivity does not take place to provide for a need or to remedy a deficiency. It does not arise from a material limitation or restriction but from the wealth and abundance of the spirit. A deficiency can be remedied only if the gift which removes it becomes the exclusive property of the recipient. But in the spiritual dialog that which is received continues to be "the giver's." A clear illustration is provided by the gift offered as an expression of intersubjective giving. The gift, as a material object, is entirely at the disposal of the recipient; but it would cease to be a gift, i.e., expression of spiritual giving, if the recipient would no longer consider it to be "the giver's." The gift is mine because I am yours, it is ours because we are "each other's."

Moreover, in intersubjective giving and receiving the emphasis does not lie on the giving of "something," but on giving "oneself" totally, so that the one subject is "of" and "in" the other. If this "giving of oneself" were to provide for a shortage suffered by the other subject, then the latter would make the self-giving subject his exclusive property. That would mean the end of the giver, for he would cease to be considered as a subject.

The profound difference between giving and receiving in the dialog of subjects as compared with that in the economic sphere of objects and services reveals itself strikingly also in another respect. The realm of economics is governed by the law of material opposition: receiving a service is distinct from delivering its equivalent or compensation. The two activities involved are different. In the intersubjective communication, however, my acceptance of the other's self-surrender means precisely my own loving surrender to him. I receive the other's *self*-communication only by giving *myself*. The giver, on the other hand, really gives himself only through his willingness wholly to receive the other. While in the material order giving and receiving appear to be distinct, on the personal level giving is at the same time receiving and receiving is giving. The characteristic feature of being-together as distinction in identity manifests itself again clearly here. Receiving reveals itself as givingly to receive, and giving manifests itself as receivingly to give.

We can see here again how defective the intentional clarification of the mystery of intersubjectivity is. It seems almost a juggling with concepts. Intersubjectivity must not be tested through preconceived univocal giving and receiving, but it is from the standpoint of the original being-together of "I" and "you" that the concepts of giving and receiving must be broadened into analogous ideas. Yet, as appeared from the preceding paragraphs, the analogous consideration cannot dispense with univocity. Univocity and analogy ultimately constitute an unbreakable bi-unity.

Personal Giving and Receiving in Daily Life. Because of man's embodied being, personal giving and receiving, which is the very essence of encounter, permeates all kinds of activities that are directed toward usefulness and service. Personal love manifests itself especially as an accompanying value in the care exercised for one another's life. The "we" is not directly known as an object but only indirectly as the driving force of human actions. The simple activities of everyday life are constantly illuminated by flashes of intersubjective giving and receiving. For this reason it is possible to point out such intimate personal contact in simple examples of daily life.

When, for example, on the occasion of a feast people give presents to one another, the dominating idea is not to see to it that the gift fills a need of the other. The main point is the *deed* of giving, through which I give myself to the other. The present, as a material expression, symbolizes this spiritual donation. The true gift is I myself; it is my own intimate self-surrender that is exteriorized in a material present. If my gift were rejected by the recipient with the remark that he "has" already the object in question, I would justly feel deeply insulted, because the remark would show that the lofty meaning embodied in the gift is disregarded. If, on the other hand, I would use the occasion to present the other with a gift which makes him dependent upon me, he would hate me for it. For in this way the act of giving becomes a refined attempt against what is most sacred and proper to the other—his freedom. If, on the other hand, the recipient accepts the present without genuine gratitude, i.e., without giving himself, he reveals that he is interested in the present itself and not in the giver. He grossly depreciates the personal value of the other and is willing to sell his freedom for the material object he has received.

Another example may serve to emphasize personal depth. When an event of importance happens to someone, he will hurry to let the person or persons he loves know about it, even if he knows that the news in question has already reached them from another source. Precisely because my friend knows about it from someone else, I will hasten to tell him about it in person. The fact that I write to him does not serve merely to inform him of the event, nor would my friend be satisfied with simply hearing the news about me. I myself want to tell him about it and my friend wants to hear it from me. From the viewpoint of news value, my action in this matter is useless, for the other knows already all about it. But the event provides an opportunity for contact which embodies our personal community.

In everyday life we constantly perform actions which, from the viewpoint of usefulness and efficiency, appear uneconomical and irrational. If, for instance, I pass the salt to my dinner companion, the important point is not the trivial object in question, which the guest could perhaps have reached just as easily himself. But through this simple gesture I express my personal respect. When, next, at his departure I help him into his coat, my action is altogether out of place from the viewpoint of efficiency, for it would cost him less trouble to put it on alone. But the simple gesture serves again to confirm his personal presence to me.

Intersubjective intimacy permeates all kinds of daily little cares. It expresses itself in the most trivial occupations because it is so sublime. It makes use of humor and of gentle mockery because it is sincere and serious. It expresses itself in foolish behavior because it is so sublime. It is artless because it presents the most profound explanation of reality. Personal love expresses itself in a matter-of-fact and simple fashion because it is so ideal and spontaneous.

5. *Bodily Being as Colloquy*

The "we" is not directly known as an object but rather indirectly as a concomitant aspect of human behavior. It is necessary to dwell somewhat upon the way intersubjectivity is embodied. The embodiment of the "I" will be touched here only insofar as it is directed toward the immediate presence of the other. Through his bodily being man is also in relation with the world. The body, therefore, mediates also between me and the *world* of the other, but this aspect will be considered later. At present we are concerned with the quasi-subjectivity of bodily being insofar as it makes the "I" appear without appearing itself.

The Body as Intermediary in Encounter. It may be said that the body acts as intermediary in the encounter with the other, at least if one keeps in mind that such an expression is deficient. The human body is not a thing used by the "I" to enter into relation with the other. There is question here only of *my* body or of *his* body, the body of a person. From this viewpoint the body reveals itself as expression of the "I." Only when this bodily being has been experienced, is it possible to consider the body as object. As expressive center of the "I," the body can never be fully objectified. We will refer to this body as bodily being.

The intimate spiritual "I" does not lie behind bodily being as behind a screen. One's exterior is not an impenetrable nature, a fence, over which one has to look to discover a person's interior. I do not know my fellow-man in his spiritual intimacy by means of a kind of analogous reasoning process. I do not conclude that he is a fellow-man on the basis of the fact that I perceive in him the same kind of behavior as in myself. Likewise, it is not a question of empathy, through which I can enter feelingly into the behavior of the other and penetrate to him. All such attempts presuppose that I first know the other in his external behavior and then only can penetrate into his interior. They introduce a dualistic separation between spirit and bodily being. Moreover, unwittingly, such procedures posit one's own "I" first and from there descend to his fellow-men.

But the inner life of man reveals itself immediately in his external behavior. We may even say that this inner life "is" the external behavior. The person exists as such only in his bodily being. As experience shows, after a personal encounter it is often difficult to give a description of the other's exterior. The personal dialog makes man, as it were, blind to the other's external appearance. Only in the first inquiring contact is the other observed and scrutinized in his external behavior for clues leading to his interiority. Bodily being, however, participates intrinsically in the spirit, so that in intimate encounter even the other's bodily ugliness becomes beautiful and attractive. When love is genuine, everything of the beloved is permeated with his personal irreplaceability. In the eyes of the loving person even the bodily defects of the beloved receive a special attractiveness, because they express in a typical way the uniqueness and the irreplaceability of the other person who is not like everyone else.

A human being is immediately present to the other and unconcealed for him.   This immediacy is the primordial datum.   Any distinction into the interiority and the exteriority of the other or of myself is to be made only from the starting point of this total human presence to each other.   Such a distinction indicates the imperfection and the resultant opposition within the one human co-existence.   However, if this unity is not lost sight of, it is possible and permissible to speak about the influence of the interior upon the exterior and vice versa.

The Symbolism of External Behavior.   The external behavior of a man as a manifestation of his interior is a special kind of sign.   An ordinary sign is based upon an agreement. We have agreed, for example, to consider a red light as a signal of danger. In this kind of sign there is a more or less extrinsic bond between the sign and that which it signifies.   One knows the sign first and only through it, that for which it stands. Moreover, such a sign always intends to indicate "something."   The external behavior, however, of man evidently signifies his internal life in a much more profound fashion.   There is an intrinsic bond here between the sign and that which it signifies. A smile, for example, is not used as an agreed signal to express happiness, but is this happiness itself in the way of a smile.   We have to do here with a so-called formal sign, in which that which is signified is perceived first and the sign itself only subsequently and indirectly.   To express it more precisely, this sign does not express happiness but the happy human being.   Bodily being does not function here in its quasi-objectivity as an instrument, but in its quasi-subjectivity as expression.   To use another example, what is important is not the meaning of the words but that it is "you" who speaks. Here the words make the "I" appear without appearing themselves.   True, human behavior can also be directed to something, and in this case the person appears through his behavior as someone who is actively occupied with something. Behavior here becomes a purposive action, by means of which man wants to attain something. Bodily being, however, as the immediate manifestation of persons to each other, is not directed to anything. Though expressive, it is not a purposive action. Through it, the person does not aim at anything but is present to the other. The expression is not a declaration that I love the other, but I love him in the expression. Such an encounter transcends the materiality and mediating character of bodily being.

The profound incarnation of interpersonal contact, compared with bodily quasi-objectivity, is not really an action which the person does either deliberately or unwittingly. It is much more the person himself. Here, too, however, an immediate correction is necessary, for even in its quasi-subjectivity bodily being still retains something of the purposive action. Mutual self-revelation always has to take place by means of "something." For this reason communication will be most immediate if it comes about with a minimum of action. For loving togetherness each other's presence suffices, and speech, which always communicates "something," is a substitute for immediacy. Lovers know how intimately persons can be present to each other in a conversation which says "nothing" and therefore is meaningful. Or, to use another example, in the face of the other's intense grief or deep happiness my words sound hollow and empty, while my silence is much more eloquent than any words. Yet even this eloquent silence harms the encounter and remains ambiguous if it is not respectfully broken by a sign of sympathy, such as a simple hand shake.

Bodily being, as expressive, is often called a symbol. Symbols, it is said, are material but express spiritual realities and values from within, which makes them intermediaries for participation. Gurvitch very succinctly expresses the ambivalent character of these symbols by stating that they deliver their content while veiling it and veil it while they deliver it. They deliver their content while veiling it, i.e., external behavior reveals the spiritual "I" immediately; but as bodily expression it remains at the same time a veil because the exterior can never communicate the entire intimacy of the "I." They veil their content while they deliver it, i.e., bodily being is only an external manifestation and therefore leaves the interior covered with a veil; but at the same time, as interiorized exteriority, it lays bare the inner life of the soul. The concealment is possible only on the basis of the unconcealment.

The sense of shame likewise indicates that the person experiences his bodily being as interiorized exteriority. A person reacts with shame when the other gazes at him only in his exteriority and considers this aspect his only value. A man feels attacked in his honor if he is valued only on the basis of his external impersonal achievements. He feels misjudged if he is looked at as an object of curiosity. Pointing a finger at someone is considered impolite because a person is not something to be discussed but someone with whom one is. Physical shame does not mean that the body, even the naked body, is impure, but that man feels shocked if he is looked at and desired as a mere object. The opposite of this form of shame is exhibitionism, which makes one want to appear to the other only as an object. Accordingly, the play of vesting and divesting oneself may manifest a revolting obscenity, namely, if a man wants to be merely a body for the other but, on the other hand, it may be also an intimate and subtle way of being together in a genuinely human fashion.

The originality of the "I" is participated in not only by external behavior but even by the objects which a man uses personally. These things share in the irreplaceability of the person. Gifts, for example, are not replaceable material objects, but constitute, as it were, embodiments of the person. They can no longer be expressed in terms of money and are not for sale. When a beloved person dies, the objects of everyday use that have served him for many years are not sold but kept as memories or given away. Even the deceased body, to which the law of matter applies so strongly, still retains traces of spiritualization. It is not without reason that we speak of the serenity and majesty of death.

Ambivalence of Bodily Being. Yet bodily being as a uniting colloquy remains also a constant contradiction, in the literal sense of this term. It unites but also separates the "I's" of the persons, and does not escape from the fundamental ambiguity of all intermediaries. Mutual understanding, therefore, is never perfect, and misunderstanding is always present.

The eminence of the symbol goes hand in hand with its abject poverty. The "loving we" is also a "fighting we." In the world of the other my words are often misunderstood. Everyone experiences that he is unable to give full expression to his inner feelings for the other and that he has to guess about the feelings of those whom he loves. It often even happens that I do not fully understand the scope of my own words. A loving word says either too much or not enough. When I declare that I love you, my words are too empty to convey my inner feelings about you. But if someone is very liberal with declarations of love, does he really love? Do not the words, "I love you," imply a promise of total self-surrender? Is it not fitting, then, that I be filled with a holy awe at the idea of pronouncing the word of love?

Intersubjective encounter constantly endeavors to pierce through the everydayness of human contact. It invents new attentions, unexpected by the beloved person. It confers a fresh meaning upon the most ordinary words. Yet man has all the time to resign himself to merely being able to point toward the ineffable.

There exists also a possibility that one will make use of bodily ambiguity to conceal himself and to profit from the resulting misunderstanding. Such a man makes his behavior a mask enabling him to appear different from what he is. How often, for instance, do people converse merely to avoid the eloquent silence of personal communication! Even speech itself, which is destined for the other, can degenerate into an egoistic dialog with oneself if one speaks merely to be heard. It is possible for someone to plunge into all kinds of social activities to avoid genuine social surrender. Such a social flight may sometimes mean a flight from authentic being-together.

The most subtle expressions of love are capable of becoming veritable incarnations of the greatest hatred and aversion. Because of the fundamental ambivalence of human existence, marriage, in which there is the greatest possibility of giving oneself in all respects, offers also an opportunity for manifesting the most bitter enmity. When a fellow human being is used only as an object of lust, he or she is humiliated more profoundly than a slave. For, a slave suffers indignity insofar as he is valued only because of his bodily strength, but in the present case the entire human person through his whole bodily being is misused as a mere object.

Correction of One-sidedness.   The foregoing considerations contain a certain one-sidedness.   The explicitation of bodily being as colloquy could create the impression that I, as a monad, address myself to you in your monadic existence. Too much emphasis has been placed upon the distinction between the "I" and the "you" and too little attention has been paid to the unity of the "we."   This consequence followed inevitably from the necessity of using language whose expressiveness is directly geared to understanding through distinctions.   Strictly speaking, everything would have to be envisioned a second time from the standpoint of the unity proper to the "we."   I do not reveal myself to the other, and he does not reveal himself to me, but the "we" reveals itself also to us.   I do not really love the other, and he does not really love me, but the "we" loves us.   However, after reaching the end of such an explicitation in which everything would be considered from the standpoint of the unity, we would have to start all over again because meanwhile the distinction of the "I" and the "you" would have become too vague.   There is no escape from the imperfection inherent in man's abstract understanding.   The difficulty makes itself felt even more here because we are endeavoring to present a "treatise" of social reality, so that we have to use prose instead of poetry. It should be possible for the philosopher to abandon his scientific reserve and to give free rein to his poetic aspirations.

6.   *The World as Human Togetherness*

Bodily being is never known directly as an object by the "I," but is known indirectly and concomitantly as the spiritual-material accompaniment of the world of objects. This world we may call peripheral bodily being. Man becomes aware of bodily being concomitantly with his conscious contact with his surroundings.   One becomes conscious, for example, of the living eye, of seeing, by looking at an object, i.e., at something else.   In seeing the object I am aware also that I see the object. Bodily being reveals itself to me through contact with my environment. One could say: there is no self-consciousness without body-consciousness, and there is no body-consciousness without consciousness of the environment or the world. However, such a trichotomy remains an artificial distinction of the person as a single conscious orientation-in-the-world.

My body is the point at which the world and my own self meet. On the one hand, bodily being belongs to the side of the subject which I am and is permeated with subjectivity. My own eyes do not belong to the visible world, but it is they which make the world visible. My living hands do not pertain to the touchable world, but it is they which make the world touchable. On the other hand, bodily being is something of the world. It is intentionality, i.e., essentially directed and related to the world; but the subject *exists*, stands out toward the world and is attached to it, yet it is also in the world, estranged from itself.

Human Milieu and Biological Environment. In objectifying thought the human body appears as matter, albeit spiritualized matter. The body is also a "nature," in the precise sense of "givenness." From the very start man finds himself equipped with a certain body. He is thrown into a certain bodily way of being. Phenomenologists speak in this connection of facticity and situation. Through his bodily being man is situated in spatio-temporal surroundings; he is anchored, as it were, in given situations, which constitute his facticity. The whole of the situations in which man finds himself could be called his "milieu" (*Umwelt*). This human world should not be one-sidedly conceived as a kind of biological environment, such as animals have. The animal knows very well how to go about in its organic environment. True, the human world contains also aspects of such an environment. Man, for example, does not feel at home if too many changes are made in his surroundings and thus prevent him from grasping the whole of the situations. One may instinctively experience that something has been changed in the environment and only subsequently discover what it is.

Nevertheless, it would be a gross mistake to identify the world of man with a biological environment. The animal's environment constitutes a closed world. The animal experiences itself only as fitting into its environment and this environment itself as wholly adapted to its own biological nature. It is fully encompassed by a network of determinations. Man's milieu, however, is an open world because it participates in the spirit. The human world is never finished, but lies in the sphere of a task to be done. Man is more than a biological adaptation to an environment; he is rather the point from which the material world derives its orientation and meaning. It is precisely the facticity of man that implies the possibility of a project. Man does not merely *find* himself in the world but he also *goes out* into the world; he is not merely *thrown* into the world but also *makes a project* of it. The world of man is never merely given *nature*, in the sense of determinateness, but also always *culture*, which reveals man's presence in the world. The human world is an undivided bi-unity of the world of nature and culture.

Unity of Man and World. Man and world together constitute a unity through their mutual implication. Being-in-the-world does not mean a sheer spatial addition to my being-man. The original spatial meaning of "in" has to be understood here in a very analogous fashion. It indicates a dimension of man that belongs to his very essence. Man is what he is in the world. He is "worldly" to the innermost depth of his being. Reversely, the world itself is permeated with humanity. It belongs to man as a human realm of presence. As Jaspers expresses it very succinctly, "There is no 'I'-less world and no worldless 'I.' "

It is impossible to conceive man as existing first in himself and then as making contact with the world. Reversely, there is no possibility of an encounter with the world of nature because every human contact with the world deprives this world of its purely physical character and changes it into culture. The world is to be understood neither in a subjectivistic nor in an objectivistic sense. The naive realistic view envisions the world as a reality independent of man. The idealistic view considers man as pure subjectivity, which arbitrarily gives meaning to the world. Both views, however, are

victims of one-sidedness.   Human subjectivity is exteriorized
in a spatio-temporal world, no matter how much it constantly
transcends this world through its existence as giver of meanings.   The world, on the other hand, is related to the subject
without, however, being entirely constituted by human subjectivity.   The world subsists, but as the counter-pole of human
reality.   As a knowable and manipulable counter-reality, the
world requires a special kind of encounter in which, however,
it does not wholly surrender its material strangeness.

The Meaning of the World.   The world is, as it were, a
further embodiment of nature by man.   Man gives meaning to
the world, so that this world always appears in a certain
perspective to me.   The human world constitutes a horizon of
meaning, within whose orientation things present themselves
meaningfully.   Here, too, one could ask the question, *Am* I my
world or do I *have* my world?   The reply can only be that the
human world lies between the zones of being and having.
Just as bodily being cannot be immediately perceived because it is prior to, and presupposed by, all perception, so also
is the world as horizon not known immediately but appears
only in the human situation.   The relationship of situation
and world is like that of profile and background.   Just as the
background appears only in the profile as a present absence, so
also I encounter the world only in a situation.   On the other
hand, the profile cannot be seen without a background.
Consequently, every situation appears in the light of an
horizon of meaning.

This meaningful world is not in a state of completion.
Its meaning opens an outlook upon further perspectives.
The meaning of the world does not lie one-sidedly in man nor
is it found ready-made in the world.   The world horizon is
not an external frame of things but imparts to them their full
meaning and essence.   On the other hand, however, the world
as horizon is not an object, but every objectification of the
world is possible only by virtue of this horizon.

Man and the world are one.   It is only within this primordial unity that two distinct poles reveal themselves.   Yet man
and the world are not identical with each other.   The identity
in question is imperfect and consists in unity through reciprocal implication.   For this reason one may and even must say

that the world influences man and that man exercises influence upon the world. Of course, such an expression is inadequate, for it represents the distinction after the fashion of things that are distinct through mutual exclusion. The distinction is not univocally but analogously real within the imperfect unity of man and the world. In other words, there is question here of oppositional identity.

Because of its "incorporation" into the activity of the spirit, the world may appear in two perspectives. On the one hand, like bodily being, it has a human meaning. It constitutes the humanized reality in which human beings are present to one another as subjects. It is the "home" in which we dwell together. On the other hand, the world constitutes an object that can be handled and render services to man. It is the material object of activity for bodily being in its objective and purposive pursuits. It therefore constitutes a workable and extraneous reality which we through our common labor have to transform into a livable space. Ultimately, however, both of these aspects of the world, meaning and serviceability, are united into a synthesis through the one reality of man.

It is not only the subject pole that points to being-together, but also the world as object pole manifests itself as a common reality. The world does not appear exclusively as mine, for the things of this world possess meanings which refer to other human beings. A book or a letter written by me points to the readers for which it is destined. A pen serves for writing because others have manufactured this little tool for this purpose. The world appears full of meanings which I have not given it but which nonetheless are meaningful for me. My world is not exclusively mine, but the world of the others likewise is not solely their world. The world is "our world" (*Mitwelt*).

7. *Conclusion*

When there is question here of the human "we," one should keep in mind all that has been said here about inter-subjectivity, bodily being, and being-in-the-world. This complex whole of aspects is present in every human communication, although the emphasis may fall more fully on one aspect than on the others.

CHAPTER FIVE
ASPECTS OF HUMAN CO-EXISTENCE

1. *Introduction*

This chapter will describe more in detail various aspects of human co-existence. These descriptions should not give the impression that the dialog of subjects is an extremely complex affair. Whatever complexity there is arises from the analytic standpoint from which the dialog is viewed. As a matter of fact, the communication of man with his fellow-man is exceedingly simple and therefore at the same time is full of aspects. The more complex the analysis is, the more simple the reality itself that is analyzed.

Intersubjectivity is not a laborious construction composed of various partial factors. The difficulty of the constructive picture arises from the procedure of analytic reason which unravels the simple wealth of being-together in such a defective and fragmentary fashion. For this reason the abstract consideration of a particular aspect must constantly be transcended by an analogous view of it. In other words, by starting from certain aspects as salient points, we must endeavor to acquire a view of the entire mystery of intersubjectivity. The implicitness and potentiality of this intuitively known mystery become more explicit and actual by means of the ever-broadening intentional ascent from the manifold forms in which interhuman communication is embodied. Or, to express the same in the formula which we have used before, philosophical reflection becomes more profound by means of its constant alternating movement from analogy to univocity.

2. *The Relation of Knowing and Loving the Other*

Man's spiritual activity is divided into knowing and willing. Phenomenological analysis points to intellectual and affective immanence in man. While the distinction between the two forms of immanence cannot be denied, it should not be conceived as similar to the difference between two activities pertaining to different orders, such as seeing and running. The two last-named activities can be performed independently of each other, even though it remains true that it is the same man who both sees and runs.

Knowing and willing constitute mutually constituent aspects of a single integral activity. Knowledge enlightens the will, and the will moves to the act of knowing. The unity of these two aspects becomes greater according as knowing and willing are directed not to things but to some person. In the personal attitude understanding and loving increasingly become more identical, in love the persons involved become transparent to one another. Although understanding and loving are really distinct, they arise from one and the same orientation of the person to being-together and to identity with the other. The imperfect character, however, of this identity is the reason why there always remains a measure of duality.

Knowing has an intentional character and is brought about in part by means of inadequate concepts. The affectivity of the will, however, constantly endeavors to overcome and transcend this inadequacy. Knowing has the character of appropriating and is centripetal, while the tending of the will goes out more strikingly to that which is known itself, so that it may be said to be centrifugal. The distinction in question is analogous and flows from the imperfectness of the identity of knowing and willing. In intersubjectivity knowing is a loving act of knowing, and loving is a knowing act of loving. Both aspects permeate each other completely. If, however, in the description of intersubjectivity the two aspects would constantly have to be mentioned, the resulting pages would assume an extremely laborious character. For this reason human immanence, as knowing and loving, will often be indicated with the single word "love."

3. *The Loving Knowing of the Other*

The understanding of the other as a subject has characteristics that differ considerably from the approach to the other as an object. Although the exchange of theoretical knowledge undoubtedly leads to a form of communication, it still lies merely in the sphere of collaboration, in understanding each other with respect to some general objective reality.

The understanding of the other, however, as a subject, requires a supratheoretical attitude. In his subjectivity the other has his own most intimate knowability at his disposal. His interior does not lie open and exposed to the gaze of every inquisitive spectator. The person has to be willing to reveal himself and does not allow everyone to share in his most intimate being. He reveals his subjectivity only to whomever he wants. Neither the desire for science nor the urge to know the unknown suffice to be admitted among the elected sharers of my innermost being.

To be admitted there, one has to respect the other's freedom in an attitude of loving reverence. The more unselfishly I go out to the other, the more irresistible and consequently the freer my invitation becomes. The less my attitude is self-forgetful, the more I make the other a mere projection or extension of myself. It is only when I am ready to respect him lovingly in his own being that I know him properly. Knowing the other presupposes his willingness to be known, i.e., to reveal himself. He must be willing to make himself present and he does so only when he trusts me. I will gain his confidence when I am willing to believe in, and hope for, his self-communication.

It is not only from the person who addresses himself to the other in knowing love that high demands are made. The same applies also to the beloved person: he must give his whole self in answering love. When he experiences the dedication of his fellow-man, he will have to be grateful for this unselfish attitude that is offered to him gratuitously. He will be able to feel the trustworthiness of the loving person only when he himself also begins to believe and trust in the self-revelation of this fellow-man. The personal attitude, therefore, appears to be wholly reciprocal. Intersubjectivity is an encounter-in-dialog in which the persons involved are *through* and *for* one another. The mutual revelation of the self is, as it were, a play of question and answer. My questioning attitude is inspired by the very reply of the other, and his reply is inspired in part by my question. For this reason it is not possible to indicate exactly what of the personal encounter comes from the one and what from the other person. Loving-knowing arises only from the "we."

4. *Love as Motiveless Choice*

Love attains the other in the uniqueness of his being, and for this reason remains motiveless. I cannot indicate any reason why I love the other. My choice cannot be explained "rationally," because there is no universal explanatory principle present. I cannot motivate my love on the basis of the good qualities of the beloved. For there are other persons with the same and even better qualities to whom love does not attract me. The qualities of the beloved person, then, do not constitute the ultimate ground of my choice. We find here a manifestation of the mystery of freedom. I do not make the choice of my love for one or the other objective reason lying beyond the proper being of the subject-to-be-loved although, of course, an objective reason can be the occasion of my love and contribute something to it.

Strictly speaking, it is meaningless to ask *why* I love. I love you because you are you. Love is its own reason, i.e., I love you for your own being. I do not love the other "in order that" he or she may love me. The relationship of love is not a "*do ut des*" proposition, an arrangement whereby I give in order that you may give. Such a reciprocity would not be a dialog but a double monolog. For this reason genuine love does not give up even if it finds no response, but remains faithful to the other. I do not even love the other because he is good but in order that he may be good. My love wants the other person to become constantly more himself. The other, likewise, in his turn wants to give full scope to my personal being. Together we surrender ourselves without motive and without self-interest to the "we" of love. We do not motivate our love, but love motivates us.

A problem that arises here is the question whether self-love has priority over the love for the other or the opposite is the case. On the personal level this question again is meaningless. Nobody can be for the other if he is not himself. Through the "we" of intersubjectivity I am the other and the other is I. The love of myself lies implied in my love of you, and the love of you in my self-love. Strictly speaking, moreover, we do not love only each other but we love each other in the love of God. Because of this harmony with the divine love, our "we" will constantly remain directed to the universal community of man.   With respect to the love of the self, of the other, and of God, the number "three" can be used only in a very analogous sense.   The fact that these different aspects of love are realized in a certain spatio-temporal opposition does not arise so much from love itself as from the material individualization of human love.

5.   *Love as Grace*

Love as a Free Gift.   I am grateful to the other when he wants to reveal himself to me, for I do not have a strict right to his self-revelation.   One cannot lay claim to responding love as if it were a contractual obligation.   For I do not constitute the other fully in his freedom, so that I do not have all rights over him.   The more the other wants to reveal himself to me, the more I experience that I do not deserve such a total surrender and that I receive his friendship as a gratuitous gift.   Even if I have shown the other great love, I do not feel his self-communication as something which I have earned.   The gift of his love surpasses mine, and I am grateful.   The other, likewise, experiences my friendship as an unearned gift.   Together we experience our friendship as a gift born of love.   We cannot make each other good, but we can merely be good for each other in the hope that the world of love will open itself for us.   Love does not flow from anything man can dispose of, it is not the result of a mutual collaboration.   No one is able to attract the mystery of being-together to himself or to possess it.   Its coming arises from over and beyond the human beings who attempt to encounter each other, it appears of itself.

While intersubjective friendship may have various occasions and causes, when it does arise it surpasses every occasion and comes as a gift.   Man can merely prepare himself for it through a humble and unselfish attitude.   In a business-like sphere I may perform actions entitling me in strict justice to compensation, but I cannot demand the gift of intersubjectivity.   On the other hand, however, the discovery of love does not make me confused, for a spiritual discovery is always a recognition.   If in the world of objects I make a discovery, the new thing is always strange and previously unknown.

The discovery unsettles me because I do not yet know what to do with this strange thing. The revelation of love, on the other hand, is not a sudden discovery, a coincidence, even though it surpasses everything that occasioned it. Even before the revelation, I lived in love. We were already united and we knew it, but now we become constantly more aware of it. Love does not come as an exchange, as a compensation earned by my humble attitude. On the personal level the deed through which I earn and the reward coincide. For in the spiritual order I can earn only through love and love is its own reward. Or rather, the sphere of earning is transcended here, and everything becomes a gift. Love is the mysterious starting point and terminus of our communicating existence. While we are on the road to love, we already proceed from love.

This spiritual gift does not lie within the range of things that are at man's disposal. If we ourselves made our being-together as we create the world through our labor, we would be able to impose certain conditions on it. We could, for example, agree to love each other only for a certain time. But the very effort to do so would at once destroy our love. Man does not stand above love like its lord and master, but love transcends man, making him its "servant."

Our Love and God. When we enter into an intersubjective union, we have accepted a common vocation. We have entered into the divine love, which is the first and proper cause of our human bond. As our intersubjectivity grows, we will recognize ever more that God has given us this happy togetherness and we will gratefully pray to Him for more love.

Trusting and hoping in each other likewise find their most immanent ground in the trusting and hoping love of God. For human certitude of each other always remains frail: our mutual surrender can be betrayed by one or the other, making us again a functional "he" for each other. Frail, however, as it is, our freedom is based upon our intersubjective bond in "being" itself, in the presence of the absolute Person. This immanent and transcendent "Thou" confers upon our mutual surrender the trusting certainty of its lasting character. The recognition of God's love drives away the fear of withdrawal and makes faithfulness more profound love.

Even as every human being has received his existence, so also have we received our being-together with our fellow-men. Although a man who is betrayed in the growth of his personality may have the feeling that he is thrown into a meaningless existence, in love we experience this "thrownness" as a happiness and a gift. Without love the other and the world become sheer resistance, and man lives in hell. But from the standpoint of intersubjective friendship the world becomes lovable for me, and everything appears in a fuller glow. Through our participation in the absolute ontological mystery of love we recognize ever more profoundly our mutual personal mystery in our growing transparency to each other.

6. *Love as Free Bond*

Freedom and Determinism. In the intersubjective encounter human freedom grows to maturity. Freedom, however, remains a mystery. Any attempt to explain freedom threatens to go beyond its goal unless the concepts used are analogously modified from the viewpoint of our experience of freedom. Nevertheless, we cannot dispense ourselves from using the dialectics of univocity and analogy. On the one hand, freedom is clarified by means of the determinism of the material world but, on the other, this determinism implies knowledge of freedom, without which one could not speak of determinism. If freedom is placed in contrast with necessity, it is easily equated with contingency. Since physical necessity consists in complete determination through external influences, freedom comes to be viewed as being freed from every external influence. In this way freedom becomes being able to do or not to do what one wants. From here it is only a short step to the identification of freedom with arbitrariness. Because of its comparison with material determinism, the essence of being-free is sought in the freedom to act. The ideal, accordingly, is sought in freedom from the bond and the facticity of the situation. But this freedom of choice or of action arises from the fact that I am an embodied being and therefore possess also an embodied freedom. The univocal approach seeks the essence of man's freedom primarily in his imperfection.

Analogous Approach. On the level of the analogous view, the essence of freedom receives a more profound explanation. From the standpoint of the *idea* of freedom the determinism of the material world is seen as an imperfect form of necessity. Freedom as self-determination is a higher mode of being-necessary. Absolute freedom and absolute necessity are identical in God. Starting with intersubjectivity, the mystery of freedom reveals itself to some extent to man. In love I experience my bond with my fellow-men. Freedom and bond call for each other in identity. Freedom without bond means blind arbitrariness, and a bond that does not arise from free will itself leads to servitude.

Undoubtedly, it is true that man experiences the moral ideal of being-together as an extraneously imposed norm and force, insofar as he depends also upon the determinism of the external world. Pure freedom, however, will increasingly spiritualize the obligatory and imposed character of these norms and change them into a privilege of love. This spiritualization is not accomplished through the abolition of the ethical law or by placing oneself above it, but by transfiguring its "extraneous" character into an "immanent" feature. The ethical law reveals itself in this perspective as the pace-maker of love.

The free mutual bond becomes even stronger when it is viewed from the free bond to the absolute Person, for in this way it appears with the splendor of free irrevocability. This divine bond of friendship likewise can be indicated only in a defective and paradoxical way. Here, too, there is question of "externality" and "immanence" but in a very elevated and analogous sense. The more loving persons freely affirm their love, the more they are conscious of the transcendency of their bond, of its "externality." On the other hand, however, this divine bond derives its form from the "immanence" of man's most free affirmation of love. The highest form of freedom equals the most intimate bond. Only from the starting point of love itself one can arrive at some idea of this inexhaustible mystery. The explanatory and artificial light of conceptual understanding does not find anything here except logical ineptitudes.

7. *Love in Its Repeatable Originality*

Singular and Plural of Love. Love touches the person in the uniqueness of his being and therefore cannot be numerically repeated. If we love several human beings, then there is always question of an original and irrepeatable affection which wholly differs from person to person, but which at the same time is characterized by the fact that in the difference there is perfect agreement. Accordingly, my loves of different persons cannot be strictly compared and I really should not use the term "love" in the plural. A comparison is possible only where there is question of partial difference and partial resemblance. This condition is fulfilled in the realm of material individuality, in which distinct individuals are opposites. In the spiritual sphere, however, strict comparison is not possible, as also there can be no strict numerable plurality, because in this sphere the subjects are wholly in agreement and totally different from one another in this agreement.

Paradoxical as it may sound, love of one person is like love of another person because the former is totally unlike the latter. The mysterious ground of this dissimilar similarity lies in the participation of intersubjective friendship in absolute Love. All love is similar because it participates in absolute Love; all love is dissimilar insofar as each participation in divine friendship is irrepeatable. However, human love occurs in oppositional situations because of man's bodily facticity, and this material individuation is the reason why in human love there is question of a predicamental and numerical comparison.

In its singularity love is universal and directed toward the entire society of all human beings. Any form of exclusiveness harms this love. The universality of love, however, does not demand that we love every human being concretely. The embodied character of man causes him to be restricted by and bound to certain persons and certain groups only. As a matter of fact, our loving togetherness does not go beyond a few human beings. Nevertheless, this love contains a readiness for, and an aspect of, a universal bond, if we do not love these persons in their exclusiveness but precisely in their orientation to the universal brotherhood of mankind. It is not so much a question of the number of persons whom we love as of the way in which we love.

Forms of Love. Love may be directed to others insofar as they also are human beings. In this case the unifying bond is still strongly biological. It is a feeling of being one with members of the same species. Love of one's neighbors is directed to fellow-men insofar as they represent an absolute value. Such love lies on a personal level, but does not yet immediately bring me into contact with this or that person. If I love my neighbors, I am concerned about them. I may even give my life for them or, as a hermit, withdraw from any human contact to bear witness to the religious aspect proper to the community of man. Insofar as love of one's neighbor finds a response in a return of love, it may be reduced to other forms of intersubjective unity.

In marital love the foreground is at first occupied by the building of the I-you attitude through the mutual revelation of the personal mystery, but later the I-you withdraws more into the background to make room for the we-orientation toward the child. Mutual love is now experienced in and through the child. If the child is loved for its own sake, marital love becomes friendship on a more profound spiritual level. Man and wife live, as it were, in a happy we-sphere.[1]

The relationship between child and parents as well as between brothers and sisters develops within the established parental intimacy of the "we." This we-sphere is not established by the children through a revelation of their personal mystery. As a matter of fact, adult children do not reveal their selfhood to their parents so much as to others. Brothers and sisters likewise do not manifest their personal mystery to one another, but have a feeling for one another without going to total intimate communication.

Friendship arises from the knowledge of being in agreement about the spiritual values which we want to realize

---

[1]For the description of the various forms assumed by love we have relied upon the article "Menselijke liefde en vriendschap" by L. van der Kerken (*Bijdragen,* vol. 7, 1946, pp. 161-199).

together. Its primary theme is not to establish an I-you relationship. The persons concerned feel themselves, as it were, united in the "we" of these spiritual values and together want to embody this "we." According as the values are less spiritual and more material, friendship gives way for mere fellowship. Friendship is less strongly directed to the parties involved than is marital love, and for this reason it is not so anxiously concerned about its own perdurance. If the conditions of life separate the friends, their mutual bond does not necessarily call for sadness. For the foundation of spiritual values, which called our friendship into being, continues to exist. When after many years of separation we meet again, our friendship appears to have grown with the growth of our own persons.

A kind of "vocational" friendship calling for the spreading of transcendent values is possible also between a man and a woman. If such a bond is sought especially because the persons involved are a man and a woman, it is not likely to last unless it is able to develop into marital love. In pure friendship, however, being-a-man and being-a-woman play a positive role because the two partners embody the we-value in, respectively, a masculine and feminine fashion which enriches both. Unlike marital love, this "vocational" friendship does not seek full embodiment of the we-value.

It is the task of the social sciences to classify, as much as possible, the various forms of human love and friendship. What philosophy does is to attempt to make explicit the ideal of love that underlies these forms of co-existence. For this reason philosophy goes beyond the univocally distinct characteristics flowing from man's human facticity. It envisions the plurality of scientifically distinct forms of love as participating, and therefore deficient, forms of the single ideal of togetherness.

8. *Intersubjective Faith and Hope*

In passing we have spoken about believing and hoping in connection with personal communication. These two aspects need to be considered somewhat more extensively here, because they are too often neglected when there is question of intersubjective encounter. Like love, faith and hope are social acts. To believe means a communication with the other's world of knowledge, to hope is a sharing in the other's affective world. These two modes of being-man evoke each other. Faith is a hopeful believing, hope is a believing hope, and both are real aspects of love.

Because human love has a spiritual-corporeal structure, a distinction can be made into love of friendship and possessive love. Love of friendship is directly oriented to the person's subjectivity. Possessive love, on the other hand, aims at the objects which the loving persons want for each other. Both forms of love are nothing else but two aspects of a single integral intersubjective attitude. They are not to be distinguished as disinterested and interested love. The subjects love each other in their value as persons and thus will also the objects which for both mean a completion of their happiness. It is only when the subjects renege their coming-to-be as persons that their condition could be indicated by the term "possessive" in the pejorative sense.

A distinction similar to that between love of friendship and possessive love applies also to believing and hoping. In the strictest sense, faith is faith in the other because of the other, and hope is hope in the other because of the other. In the terminology of scholastic philosophy one could say that, as in love, the formal object of faith and hope is the other person and that the material object likewise is the other person. Alongside this form of faith and hope there is also desirous faith in "objective" truths on the authority of the other and desirous hope of obtaining objects through the other. Both of these forms of faith and hope are aspects of a single interhuman activity.

Even as love of the other and self-love evoke each other in heterogeneous identity, so also are the acts of believing and hoping directed to the personal value of both the other and myself. Man believes in himself because he believes in the other, and he believes in the other because he believes in himself. Hope in the other, likewise, includes hope in oneself, and vice versa. As we experience love as a gift, so also we believe and hope in each other by virtue of our believing hope in the absolute Thou. If, for example, I really hope for my friend's recovery, I express my prayerful trust in a higher power which is capable of realizing my hope.

9. *I Believe in You Because of You*

The entire life of our civilian society is based upon a constant faith in one another. This mutual social faith is directed to the realm of "having." I believe here in "something" upon the authority of someone. Without this faith it would not be possible to live together in society, for in our purposive search for the necessities of life we depend wholly upon one another. Such a "functional" faith is justified by the objective testimony of the other. My faith finds its foundation in the function itself which the person fulfills or in previous testimonies whose veracity I have experienced. This form of faith can be justified in a "rational" way.

Man is inclined to consider care-conscious being-in-the-world as most authentic. The togetherness experienced in the mutual exchange of services is easily taken to be the yardstick of existential communication. For this reason the most authentic act of faith is often sought too much in this realm of things and given too scientific a foundation. But when there is question of believing in the "being" of the person who gives himself totally, then all such criteria fall short. The economic-social and verifiable trustworthiness of a person can never guarantee that he will give himself to me in his very "essence." All criteria lying outside this person himself fail to suffice. In this kind of belief I am not concerned with objects or services but with the person himself. Existential faith in the other finds its suprarational foundation in love. It is love which is the mysterious starting point and terminus of inter-subjective faith. Because I know the other already lovingly, I believe in him, but on the other hand, it is just as true that I lovingly know the other because I believe in him.

With respect to "objective" reality, believing and knowing exclude each other. In the "objective" realm I no longer believe what I know, and that which I still believe I do not yet know. My capacities are limited and for this reason I cannot discover everything for myself but have to admit many things upon the authority of a fellow human being. This faith does not arise from the character of the reality to be known, for in principle I, too, could discover what the other has found out.

On the spiritual level, however, faith in the other arises from the mode of being belonging to the person to be known. For the other has at his disposal his own intimate knowability, which he will reveal only to one who is ready to believe in him. It is not possible to know a spiritual subject without an act of faith. Faith in "objective" reality is a consequence of the fact that I myself know only very little. But faith in the other persons arises precisely from the fact that I know very much. The more intimate my loving knowledge of the other is, the greater my faith in him will be. And the more my faith grows, the more my loving knowledge gains in depth.

Such an existential faith in the other cannot be patently explained in a rational fashion and therefore has the character of an adventure—an adventure, however, which is "superjustified" from the standpoint of love. The other's credibility is so great that I do not feel any need to undertake objective verification, as is needed in the case of economic-social trustworthiness. Accordingly, I experience everything that bears witness to the other's credibility not as a *proof* of this credibility but as a manifestation *emanating from* his present credibility.

We may add again the usual correction—namely, that faith is a communicating act. I do not merely believe in you because of you, but we believe in each other because of our being-together.

10. *I Hope in You Because of You*

Socio-economic society is based also upon mutual trust. In trust I rely upon the butcher, the cab driver, and many other citizens. I trust that the engineers have constructed the bridge solidly. This form of hope is directed to the obtaining and having of something. My "functional" trust is rationally justified because it is the other's interest also that he acts in a reliable way. Our relationship here is of the *"do ut des"* kind, "I give in order that you may give." Here, again, however, with respect to hoping in the "being" of the other, all the usual criteria of reliability fall short. This is true even of the proofs of reliability given on previous occasions by the one in whom I hope. Nevertheless, my existential hope in the other is justified because through love I am already certain of his self-surrender to me.

Hope which is directed to "having" substitutes for my own willing and being-able-to. If I myself am able to attain the object, I no longer hope for the help of the other. But when there is question of hoping for the love of the other, I hope because I love him already, and I love him because I hope in him. Hope which is oriented to an object does not arise from the character of the desired reality, for what lies here within the reach of the other is in principle attainable also for me. But insofar as the self-surrender of my fellow-man is concerned, I can only trustfully hope, for his self-surrender is at his own free disposal. As compared with hope on the level of having, hope in the realm of being does not mean any impotence. In the spiritual order my hope arises precisely from my selfhood. The more I as a person know how to give myself to the other, the more intense my hope will be. To hope here does not mean merely to enter the road toward the hopeful future of being-together but to be already together in intersubjective unity. Because of this love my trust in you is so "superjustified" that I do not uneasily and doubtingly search for proofs of your reliability. I hope in you because of you, because we hope in each other.

It may not be amiss to make once again the remark that in intersubjective faith and hope objective proofs also play a role. All aspects of man as a spiritual-sensitive being remain present in his intersubjective growth. The accent, however, does not always fall on the same aspect. In the dialog of subjects man's behavior assumes the nature of a manifestation of trustworthiness rather than its proof, although this behavior itself will lead to more intimate faith and hope. My business-like attitude to the other, however, is based upon the fact that I have verified his reliability through proofs, although here also I rely on an original existential bond.

11. *Disbelief and Despair as Self-Destruction*

Belief and hope in each other's togetherness imply a constant fundamental task of life. Man experiences how heavy this task is especially because there is question here of situated belief and hope. When he experiences the inevitable facticity of life, e.g., in the incurable disease of himself or of a friend, he faces the task nonetheless of expressing his faithful trust in life. The very moment which constitutes the gravest temptation to unbelieving despair often sees also the birth of the purest hope. The darkness of inescapable and absurd situations is often pierced by the blazing light of intersubjective faith and hope. We do not mean to say that I continue to hope against hope. I do not hesitate to realize with all clarity that the situation is inevitable. Yet I continue to hope in faith from the perspective of love, which is capable of giving meaning to every situation, no matter how inescapable it be. For hoping in faith is not primarily concerned with the attainment of something. It is not without reason that in expressing the hope that someone's wish be fulfilled we add "if it is for his own good."

While despairing unbelief capitulates to the situation and undergoes it as a meaningless fate, hopeful faith is willing to see the positive side of reality. It constantly realizes more and more that there is question of a supratemporal and suprasituational "good." The intersubjective man will not attempt to modify the facticity of life through inhuman will-power, but he will accept the inevitable in all serenity. According as his faith and his hope grow, he will come to realize more and more that many situations of life are inevitable and beyond explanation. Though he will be tempted to disbelief and despair—a temptation which arises from his very faith and hope—he will overcome it through a more profound attitude of believing and hoping.

The unbelieving and despairing man undergoes life as an inescapable facticity and is resigned to its meaninglessness. He lives in a fixed, futureless fashion. Despair no longer even knows fear. Fear still implies anxious expectation, but in despair life itself comes to a standstill. Unbelieving man lives in "closed" time. For him life is without history, it lies scattered in dispersed moments of time, past, present, and future, which do not show any coherence. The man who is hopeful, on the other hand, gives meaning to time from the standpoint of eternal togetherness. He creates his time and

makes history. He lives in an "open" time, for past, present
and future constantly throw light on new aspects of his salvation. Such a man is already rooted in the eternity of love,
although he still undergoes eternal salvation as a task to be
performed in time. The unbelieving and despairing man is
exteriorized and reduced to loneliness in fleeting temporality.
He lives without meaning. Choked in the vise of his despair,
he is on the road to self-destruction.

12. *I Accept You*

Meaning of Acceptance. In every human encounter we
experience the world as a real and potential fountain of possibilities, but on the other hand, the world undeniably excludes
certain possibilities. Human facticity is both positively and
negatively colored, it means both wealth and poverty. Idealistic thinkers deny the problem of facticity because they one-
sidedly derive all possibilities from the spirit. Materialistic
trends think that all actual determinism can be eliminated,
neutralized entirely in the course of history. A realistic philosophy can hardly deny the obstructive and oppositional aspect of the "human condition." The determinism of human
existence reveals itself especially in inevitable and painful
situations, such as the death of a friend or the difficult
character of one's beloved. Such situations, however, always
still imply the possibility of accepting them or of cursing
them. A man is unable to escape from the existential
dilemma—either he meaninglessly resigns himself to absurdity and thus falls into an inauthentic attitude of life[2] or he
places himself on the standpoint of acceptance and "lives" the
wealth of personal togetherness.

The first superficial impression one gets of acceptance is
that it means a passive undergoing of the situation. This
affective value of the concept "acceptance" arises because too

---

[2]A distinction may be made between the authentic and inauthentic
aspects of human existence, but both are aspects of one and the same
human togetherness. The anonymous sphere of the impersonal must
constantly be taken up in a personal fashion. Without the potentiality of
this anonymous "we" there would be no possibility of personal communication. Only when man's being is lowered to such an extent that his life
is wholly submerged in the sphere of the anonymous group may his condition be referred to as "inauthentic" in the pejorative sense of this term.

much emphasis is placed upon man's freedom of action. Even if my freedom of action is determined by foreign influence, it does not mean that my spiritual freedom, which consists in the giving of meaning, has been uprooted. Acceptance demands a personal initiative and a personal effort. Such an attitude of life is required with respect to situations which do not motivate my attitude in an objective fashion and in a way that can be rationally understood. The situations in question are no longer only inevitable crises, such as an incurable disease. We speak of acceptance also with respect to a function or a decision, because here also my attitude is not motivated in a rational way through the situation itself. If the situation itself with logical clarity inspires the decision, it would be out of place to speak here of an acceptance. For example, if someone has been out of work for a long time, it would be arrogant for him to speak of "acceptance" when he is offered a job, because the decision to be made in such a case is wholly indicated by the situation. With respect to marriage one could use the term "acceptance" because such a vital decision has far-reaching consequences stretching over a length of time, which man cannot sufficiently grasp to calculate its implications. The attitude of acceptance does not refer to the everyday events in which man acts generally as "everybody does," but applies only to existential decisions demanding a very personal dedication.

Ground of Acceptance. The foundation of acceptance does not lie in the rationality of the situation but in freedom as love. I accepted the situation for you. I go beyond the realm of the foreseeable and no longer rely upon my own controlling grasp. Man surrenders himself to the incalculable power of love. The more my life situation defies calculation and escapes comprehension, the greater the demand that I assume an attitude of acceptance. Through the intersubjective bond, even the most absurd situation of life receives a value which escapes our understanding as viewed from the standpoint of the situation itself and of everyday values. The death itself of my beloved remains acceptable from the standpoint of a love that is stronger than death. From the viewpoint of eternal intersubjectivity you, though dead, remain alive and present to me in a mysterious absent pres-

ence.   Acceptance cannot be learned through any kind
of objective cognitive intermediary, and in this sense it is
incommunicable.   In the interhuman encounter, however, we
communicatively share with each other the uniqueness of this
attitude of life.   I accept you because you accept me.   We
gladly accept each other because of our love.

Unauthentic Man.   When man's being falls away from its
authenticity, the world assumes a fully determined character
and our fellow-men themselves are absorbed by its absurd
inevitableness.   Facticity becomes wholly opaque.   One who
has the attitude of acceptance knows how to make the hope-
less profile meaningful against the horizon of togetherness.
One, however, who cannot accept determines the horizon by
means of the profile, so that the absurd situation constitutes
as its background a world that is of necessity meaningless.
Such an unauthentic man tries to conquer his world through
aggressive resistance or to escape from it in fearful flight.   He
vacillates between these two extremes of resistance and flight.
Every victory over the oppositional world causes a new and
even more choking boundary to appear, because being-in-the-
world is an essential dimension of man and therefore cannot
be eliminated.   Flight from the inescapable world is likewise
meaningless, for it means flying to an unreal world, which
nonetheless becomes constantly more and more oppositional.
Worn out, man can give up the battle and passively resign
himself to inescapable facticity.   But even such a resignation
is ultimately a masked form of meaningless resistance or
flight.   It is true that in the spirit of certain existentialist philosophers, such as Sartre, one may attempt freely to accept
this absurdity of life.   However, this Sartrian authenticity remains something negative, because it is based upon a wholly
absurd choice.   Acceptance, on the other hand, is the positive
taking of a position from the standpoint of intersubjectivity, by
virtue of which I am able to give meaning to human facticity.
This giving of meaning has also an aspect of resignation,
insofar as it freely consents to accept the limitations of
man.

13.   *You Remain the Other for Me*

All friendship and love live by the grace of the mystery which one person remains for the other.   Every communication remains an incomplete communication of this mystery, because the inner nucleus of the person is ineffable.   On the other hand, however, it is precisely loving familiarity with each other's concealed intimate being which supports the intersubjective bond.   There is no one with whom I am more familiar and at home than with the person I love.   Nonetheless, it is also precisely the beloved person who, more than anyone else remains for me the "other," and a "stranger."   On the personal level we meet here the paradoxical truth that the more intimately persons are familiar with each other, the more they affirm their distinction.   In the strict sense, they are *other* for the other.   The more I know the other lovingly, the more the mystery of his person delineates itself to me. Knowing in this order consists of a profound awareness of not-knowing.   Yet if my fellow-man is a mystery for me, my knowledge of him is at the same time very profound.   Not-knowing on the level of intersubjectivity therefore means simultaneously a high degree of knowing.

An encounter which does not experience the trial of not yet knowing each other hardens into a purely business-like relationship.   A relationship, however, which grows in intimacy with each other consists in a dialectics of unknownness and knownness, but in such a way that the negativity of the unknownness is part of the foundation on which the positivity of the knownness is based.   In the interhuman encounter the other's strangeness has the character of a strangeness that is already overcome, it is a being-on-the-road to a more intense degree of familiarity.   The negativity in question is a "surpassed negativity" (*négation dépassée*) and not the "static negativity" (*négation statique*) which characterizes the fallen state of human existence.

In the world of objects there is contrary opposition between the known and the strange.   The more something is strange to me in this order of things, the farther it lies from my world of experience.   In this realm I can take something into the world of my life only by making it "predictable" for me and by reducing it to the "ordinary." On the personal level, however, the subjects respect and confirm each other in their heterogeneity and in this way become most intimately familiar with each other.

A one-sided rationalistic attitude divests the fellow-man of his mysterious otherness and reduces him to something common and ordinary. Although in this way the other person becomes ordinary for me, I am nonetheless estranged from him. I may have many acquaintances, persons I "know," but they are precisely persons whom I do not know. I have not penetrated into the sacred and fascinating nucleus of their personal being. Instead I have deprived these fellow-men of their dignity by identifying them with impersonal roles or functions. In this "fallen" world acquaintances bore me because they are so ordinary. The loveless man is nihilistic but may retain the illusion that he is able to escape the meaningless routine of life in sexual encounters. Yet every sexual adventure leaves him still more estranged from the other and in even greater loneliness. It is only genuine love that is capable of discovering the mysterious inner sanctum of the person and of overcoming his strangeness.

14. *I Feel Lonely With You*

Loneliness and sociability, like strangeness, are ambiguous realities. These concepts can be applied to both the spiritual level and the external physical realm, but they assume quite different meanings in these two contexts. For instance, genuine being-together does not necessarily have anything to do with all kinds of social activities. All too often plunging into social work is really a flight from genuine togetherness. On the other hand, it is possible that someone will leave society because of his great love of mankind. In this way the most "social" human being may be very "asocial" and the most "asocial" man may be exceedingly "social."

Solitude likewise may have the same ambivalent character. Sociologists duly note that modern man no longer has a possibility of being alone. Modern means of communication and sources of information have increased social contacts to such an extent that there is neither room nor time for being alone. The psychologist, on the other hand, will say that the loneliness of modern man leads to all kinds of neuroses. It is, indeed, a general complaint, which manifests itself in all kinds of artistic expressions, that contemporary man suffers from loneliness. Even he who is least alone may apppear to be most lonely and, reversely, he who is most alone may be the least lonely.

In intersubjectivity, solitude possesses a positive value. Finite interhuman fellowship constitutes also a dialectics of solitude and togetherness. The negativity of solitude is here in part the foundation of the positivity of being-together. A togetherness which does not experience solitude as an aspect of the persons' total absorption by each other is in danger of hardening into a purely physical presence. The foundation of this experience of solitude lies in the finiteness of human intersubjectivity. The being of my fellow-man can never become fully mine nor mine his. No matter how much we are interrelated and how more intimately we constantly fuse, we are never able to reach the fountain from which we both originate, although our entire growth in togetherness points all the time more profoundly toward this fountain. The higher the degree of being-together, the more profoundly it reveals the lack of reciprocal identity. It is precisely this experience of solitude which makes us more mature and ready for a more intimate experience of the personal "we." As Binswanger expresses it very strikingly, "I 'alone' am not lonely, but I am and can be lonely only in loving reference to you." Solitude is the nostalgia for eternal dynamic rest, to which loving persons restlessly look forward in their finite and temporal existence. Solitude has nothing to do with loneliness as the permanent absence of the other. It is not a "static negativity" but a "surpassed negativity."

Togetherness and solitude are the rhythmic succession of forever increasing love. This dialectic rhythm does not primarily consist in spatio-temporal interruptions, although such an oppositional dimension is always present because of the bodily aspect of the "we." The rhythm in question should be understood as growth in a highly analogous sense similar to the eternal dynamism of love itself.

Because of his embodied character man will often also feel the need to flee from social activities and to withdraw

into privacy. This need does not mean that he gives in to an
asocial inclination. Man needs this form of solitude precisely
for the sake of keeping alive his spiritual belonging-together.
One who hates physical solitude flees genuine togetherness.
Such an unauthentic man does not experience being-alone as
rendering being-together more profound but as underscoring
his loneliness. He is afraid of being spatio-temporally alone
and seeks refuge in collectivity. But going underground into
the anonymous mass can only serve to increase his loneliness.
It is only an authentic encounter with a subject which can
deliver him from his fatal spiral dive.

15. *The Idea of Loving You Fills Me With Awe*

Another important aspect of the interhuman dialog is
awe. One who has not yet experienced that the person is
something sacred, something mysterious, which may not easily
be revealed or approached without risk of being desecrated,
will have great difficulty in feeling the fine shades of meaning
implied by awe.

Awe is primarily a spiritual mood on the high level of
intersubjectivity. Who does not feel awed when he has to
reveal his love to the other or to express his sympathy with
the other in his deeply-felt personal grief? Awe is an interhuman phenomenon. I feel awed not only by the idea of expressing my intimate feelings to the other but also by the
thought of entering into the inner sanctum of the other person.

Awe does not mean that the loving persons are ashamed of
their intimate bond, but means that they experience every
exteriorization and objectification of their love as both wealth
and poverty. Because these aspects of wealth and poverty are
materially individualized and therefore embodied in spatio-
temporally distinct forms, awe is very often misinterpreted.
One could think, e.g., that it consists in building a shell
round man's inner being. But awe does not refrain man from
revealing himself. Awe is a finely attuned mood which makes
man aware of the fact that words are really too poor to
express his inner feelings of love. But awe does not erect a
facade behind which man's inner being conceals itself. On the
other hand, the awed person is aware of the poverty and

everydayness proper to human expressions and for this reason he will reveal his innermost being only at selected times and in a subtle way. When, however, loving persons at privileged times reveal their sacred mystery, it does not mean that awe overcomes itself. On the contrary, awe demands these expressions of love, because spiritual intimacy remains formless without exteriorization. In a subtle way the loving human being knows how to neutralize the tension between enrichment and impoverishment which characterizes every exteriorization of human subjectivity.

It is difficult to find a suitable word in English for this finely attuned mood. Awe and shame seem to come closest to expressing it. Shame guards man especially against cheapening his inner being. One could say that shame reveals by concealing and conceals by revealing. Reverence and shame are intimately connected. That which in reverence is experienced as a distance assumes in shame the form of concealment or cover. Shame has the mysterious character of leaving the person transparent in his concealment. In the concealment one sees the inner being, and this even in such a way that the concealed inner being receives a greater revealing value than it would have had if it had remained unconcealed. For the respectful and shame-ful regard, the other's interior becomes visible as something sacred precisely in and through its concealment. The opposite occurs with respect to the everyday gaze, for here concealment protects the other's intimacy.

Awe and shame stand mid-way between two extremes. On the one hand, they prevent man from objectifying his subjectivity too much and, on the other, they guard him against being too closed. In this way they prevent him from delivering the mystery of his person in a vulgar way to everyone or from shamelessly penetrating into the other's personal mystery.

Awe and shame have nothing to do with prudery or an excessive feeling of shame. Prudery is not a concealing revelation but does not go at all beyond mere concealment. For prudery the conventionally established forms in which shame expresses itself are a goal in themselves. It uses concealment as a frozen facade and not as a refined exteriorization of the

inner mystery of the person.   In genuine shame the concealing
cover is "flexible," i.e., it participates in the originality of the
self-revealing person.   Prude shame shrivels the external forms
of shame, so that they are no longer a subtle expression
of the person's mystery. Existential shame, which is born from
reverence for each other's subjectivity, is the foundation of all
other feelings of shame, such as modesty of the body.

The more intimate the persons' sense of belonging together is, the greater the awe and shame which they have with
respect to each other.   On the one hand, they want to remain
sheltered together in love and to abstain from leaving this
shelter through a revealing objectivation without having first
refused to reveal themselves.   On the other hand, however,
this bashfulness to reveal themselves constitutes the most
subtle self-communication.

Respectful awe for the other implies also that I show
reverence for the beloved's sheltering in God and that together we envelop our sheltering in Him with a delicate shame.

16. *The Eternity of Love and the Temporality of Care*

Temporality is a typical characteristic of human existence.   Time does not exist in an objectivistically conceived
world nor does it apply to pure subjectivity.   It characterizes
the mode of being of a subject in the world.   Temporality is
an essential dimension of a situated subject.   The primordial
experience of time is the experience of a subject which in its
project becomes involved with the world.   It is only upon the
basis of this "lived" time that it is possible to consider physical or cyclical time, which is measured by the course of
events.   Man does not dwell in time as if time were something
absolute, but man is essentially temporal.

When someone renounces his vocation as a person, he
experiences time in fragmentary and dispersed moments.
Such an anonymous human being is carried away by the flow
of time.   For him today is like yesterday, and the future is
nothing but a meaningless repetition of the present.   This
colorless flow is marked by boredom and restless agitation.
Here also the extremes evoke each other.   Boredom makes
man restless and restlessness results in boredom.   On the one
hand, man no longer lives because he has become fixed in the

petrified past, but on the other, he does not yet live because he wants to seek his abode in the still-absent future or rather in a totally new future. One who, as it were, undergoes life in boredom does not succeed in living in the present as issuing from the past, and one who is restless runs "ahead of himself" by trying to build the future in disregard of the present.

The bored man experiences life as a meaningless repetition, and the restless man strives in a utopian way for an unattainable originality. In this way the man suffering from boredom becomes restless and the restless man begins to be bored, because neither one nor the other knows the present. They live in an unreal world, in which they try to throw a bridge from the past that no longer is to the future that is not yet, without anchoring it in the present. The person, however, who has entered the world of love does not experience time in fractional moments. The mutual presence of loving subjects knows sublime moments of eternity, no matter how short these moments may be in time. The "no-longer" of the past and the "not-yet" of the future are meaningful moments of intersubjective presence.

Eternity does not lie in the line of constantly succeeding moments of time, for otherwise eternity would be in time. It would go on and on in desert-like monotony, as is the case when one lives in an infrahuman fashion. Spiritual being-together, on the other hand, transcends the flow of time and is timeless. Eternity is not in time, but time is a form under which eternity appears. The eternal intersubjective encounter becomes embodied in the flow of time as duration. For this reason faithfulness is an aspect of the embodiment of love in the temporal world of care.

Although the eternity of love reveals itself in the temporality of care, it is not necessarily affected or even eliminated by this temporality. The supratemporal happiness of being-together cannot be built upon the basis of time. We cannot decide at a given moment to enter into the eternity of love. Searching for this sublime encounter does not suffice to reach it, for searching does not go beyond the order of what is not yet or no longer. The supratemporal encounter is simply received as a grace, of which I cannot exactly indicate "when" I obtained it. It has the character of "having always been and being forever." With the growth of our being-together we become also increasingly more present to each other in this eternal way. The eternity of love shows itself inversely proportioned to the temporal dispersion of the world of care. Nevertheless, for embodied man this eternity remains, as it were, a contemporary of temporality. The boredom and restlessness of caringly-being-busy are increasingly more and more transformed into lasting and faithful service.

17. *Man and Woman in Intersubjectivity*

Person and Sexuality. The irreplaceable proper being of every man, in which he differs from the other person and at the same time is similar to him, is characterized also by sexual otherness. Because the human body participates in the spirit, man is an original being even in his bodily being. Thus the body's sexual mode of being goes to the very heart of the person. It permeates the entire human person through its participation in the spirit. The human being, therefore, is a man or a woman. A so-called "neutral" human being, who could be masculine or feminine, is not a starting point but the terminus of a far-reaching process of abstraction. It is not possible to be human without being either a man or a woman.

Accordingly, it is from the proper being of the person that the sexual character arises. Human sexuality, then, is not biological but a personalistic event. It is concerned with the personal encounter of this man with this woman and not with making contact with an anonymous entity pertaining to the other sex. Sexuality participates in the original proper being of every person and for this reason is a sacred mystery which no one can ever fully exhaust although he may experience it ever more intimately. Even as the human being is concomitantly known in all his behavior and nonetheless is also absent from this self-expression as an fathomless mystery, so also being-man or being-woman accompanies all human actions without being totally identified with them. The sexuality of every man remains an absent presence in all sexual characteristics. Like being-a-person itself, it can never be described in a fully objective way. Just as a human being cannot place himself in front of his own existence to consider it as an object, so also is he unable to take a position outside his own condition of being either a man or a woman.

It is undoubtedly possible to consider sexuality as an object, but in this way the sexual mystery does not even fall within the range of our view. We may even say that it is obscured when one endeavors to describe it purely in an objective fashion. Only from the standpoint of one's own being a man or being a woman is it possible to objectify sexuality in a meaningful way. From the viewpoint of sexuality as an aspect of subjectivity, objective sexuality becomes more and more intelligible and open to understanding as a sexual characteristic. For this reason it would be wrong to identify sexuality with these characteristics, which merely serve to make man's sexual being known. As symbolic signs, they make the sexual mystery tangible, but as material signs they also conceal it. They attempt to make man's inconceivable and inexpressible sexuality conceivable and tangible. The mutual attractive power of the sexes, therefore, is not based solely upon their biologically different structure, but also and primarily upon the irreplaceable proper value of each human being. Sexuality is determined from the inner core of the person, i.e., from his love. It lies therefore in the sphere of the gift and the task. No one is capable of definitely possessing its secret or of drawing it to himself by his own power. It cannot be communicated to another as an object of knowledge. It is not "something" but "someone"—namely, this or that man or woman. The mystery of sexual being comes to the two lovers as a gift, because the meaning of being a man and being a woman lies in love.

Sexual Encounter. Man's entire life is an encounter of the sexes. Man is orientated to discovering his "I" in the "you" of the woman, just as the woman wants to see her "I" confirmed in the "you" of the man. Marriage is primarily the specifically sexual encounter between two beings. The most proper possibility of expression lies here in the caress. Here the body loses its purposive activity, it is no longer an instrument for handling the world but becomes wholly expression. Bodily behavior loses its functionality and assumes the character of a play—the play of love. Its motions express sexual desire, which is not primarily a thirst for lust but an intense longing to let one's person fuse with the other. The other's body is not grasped in the caress but fondled. The hands slide over the body of the beloved to be together through the body as an expressive medium. Because the hand is still too much an instrument for grasping, the fleshliest parts of the body play a role in the caress. By mutually fondling each other all over, the loving persons experience their immediate presence.

The caress is tender. It is not directed to anything, it has no further aim but is simply for the sake of the other. In caressing the other, I feel myself becoming present in your bodily being and you in mine. At the climax of this encounter there is question only of "our" body, experienced as our mutually becoming-present. It is the experience of becoming one. At this moment the "world," i.e., the world of purposive activity, disappears; it has become condensed into a participation in each other.

Bodily being, however, is ambiguous. On the one hand, it makes it possible for my intimate being to fuse with yours into a single intimacy, but on the other, it is a barrier and prevents our persons from becoming totally one. For this reason sexual embodiment is never complete, but remains a constant tender desire for a more intimate fusion of our existences.

Unauthentic Man and Sex. When man falls from the level of authentic existence, sexuality becomes a blind force which breaks away from the person. The mysterious sphere of the sexual encounter becomes merely a meeting of two bodies. It is a contact of two anonymous beings who deceive themselves, soon get bored with, or even hate each other, separate and go to seek their happiness elsewhere. Sexual encounter is capable of being an infinite joy for man, but also the most wretched death and loneliness. In the sexual union man can embody himself as loving presence but also as a being full of hatred and aversion. In unauthentic sexual life the attitude vacillates between the extremes of sadism and masochism. In sadism man attempts to experience his existence solely as power by endeavoring to master the other as an object through the brutal force of his body. In masochism man flees from himself, but attempts to maintain himself by estranging himself as an object.

In authentic love sexual otherness is an invitation to leave oneself and become the other. Sexual attraction invites man to surrender himself to the other, which includes at the same time a hospitable reception.

18. *The Social Feast as Meaningful Waste*

Work and Feast. Our caring and working being-in-the-world is an existential aspect of man's being. The material possibilities of the world must be transformed into things of service and usefulness for man through the person's projects and activities. Work is an all-pervading human mode of existence. But man's working existence is surrounded by an atmosphere of agitation and rush: he is very busy. While working, man "undergoes" life as an onrushing colorless flow of temporality. When the person is totally absorbed by his labor, he has a feeling of aimlessness because he lives meaninglessly. For work, as a utilitarian activity, is directed to something else so that, if life is wholly reduced to work, one is constantly searching for this "something else" without ever finding it. A man who does nothing but work is nowhere "at home," because he does not know the tranquillity of meaningful togetherness.

The working aspect of man does not encompass his entire human existence. Work appears meaningful only when it is done for someone with whom we are united into a "we." Work contains a destructive element because it turns man away from himself toward matter and to a world which estranges him from himself. Nevertheless, if human beings labor in the unity of a "we," work assumes a lasting value because they spiritually know themselves to be present to, and in communion with, one another.

Feast days are periods of time which man sets apart to reflect upon his working and caring existence. Because of the element of self-loss proper to labor, the more profound human dimension of togetherness runs the risk of being disregarded in the profile offered by man's caring busyness. Being-together, which is the fundamental inspiration of man's working existence, demands that now and then a time be set apart for itself. It is in the feast that this togetherness assumes its embodied form.

When man wants to celebrate a feast, he cleans his shop, stores his tools, or puts his books back on the shelves. He does not do this to make it easier to resume his labor after the feast. But it seems to him that his working existence is definitely over, so that he can rejoice without any thought of work. Putting on his Sunday clothes, it seems that he puts on "a new man." He enters into a new world, in which everything is permeated with happiness and festivity.

"Wasteful" Feasting. In this way the being-together of the "we," which because of its inner meaningfulness has no goal, assumes a meaningful form in the feast. The intimate togetherness transcends the rushing flow of temporality and contains moments of eternity, rest and unworriedness. During the feast the passing of time is forgotten. When it is "over," man is not sad to see that the time to return to work has come, for the feast lies outside the passage of time. It is a permanent and eternal being-together, which is not suspended during the time of labor. Man does not feast merely to relax and thus be able to return to his work with renewed energy. Such a relaxing celebration could still find place within the framework of a working and caring existence. From the utilitarian viewpoint the feast is a useless waste and squander. It does not serve for anything. Yet this is what makes it so valuable, for it reveals itself to be a meaningful expression of human togetherness, which does not consist primarily in usefulness but in an unworried and "wasteful" love. The material abundance that characterizes the feast meaningfully expresses the care-lessness of our being-together.

It is quite correct for man to interrupt his working existence with "wasteful" feasts. As a worker, man may not be able to appreciate the loss of so many hours, but as a human being, the worker will view the feast as a meaningful understanding of his caring existence. For all working activity derives its value from the act of the "we" that constitutes our togetherness.

The feast manifests the original tradition of friendship and love. Our togetherness is celebrated in a repetition of feast days. The feast is not merely a custom but pertains to the serene sphere of values. For this reason it is "celebrated" and not merely "held"—its unworried, joyful and playful sphere contains also something which makes it solemn. To celebrate a feast is more than merely to make merry, it requires culture and demands a high degree of wisdom of life. A feast is full of meanings created by the bond of friendship, but, in addition, it obtains a sacramental value, because in man's togetherness a glimpse of divine love makes itself transparent. For togetherness is not a product of our labor, resulting from our contractual collaboration. It is a gift which is not earned by work. For this reason the religious man begins his feast with a participation in the divine Communion, in which our human communion encounters the "Thou" of God. The feast is then continued "at home" in a festive meal, song, and dance.

One who does not know how to feast, because either he views it merely as relaxation or he assumes an air of aloofness, shows lack of comprehension, i.e., of partaking in man's being-together. He does not see the meaning of the human encounter with his fellow-men which has its first feeble beginning in our working existence. A feast that is celebrated in genuinely good style is not an economic loss and does not make it more difficult to return to work. On the contrary, it makes man happy that he is able or rather "privileged" creatively to unfold a new aspect of festive togetherness—namely, being of service to the other through his work.

CHAPTER SIX

THE FAMILY AS A PERSONAL COMMUNITY

1. *Introduction*

A One-sided Approach. At the end of this study of the human encounter we must devote our attention to the community which is the family. For the family is the community *par excellence* in which human togetherness can and must develop creatively. The traditional studies of marriage and the family are strongly colored by the rationalistic attitude of mind. The main effort appears to be directed to deriving from the "nature" of marriage the laws which man must observe. In this objectifying approach nature is unwittingly considered as a biological-physical datum, and the morality deduced from it receives an exaggerated physicalistic imprint. From the sociological or juridical viewpoint there is full justification for such an attitude which scrutinizes marriage and the family as a scientific object. In the reflection, however, of ethical philosophy man may not remain an "objective" spectator, but has to endeavor to discover the value of family togetherness from the starting point of the being-with-others which he himself is.

The exaggerated conceptual approach has the result that, on the one hand, too little attention is paid to the inspiring ideal of love and, on the other, the bodily aspect receives a strongly distorted meaning. For the subjectivity of love escapes an observer who studies the reality-to-be-known from a distance as an object. Moreover, man's bodily being is one-sidedly viewed in its objective character as a biological nature. It is not envisioned as the tangible presence of love, as the soul rendered visible. In this trend of thought the moral ideal of the personal encounter in marriage and the family is broken down into a number of normative laws, one-sidedly founded by scientific reason. It stands to reason that such a rationalistic interpretation of marriage and the family is not a source of inspiration for modern man. Moreover, this purely conceptual foundation of marriage and family ethics lacks force of conviction. Spiritual values are not unqualifiedly

110

subject to scientific demonstration, but demand above all a believing and unselfish attitude. What such proofs attempt to demonstrate becomes meaningful only from the viewpoint of love. The convincing power does not lie in the scientific argument but in love itself. This assertion does not mean that a personalistic philosophy wants to deny eternal and incorruptible values, but it does mean that the absoluteness of the moral ideal lies primarily in the total claims of love, in a spiritual "law of nature." The demands which bodily being makes upon man receive a greater stringency from these spiritual values. The spiritual perspective renders the moral norms more profound by raising them to the level of "being privileged to" and relegating their obligatory aspect to the secondary rank.

Dangers of the One-sided Approach. The one-sided conceptual approach to the reality of marriage leads also to the use of expressions which cause a feeling of dislike when they are viewed from the standpoint of this spiritual level of man's being. It sounds out of place in this sphere to speak of purposes, reproduction, or sexual satisfaction. It is ridiculous to divide the human body into "decent," "less decent," and "indecent" parts. Such expressions are the consequence of an approach that is too rationalized and therefore too thing-like.

The same one-sided approach leads to the narrowing of the term "social" to collaboration in the realm of common welfare and to neglect the community which the family is. Insofar as the family is at all considered, it is evaluated far too much from the standpoint of the society which is the state. This mentality manifests itself, e.g., in such expressions as "the family is a cell, the first structural organ of the state." Biological comparisons of cell and organ belong characteristically to the sphere of such a physicalistic approach. The so-called corporate concept is a dangerous basis of comparison. It places Christian solidarism unwittingly upon the sloping road of a collectivistic view of the family, on which it manages to prevent its fall only by means of the principle of subsidiarity. The family does not derive its value from the fact that it produces good citizens, but the state owes its role to the fact that it performs a useful and subordinate function with respect to the family. If biological comparisons are to be used here, they must be understood in an analogous sense. Far too often, however, the analogous character of such expressions is neglected. For instance, the term "social" is understood in a very univocal fashion as mutual collaboration based upon man's need of assistance. In this way the family and the state are viewed as lying in the same line. According to the personalistic view with its analogous conception of social reality, every group lies in a different perspective. Every social group embodies in its own distinct way the sociality of man.

The personalistic view leads to a shift in the following aspects of marriage and the family: from a more negative and defensive standpoint to a more positive and ideal viewpoint; from an apology of marriage to a spirituality of matrimony; from a one-sided morality of obligations to the mysticism of wedded love; from the patriarchal to the democratic family; from a community dominated by authority to a community of love; from a subservient woman to man's partner in life; from the closed to the open family. This shift in mentality does not arise, of course, solely from the difference in philosophical approach, but is connected also with the changes that are taking place in the contemporary pattern of culture.

2. *The Family in the Changing Picture of Culture*

Functional Losses. In our contemporary dynamic society the structure of the family undergoes far-reaching modifications, which may be indicated by the term "functional losses." This term indicates that the family must now leave to the state several tasks which it used to fulfill. The family undergoes especially the influence of the increasing tendency to differentiation which marks the various realms of life. The stable society of yesteryear with its primitive economic relationships was composed mainly of establishments aiming at farming and crafts or trades. Family life and labor were intimately connected in them. The family was both a producing and a consuming group. The family structure served as the model of all secondary groups. The hierarchy of master, assistant and apprentice, for example, owed its inspiration to the family sequence of father, older and younger sons. Even during the time when industrialization began to grow, the patron remained somewhat a patriarch with respect to his laborers. The family continued to provide for the prime necessities of life. Work, education, relaxation and culture had their place within the framework of the family.

According as society was increasingly more divided into all kinds of groups and associations, the task of the family became narrower because many of its functions were surrendered to one or the other group. One of the most profound modifications that has taken place is that which separated family life from work. Modern technology required that labor be performed outside the family. The functional environment of labor acquired a moral pattern which differs greatly from that of the family. The patriarchal type of family demanded above all obedience and submissiveness. But in the modern environment of labor the young have to conquer a place and see to it that others do not push them aside. Actions which would be suitable in the context of a family would be branded as signs of weakness and lack of character in this business-like atmosphere.

So far as training and education are concerned, the family has likewise suffered a loss of function, because part of this task is now performed by professional teachers. Man dwells in ever increasing agglomerations, huge cities, so that the family begins to lose the external stabilizing factors proper to a closed society. The city divides life into functions; it has its separate centers for industry, relaxation, education, and residential quarters. Both spatially and temporally life goes on less and less within the confines of the family. The dwelling is less than formerly a symbol of family stability. In modern society man must remain mobile, so that the home becomes a functional, exchangeable space in which the family dwells. Contemporary man is less rooted than before in the soil and his surroundings. The home is much less the focal point of the family's coming and going.

A similar loss of functions may be observed in the realm of mutual care. Sickness, old age, unemployment, inability to work, etc., need no longer be taken care of by the family alone. Social insurance and social organizations largely assume responsibility in this respect. Formerly one had to rely upon the family to cope with the contingencies of life, so that the family often included several generations dwelling under the same roof. Nowadays a family is increasingly more limited to parents and their unmarried children.

Evaluation of the Changed Pattern. On first sight one could easily suspect that the transfer of functions to society must imply a dimunition of family values and therefore contribbutes to its disorganization and break-down. But loss of function and disorganization do not necessarily go hand in hand. In other words, one may not simply take it for granted that the so-called loss of functions does necessarily mean a real loss for the family. It is quite possible that the various tasks which the family must now leave to the state and society are marginal functions that do not touch the real value of the family. Now that the development of society constantly produces new organizations, each of which takes care of a special human function, it may very well happen that this specialization means even a gain for a family. It is possible that in this way the family is better able to realize in a purer and more intensive fashion its essential value as a personal community transcending the functional level. At any rate, an earnest effort has to be made to find and promote the positive aspect that is present in every social evolution.

The disappearance of the patriarchal type of family has many favorable aspects. The preponderant role which his labor gave to the husband is disappearing. The wife, who formerly saw herself assigned only to housekeeping, begins more and more to play a role also in public life. In this way husband and wife become partners also in additional sectors of life, capable of making decisions in mutual consultation and harmony. In the patriarchal family the child was strongly controlled by a paternal authority which was rather impersonally business-like and much less attuned to personal feelings. The father, or at least the two parents together, would exercise a strongly determining influence upon the future of their children, including even the choice of a marriage partner.

The growth of self-determination, especially with respect to marriage, has various social reasons. The greater mobility of life means that there are more opportunities of meeting others which may eventually lead to marriage. The children, moreover, are more independent in a material respect: they have jobs outside the family and earn their own wages. In former times the marriage partner had to fit in more closely with the family, because the parents and other members of the household depended upon him in case of illness, old age and other contingencies. Thus the choice would preferably go out toward someone exercising the same trade or profession, so that he could eventually take over the family business. Moreover, he or she had to be economically desirable, not a burden to the family finances but, if at all possible, an asset. Nowadays such business-like motives play less and less a role. In our days couples get married because they seek love and inner security with each other to counterbalance the functional sphere of their profession. Property and class are no longer decisive factors. Class, however, remains an important factor insofar as it implies a cultural development which may promote genuine mutual understanding.

In former times the wedded couple accepted the child without any further ado. This unqualified acceptance was fully in line with the cultural picture of the age, in which the natural situation constituted the basis of life's security. Man adapted himself to the rhythmic order of nature. The child was viewed as the necessary consequence of the married state which the couple had entered. Social conditions, moreover, made the question of fertility much less a problem. Society, which knew the decimating force of illness, disease and poverty, demanded that marriages be as fertile as possible to secure its own stability. The increase of welfare, making it possible to almost everyone to get married, and the progress of medicine have made the population increase a social problem which can be solved only by means of advanced technico-economic planning. In former times, moreover, the child was cheap labor in many family enterprises. In modern society, which is based chiefly upon salary and wages, each child means a financial burden. Besides, the parents no longer depend so much upon the children in case of sickness or old age. All this means that human fertility loses its unquestioned accept-

ance. It becomes a task demanding man's personal reponsi-
bility and dedication.

In a personalistic society with its democratic type of
family the emphasis falls upon the independence of the child,
while formerly the general interest of the family stood more in
the center of attention. The young person's freedom in the
choice of his friends, his career and marriage meets with
respect. As this brief sketch shows, in former times family
life possessed a fixed sociological pattern. Its structure was
given, as it were, as a furnished dwelling in which the family
had merely to settle down. There was far less appeal to
personal initiative to erect a new structure. The accent of
morality with respect to family life fell upon faithful conformity with social norms imposed from without.

3. *An Erroneous Kind of Personalism*

The emphasis which the modern mentality places upon
the individuality of the person sometimes threatens to go too
far in the opposite direction. It then replaces the law by love
alone, the obligations of the married state by absolute freedom, and marriage itself by free love. Moreover, the former
puritanical fear and underevaluation of bodily being threatens
to become overevaluation. The so-called "trial marriage" is
defended because the couple wants to know if they are sexual-
ly adjusted to each other. Such an exaggerated personalism
believes that love is the autonomous property of man himself.
It forgets that love is a gift, demanding a corresponding
surrender. Moreover, man may not deny the proper character
and destiny of his sexual nature and modify it arbitrarily in a
technical fashion, for otherwise he falls back to the purely
biological level by treating it as a mere thing. It is a false
kind of spiritualism, and consequently a refined kind of materialism, to demand free love without moral obligations and
fixed norms. For otherwise the love of man and woman
becomes again a mere contract, albeit perhaps less institutionalized than before. Free love is a kind of two-headed egoism
to satisfy each other's subjective desires and needs. Love is
reduced to a one-sided bond of solidarity in the daily struggle
of life. It becomes a *"do ut des"* relationship—if the other

satisfies my need for feeling secure and loved, I in my turn will satisfy his.

In such a false spiritualism the child is in danger of becoming merely a means to satisfy the parents' subjective needs. It is not viewed by them as a gift of love. It is accepted merely if they feel the need of a child. Such an egocentric desire may be based upon a variety of motives. For example, the couple may not have found each other in love and want to seek compensation for it in the child. In such a case they will prevent it from growing up and going its own way, for they are unable to love the child for its own sake. It may often happen also that the child has to satisfy the social ambitions of calculating parents. They want to secure a better standing for themselves by means of their child.

4. *Fortunate Irrevocability*

Pure personalism has a balanced marriage ethics. It integrates meaningfully the values of the spirit and of bodily being. Spiritual freedom does not mean arbitrariness but being-bound by love. This bond is not experienced as a restriction but is freely willed from within. On the other hand, however, wedded love, which runs its course in a spatio-temporal world, demands to be embodied in an institutional form. This love includes a common task, which the partners want to accomplish in union. The human love in question is a spontaneous institution, as also this institution is an orderly love. The great merit of the personalistic view is that, on the one hand, it rejects the false spiritualism of free love but, on the other, emphasizes also that the idea of considering matrimony as a mere contract, no matter how *sui generis*, is a false materialism. The marriage contract not only serves to protect husband and wife against each other, but constitutes also a permanent expression and a constant sign of their mutual self-surrender.

The eternity aspect of wedded love assumes the form of indissolubility when this love is consummated in spatio-temporal reality. The originality of the mutual bond receives an exclusive character by means of man's bodily being. For the sexual encounter means that man and wife enter most intimately into the irreplaceable mystery of each other's person, and for this reason their union cannot be replaced or exchanged. The love of a person who envisions a return to himself and imposes conditions to make such a return possible has an egoistic character and is no longer true love. Conditions do not belong to the realm of self-surrender in love but to surrendering to a superior enemy when one attempts to save at least something from the disaster. Wedded love does not want to save but to give its all, to deliver its entire life. The unbreakable marriage contract visibly embodies this unconditional mutual self-surrender in love.

5. *The Child as the Gift of Love*

Marriage is essentially directed toward the child. The exclusive bond of man and wife manifests the universal openness of love in the desire for new life. The child is the most adequate and unique expression, both spiritual and corporal, of the mutual self-surrender. The wedded "we" experiences the greatest intimacy when it becomes itself in the child. It receives its expression and mediating incarnation in this spiritual-corporal gift of love. The blessed irrevocability of wedded love becomes even more shining through the child. A marriage which, for arbitrary and subjective reasons and not out of love for the child itself, refuses to create new life rejects the expression of its own love.

Because man and wife love each other not as anonymous sexual beings but as persons, i.e., as this man and this wife, both do not want merely *a* child. They want this unique child as the irreplaceable expression of their mutual love. Human sexual being is lowered to the biological level by any practices and means to procure artificial insemination, for such means aim at producing *a* child and not *this* child of you and me, the issue of a unique sexual expression of our unity in love. On the human level, therefore, one should abstain from using too freely the term "reproduction." For the same reason it is less correct to speak here, as is often done in moral treatises, of sexual satisfaction and sexual pleasure. For through love these bodily feelings are spiritualized into creative joy and creative happiness.

Catholic marriage literature often speaks about the goals of matrimony. The first goal, it is said, is the preservation of the human race and the second, mutual love. There exists a controversy over the rank to be assigned to these two goals, which is largely based upon the rationalistic approach to the spiritual reality that marriage is. Far too little attention is paid to viewing human sexuality from within. Personalistic thinking objects even to the terminology used in this controversy. The term "goal" has too many associations with the extrinsic finality of a functional or operational society. As we have seen, such a society bears strongly the utilitarian imprint of being a means to reach an external goal. Using such expressions in reference to the reality of marriage will very easily lower the personal relationship to the functional level. A person, however, may never serve as a means. This rule applies equally to the parents with respect to their children as to the children in reference to their parents. Wedded love, on the one hand, possesses an ultimate and irreplaceable value, so that it may never be used as a means to anything else, not even to the child. On the other hand, marriage is not directed to the preservation of the "species," but to the creation of free beings endowed with an unrepeatable personal value.

Instead of speaking of "goals," personalistic philosophy prefers to speak here of the "meaning" of marriage, for this term points to the proper value and immanent importance of this reality. In other words, personalism reflects upon marriage from within. Man and wife endeavor to build the most perfectly human I-you relationship, but nonetheless, in their care and their love for each other both remain somewhat alone. Although the man cares for his wife and the wife is fully dedicated to her husband, in their dedication to each other they experience the limitation of their mutual orientation. They desire not only to love each other and to be one in love, but also to love again in union and as a unit. All reciprocal love tends to love itself in a third. The expansion of this unity of love is brought about for the parents in the child. Henceforth the couple is able together to love the child and together to care for the same person. In personalistic thought the child does not mean one or the other purpose or effect of marriage, but it is the meaningful unfolding and the internal bloom of the unity of love between two persons. The so-called primary purpose of marriage, the child, is really the same as the secondary purpose, mutual love, in its unfolding and perfecting form.

6. *A Plea for "Adventurous" Parenthood*

The patriarchal type of family with its manifold external stabilizing factors accepted its number of children quite naturally without any further ado. Conscious personal responsibility may perhaps have been absent in some cases. Yet there was much moral greatness in the faithful acceptance of the obligations attached to the married state of life. The growth of personalism in our days, which concentrates especially on the aspect of love that constitutes, as it were, the "supernature" of the marriage union, realizes that love as the highest free personal act demands also deliberate and justified parenthood. One has to take into consideration whether or not the necessary material and psychical conditions for raising and educating the child are present. Parents who remain unconcerned with the fact that their child has to be raised in a spatio-temporal world are guilty of a false spiritualism. The child cannot be raised on "love" alone, which is nothing else but immature sensibility. Genuine love will not lose sight of any aspect of life's entire reality.

Here, too, there is a tendency to go to the opposite extreme. The motive of justification is sometimes too one-sidedly sought in material factors. Exaggerated demands are made with respect to the material possibilities of the future. But justification has to be made especially from the standpoint of love. For one who assumes one-sidedly a calculating attitude, such a suprarational justification includes an element of irresponsibility. When there is only a low degree of love, parents will easily take a pessimistic view of the future facing the new life they could create. They have no idea of the adventure which life is from the standpoint of love. They are able to march only along well-appointed paths and do not believe in original and unforeseen possibilities opened up by the unique character of their bond-in-love. Genuine love, however, is creative and resourceful, it knows how to exploit the chances offered by the facticity of existence. Even as marriage itself and the uncertainty of the future are justified and accepted as such, so also must the child's conception be justified through the parents' mutual bond, and the risk of life be accepted. Paradoxical as it may seem, such an adventurous parenthood will carefully and maturely weigh the conditions of life and the possibilities of education.

Because parental love is directed to the irreplaceable mystery of being which the child is, it experiences a new and unrepeatable happiness at each new birth. Each child is unique and without substitute, no matter how many they may have. Parents who do not experience their most intimate happiness in their children have not yet discovered the meaning of the state of life upon which they have embarked.

7. *The Contemporary Marriage Crisis*

In former times matrimony was determined by many external sociological factors and thus assumed a one-sidedly institutional aspect. With the growth of a greater awareness of man as a person the emphasis began to fall upon the aspect of love. The difference in mentality is sometimes expressed in a very succinct and, therefore, somewhat exaggerated way by saying that formerly people loved each other because they were married, but now they marry because they love each other. The transition from the old to the new view of marriage has led to a certain crisis. Divorce is on the increase, and likewise complete sexual intimacy before marriage. Birth control through contraceptives threatens to become a general custom. Nevertheless, it would be wrong to view these phenomena in a purely negative way. Undoubtedly each era has always had its own particular form of crisis in this realm. Moreover, it would not do to devote attention to these phenomena without considering their background. This background consists, on the one hand, in a convulsive reaction against the preceding phase of culture, in which marriage was strongly controlled by the forces governing society. On the other hand, the reaction is codetermined by contemporary man's desire for personal security. It is against this background that such behavior must be evaluated. This remark does not mean that these aberrations can be approved. Otherwise one would disregard the profiles to concentrate upon the background and forget that the background finds its expression only in these profiles.

The phenomena in question are often unconscious and inept efforts to find the happiness of love. For this reason it is now more important than ever before to display the ideal perspective of marriage. Contemporary mentality inquires especially about the meaning of the moral obligations. It would not do to reply: there are laws and obligations, and therefore the moral "ought" is meaningful. Marriage ethics are to be described from the standpoint of love as a meaningful and joyful task. We do not mean, however, that man does not have any obligation before he sees the meaning of some technical law. For the discovery of spiritual values demands above all an unselfish and believing attitude of mind and for this reason it is not always given to everyone to see immediately the inner meaning of a moral obligation.

Marxism attributes a positive value to the crisis of marriage and the family. It sees free love as a necessary transitional stage from the capitalistic marriage, as an institution of possession, to the monogamous marriage of love. In this transitional time free love must be promoted and defended to expedite the ruin of the capitalistic marriage in which the woman is the property of the man. This idea flows logically from the Marxist theory that love is not a divine gift. For the Marxist, love is made ultimately by man himself and therefore represents actually only a higher form of work. Thus man may, as it were, by means of free love "technically" learn unselfish wedded love.

Sometimes Catholic politicians think that their faith prevents them from aiding in the codification of the reasons for divorce, because it would make them guilty of cooperating in evil. Such an attitude is inspired by a wrong distinction between law and morality. It attempts to make a clear-cut conceptual division between the two domains and thinks that law is concerned only with man's external activity. Thus law is assigned the task of formalizing moral norms in the external life of society. In this way the problem is simplified by dividing man, as it were, into the inner and the outer man. But such a view loses sight of the fact that both the juridical and the ethical dimensions are authentic modes of man as a whole. Only if this fact is kept in mind is it possible to penetrate into the proper character of law and morality. As for the particular problem raised above, our standpoint means that in the realm of law it is good to create order in a chaos. Precisely when divorce is everywhere on the increase, this social phenomenon cries out for order. Accordingly, it is consonant with morality that the moral ideal be embodied on the juridical level in a fashion that is appropriate with this state of affairs.

8. *The Family as a Suprafunctional Reality*

When sociology discusses the family, it speaks in terms of structures and functions. In general, three fundamental functions are attributed to the family. They are the creation of a community of life ruled by intimacy, love and familiarity; the transmission of human values by means of education and training; and the satisfaction of certain material and psychical needs. Sociology as a science pays attention to objectified and institutionalized social relationships and therefore correctly speaks of family intimacy in terms of functions. It is concerned with the way in which the spiritual togetherness of the family is embodied in spatio-temporal reality. In the view of social philosophy, however, the essence of marriage and the family lies on the level of the suprafunctional. The so-called function of the intimate community is nothing else but an expression of suprafunctional togetherness on the level of collaboration.

The Intimate Community. When it is said that in modern society the family hardly retains any other function than that of being a "safety island," this expression touches precisely the vital core of the family. It is the family which constitutes *par excellence* the intimate community in which the members can be free and open with one another and do not have to assume a pose or to play a role. The many free or forced business-like contacts of daily life often oblige man to hide his true being behind the functional activity expected of him. This functional tension can and should be released in the artless sphere of the family. Contemporary man seeks this we-familiarity more and more in marriage and the home, for the artificial world built by modern man makes him lose

his cosmic sense of security and constantly brings him face to
face with man himself.

We may see here very clearly the tendency of human
culture toward an ever increasing differentiation and diversity
of the various aspects of life within a growing unity and
interconnection.   In the preceding centuries the idea of a
closed society prevailed in which man was closely connected
with the soil and his local environment.   Family and society
were far less distinct than is the case in our time.   On the one
hand, the boundaries of society coincided with the locality
surrounding the family.   Thus society was less functional and
assumed the familial character of a neighborhood.   On the
other hand, the family atmosphere was more business-like
than in our days because of the close relationship between
family life and labor.

Contemporary society, however, becomes constantly more
functional, and in marriage and the family there is a growing
desire for personal togetherness.   At the same time this increasing diversity of life's levels gives rise to a greater interconnection.   In the life of society man becomes increasingly
more aware that all human beings are equal, because all feel
that their labor contributes something of value and because in
our artificial world no one can be self-sufficient.   Moreover,
the growth of general prosperity offers more and more possibilities of guaranteeing to all a life worthy of man.   In this way
the functional character of the labor order both gives rise to
the desire for the home-like sphere of personal encounter
and lays the material foundation required for the creation of a
family.   The family, on the other hand, manifests a greater
relationship with society.   The more family life is really
home-like, the more its members will be willing to fulfill a
function in the life of society.   Being-together inspires working together.   Typical in this respect is the fact that dwellings, education, family rules, etc., show an increasing openness
for the outer world.   The growing functionalization of man's
various needs reveals very strikingly the proper value of the
family as the intimate community in which man can be himself.

dience instead of a loving boldness.   But the moral level of a child should not be measured by the ease with which it spinelessly adapts itself to the views of the parents but by the extent to which it has meaningfully accepted the norms of conduct and assimilated them as its personal possession.   The true educator therefore is someone who knows how to make himself superfluous as quickly as possible, just as the true teacher is one who makes his disciples truly master of the subject matter.   Because of an incorrect idea of the person, the reaction today often makes the pendulum swing too far in the opposite direction.   There are educators who think that they should leave the children "full liberty." They forget that freedom does not primarily consist in a liberty of action but in a liberating bond of love.   On the other hand, for an embodied being such as man, it remains true that this freedom-in-bond demands a constantly adapted realm in which there is freedom of situation or movement, if it is to reach maturity.

Undoubtedly education does not consist primarily in giving counsels but in a loving care of the child.   Such a caring love will evoke counter-love in the child and it is precisely this responding love which leads the child to moral freedom and moral greatness.   For, the genuinely human personality, the genuinely moral man, is nothing else but love, care and disinterested orientation toward his fellowman.   The self-forgetfulness of the parents will usually be the measure of moral success in the education of the children.   The parents' disregard of themselves will evoke a loving respect in the child and will ultimately stimulate it to imitate the parents in this respect.   For this reason education is not so much a separate fundamental function of the family as an implication contained in the mystery of loving togetherness.

In former times the traditional socio-economic society, in which family relationships were to a certain extent continued in a different context, offered security through detailed patterns of life learned in the family.   The rhythm of life was adapted to nature, considered as the exemplar and model of order.   In our time, however, it is the artificial that is experienced as orderly, while former nature impresses us as disorderly and chaotic.   The order of this artificial world arises only through man's creative and constructive activity and

The Educational Function. The second important family function enumerated by the sociologist is education. As long as education is thought of outside its connection with family intimacy, one does not yet have a correct picture of this human community of life. Education also lies primarily on the suprafunctional level of existential togetherness. The child develops into a person most of all by dwelling in the tender sphere of the we-community. If education is viewed too much from the functional standpoint, there is danger that the child will be made subservient to the function. This will happen when the parents are concerned with teaching their children everything pertaining to a so-called "good" education. For in such a case an educational scheme which is sociologically determined by class and fortune will occupy the center of attention and the child's own being will be disregarded.

The educational relationship may be conceived as the relation of a subject to an object which has to become a subject. We see here at once the ambivalent character of education. The parents will have to teach the child moral norms and moral behavior; they will have to make heteronomy and compelling authority prevail in order to give autonomy and freedom a chance to develop in the child. This subject-object approach will lead to an encounter of subject with subject if the parents' authority, force, counsel, etc., are permeated with loving concern. For then their embodied love will harmoniously integrate freedom and authority, autonomy and heteronomy. If the subject-object approach does not radiate love, the formation of the person is lowered to the rank of mere training. There is an atmosphere of torturing compulsion, from which the child seeks to escape by the rejection of all authority. If, on the other hand, the parents want to educate their children merely with tender love and without any appropriate strictness, they likewise show themselves bad educators. Their love is not yet mature and shows signs of weakness. Such a formation would also lead to the rejection of all authority and all restraint, in such a way that only harsh force can succeed in imposing any kind of restriction on it.

In the patriarchal family structure authoritarianism usually prevailed. The child was expected to be meekly subservient. Being "good" thus acquired a content of servile obe-

remains subject to constant change. For this reason, the family can no longer provide the children with a fixed attitude of life. If strongly situated patterns of behavior are nonetheless imposed upon the child, it becomes incapable of finding its way in modern society.

There is no need to bewail this new status of the family, for it implies a real gain. Education has no longer to be directed to adapting the child to its environment, but should now aim at promoting its personal autonomy. The child has to learn how to find, from within, the principles guiding its life, so that it will become personally able to determine its attitudes in a diversity of situations. It is love which clarifies man's views, makes him adaptable in his behavior, and creative in his situation.

Providing for Material Needs. The third fundamental function of the family, to provide for the various material needs, likewise possesses a suprafunctional value from the viewpoint of social philosophy. It is not so much a matter of what kind of material activities the family exercises as of the spirit with which they are performed. Not the achievement, but the caring love of which achievement is an expression counts first. For this reason loving clumsiness may have a greater value than cold-hearted skill. Even when someone is permanently crippled and cannot perform any work within the context of the family, he will still perform meaningful "work" if he allows himself to be cared for with a smile on his lips.

There is reason to be grateful for the fact that socio-economic development of society has taken away various economic functions from the family, for the over-burdening with material concerns caused a neglect of its intimate togetherness. Formerly members of the same family could easily live side by side without any real encounter because they could be absorbed by their functions. The contemporary family, however, is constantly confronted with its fundamental value. It hardly manages to survive as a family unless the various members really meet as persons and confirm one another's personal existence.

9. *The Open and the Closed Type of Family*

Contemporaries often speak about the closed and the open family. This terminology easily gives rise to confusion because the terms "open" and "closed" may be understood in different senses. In the spatial order of the human encounter openness and closedness are contrarily opposed. No one will applaud the openness of the "asocial" family which does not know any sphere of privacy or the closedness of a family which avoids all contact with outsiders. From the standpoint, however, of human togetherness this opposition between openness and closedness is harmoniously overcome in meaningful unity. Family life demands a private sphere in the external world, and in this sense one may speak of closedness. On the other hand, love makes this private closedness an expression of universal openness. In other words, as a community of persons, the family demands a closed openness or an open closedness.

The fact that in our time a plea is made for the open type of family is connected with the former structure of the family. Its reaction against its constantly diminishing functional importance consisted in a negative attitude toward the absorbing influence of society. This closed and supposedly intimate type of family, which the nineteenth century considered sacrosanct, has nothing to do with the intimacy of the personal community. It may even be called a decadent form of authentic togetherness. Even as parental love may degenerate into an egoistic attachment to the child, so also family togetherness may become petrified into a solidarity of egoistic defense against other families. All this has very little to do with genuine love. What the defenders of the open family want is a more positive dialog between family and society. Understood in this sense, the openness of the family is, of course, wholly laudable. At the same time, however, this openness implies also a private closedness. For a family whose members are never able to be themselves in a private sphere does not know any genuine togetherness.

10. *Conclusion*

As we have pointed out before, the value of the family must not be defended by describing it as the healthiest cell and organ of the state.   Such a defense runs the risk that the family will be sucked into the vortex of state absolutism, which is all the more dangerous because modern despots no longer attempt to subdue the people by brutal force but endeavor to gain them through sympathy and love.   Likewise, the family may not be described as a part of the "general prosperity" which the state has to take care of, without depriving the family of its autonomy.   For the state is not the society which includes and perfects all communities and groups, but only the society which creates the necessary conditions for the flourishing of other social groups and especially the family.   As a personal community, the family transcends the state, which is the functional society.

It is an essential characteristic of love to communicate itself.   The moral excellence, for instance, of a good family will radiate over the society to which it belongs.   But if the value of the family is emphasized solely because of its importance for the state, as is the case in collectivistic systems, one overlooks the intrinsic goodness of the family too much and attaches supreme value to business-like relationships and the exchange of services.

EPILOGUE

In one of his works, Albert Camus writes, "The spectacle of the years we have gone through has destroyed something in us. This something is the belief that one may expect the others to react in a human way as soon as they are addressed in the language of humanity." The eminent author is not the only one to speak in this fashion. We ourselves have often heard the same idea expressed by young men and women. They managed successfully to pass their examination in social philosophy but candidly declared that they did not believe in the joyful mystery of man's togetherness with his fellow-men and consequently neither in God. Yet they were not the worst of all, for they eagerly desired a personal encounter, but could not find anyone inviting them to dwell in the house of love.

Those who today complain so easily that the sense of guilt is disappearing would do well to examine their conscience to see whether their complaint does not apply also to themselves. Though they may perhaps have observed the moral norms of the common man, they may be guilty of having no love for those who have gone astray but continue to make hesitant, albeit inept, efforts to find their way toward their fellowmen. Such people think that they are practicing love by speaking of God, but forget that contemporary man cannot recognize the love of God if he has not experienced a loving bond with his fellow-man. It would be a sign of unloving callousness to speak about the marvellous beauty of color in nature before an audience of blind persons, and the same applies to speaking of God to such disoriented contemporaries. God does not reveal Himself most profoundly in nature but in the intersubjective surrender to each other in love.

The encounter with the other as a subject is the central orientation of the person. This idea has not yet sufficiently penetrated our ethics. Morality may not be primarily directed to my own ego in a one-sided action against my own evil inclinations. One who in this way wants to acquire an iron will is actually engaged in a mere process of frustration. Even mortification often constitutes a narcissistic preoccupation with oneself. Modern man, however, is no longer as capable of bearing such a frustration as he was in former ages when he was physically more vigorous. What is needed now is a greater awareness that the ethical ideal consists in lovingly letting the other grow in his own being and helping him to be himself. Self-denial and self-mortification become a meaningful task if they are viewed as happiness over the privilege of being allowed to do something for the other, as joy over being allowed to confirm the other as man or wife.

Living our Faith does not demand of us, modern men, that we build again giant cathedrals and search for all kinds of external religious practices for the alleged purpose of christianizing public life. Such an attitude belongs to the Middle Ages and in all probability is definitely past. In the Middle Ages external religious practices played a role in controlling a way of life which remained barbarous in many respects. Our time, on the contrary, demands above all an immediate manifestation of friendship and love. It is no longer the cosmic dimension but the ethical dimension that must point toward God. When persons find one another in a constantly increasing way through a horizontal friendship and love, the vertical solitude and estrangement with respect to God is bound to melt away like snow in the shining rays of the sun. For human friendship and love will evoke a nostalgia for the absolute friendship and love of Him whose Fatherhood remains the foundation of all human bonds.

PART TWO

MAN IN SOCIETY

CHAPTER SEVEN

PHILOSOPHICAL ORIENTATION

In this second part, which we are now beginning, the person will be considered in his social relations. After devoting our attention in Part One to intersubjectivity as a community of love, we must now consider especially the worldly dimension of man's bond with his fellow-men. Wherever there will be question here of social reality, this term refers primarily to the world in which I co-exist with my fellow-men. Man's social dimension, however, remains an analogous entity, which as such assumes in every particular social group its own appropriate form. If, then, in Part Two the term "social reality" refers here or there primarily to the intersubjective bond of man with his fellow-men, the context itself will make this sense clear.

1. *Introduction*

When social philosophy reflects upon human society, its very approach to the subject of its interest differs from that of science. The scientific approach is characterized by an attitude that tends to control. He who adopts this attitude manipulates reality. He "artificially" isolates a certain aspect of the "lived" world and considers this in itself. Moreover, science proceeds to a certain extent in an aprioristic way. It thematizes the world and makes it its object from an *a priori* selected formal viewpoint. To express the matter in Heideggerian terms, science considers reality-as-given-in-the-world ("*Zuhandenheit*") from the standpoint of manipulability ("*Vorhandenheit*").

Philosophy, on the other hand, endeavors to understand the "lived" world of man in its concreteness and totality. It seeks to encounter reality. While science views the "lived" world as an object and consequently has to proceed in an abstractive and aprioristic way, philosophy attempts to penetrate this world in its integral original givenness. Philosophy and science, therefore, do not follow the same line. Philosophical knowledge is not the foundation of scientific knowledge,

135

and, conversely, scientific knowledge does not provide philosophy with its subject matter. The two are essentially distinct because they arise from different attitudes toward reality. The scientist tries to acquire *control over* reality, but the philosopher desires to *surrender to* it.

The assertion that there is an essential distinction between philosophy and science because of their difference in attitude, does not mean that no connection exists between them. Both science and philosophy are endeavors of living human beings and in these beings everything is connected with everything else. Philosophy helps the scientist, for instance, not to absolutize his univocal approach but to place it against the background of integral human reality. Conversely, without science, philosophy runs the risk of getting lost in endless horizons. Science cultivates a restricted but very real aspect of the "lived" world. It is the task of philosophy to take notice of what science discovers in this respect and to integrate the investigated aspect again in the whole of reality.

2. *Understanding Society from the Standpoints of Philosophy and of Social Science*

Social philosophy and the social sciences are both concerned with social reality, but this reality is not univocally the same for both groups of intellectual disciplines.

The Aim Pursued by the Social Sciences. The aim of science is to observe reality as a fact and to explain it as such. Science wants to base itself on facts and to remain within the framework of given facts. It tries to find inter-objective connections between the facts and to arrive at general laws and theories. For this reason the social sciences attempt, on the one hand, to deduce empirical laws from social facts, and on the other, to explain social facts by means of empirical social laws. This inductive and deductive procedure on the univocal level is characteristic of science.

The procedure in question contains two moments or aspects which should not be separated from each other, although they may be distinguished according as the emphasis lies more on one aspect than on the other. By virtue of its method, science makes a given reality a fact, but on the other hand, this particular reality invites science to use this particular method. Scientific truth implies not only a conforming of the subject with the object but also a conforming of the object with the subject. Differently expressed, theory and fact constitute a dialectic unity: the theory is based on the facts, but on the other hand, the facts are inspired by the theory. It follows, therefore, that a certain restriction is necessary when the claim is made that science is based on given facts. This claim is valid only insofar as it intends to express that science remains within the realm of the empirically observed world or within the realm of reality-as-"object."

The Aim Pursued by Social Philosophy. Philosophy does not want to consider reality in a horizontal fashion, but tries to penetrate it vertically. Unlike scientific reason, philosophy does not argue so much from one thing to another, but penetrates given reality with a certain immediacy, i.e., intuitively. It is concerned with human reality as integrally human, in other words, with the meaning of this reality. This assertion should not be misunderstood. It does not mean, for instance, that the social sciences deal with data bereft of any meaning, but that they consider meaningful reality as a fact.

The philosophical discipline which endeavors to penetrate the meaning of the "lived" world does not view this world from an abstract and general standpoint but precisely in its original concreteness. Unlike science, it does not make a horizontal cut through reality but a vertical cut. More accurately expressed, its crosscut is reality itself. The meaning of human reality as orientation to the absolute is identical with what is given in its integrity.

The Two Phases of Philosophical Reflection. Man's imperfect knowledge constitutes a bi-unity of intuitive and conceptual knowing. For this reason two phases may be distinquished, but not separated, in philosophical reflection. This distinction is justified because, despite the fact that the cognitive activity exercised in philosophy is "one," emphasis may fall either on the intuitive aspect or on the conceptual aspect. The two phases in question are the following. When reality is understood as having meaning, observed reality is viewed in the light of its absolute meaning, but on the other hand, the ideal of absolute meaning is clarified through the observation of that reality. As we have explained in this connection in the first part of this book, the analogous consideration is clarified through the univocal view, and conversely, the univocal view is rendered more profound through the analogous consideration. In his explicitations the philosopher will experience this circular procedure as meaningful, because it takes place within the unity of one spiritual reality which is evident to itself with a certain immediacy.

To clarify the procedure of the two philosophical phases, which is logically not easy to understand, it is perhaps best to refer to the dialectics of figure and horizon. The analogous ideal of meaning, as horizon, is not known immediately but makes itself felt only in that which is observed as an actually given fact. The background appears in the figure only as a "present absence." On the other hand, however, it remains true that the perceived reality cannot be understood as having meaning, i.e., as figure, without the background. The figure receives its contours from the light of its background.

In his spontaneous knowledge, man does not distinguish between fact and meaning or between observing and understanding. Critical analysis, however, demands to a certain extent such a bipartite complex consideration. Yet the more complex the analysis is, the more simple is reality itself. While it is true, therefore, that philosophy must start with given facts and cannot dispense with univocity, nevertheless, from the very beginning its perception and observation differ in character from those of positive science.

Science abstracts the figure from its background and wants to observe it solely as a fact. It endeavors as much as possible to arrive at a univocal formulation of its data. The reflection of philosophy begins likewise with the figure, but from the very beginning wants to understand that figure in the light of the background which gives it meaning. The philosopher is forced to make use of univocal clarity, but from the very start he attempts to break through this univocity and transform it into an analogous meaning. For this reason, philosophical knowledge cannot simply base itself on the facts gathered by positive science and entrust to the latter the task of observing and establishing the data needed by philosophy. On the other hand, philosophy indirectly profits from the results of scientific thought—namely, insofar as even mere facts remain an aspect of integral reality. Yet the philosopher can use such facts only after making a certain change of perspective, a change which arises from the bi-unity of understanding observation and observing understanding.

The Univocal Phase of Social Philosophy. When in the subsequent chapters we will consider various topics of social philosophy, our study will have to pass through the above-mentioned twofold aspect of philosophical thought. We will have to begin with an understanding observation of the reality to be considered; we have to describe that reality by means of concepts. Philosophical reflection on the reality of society should all the more begin with such a conceptual description, because it deals with activities which are embodied in a material and worldly structure and consequently lend themselves more easily to an understanding in terms of categorical concepts. As we have shown in the Introduction to the first part of this book, concepts such as work and possession lie more on the level of improper logical analogy than concepts which express purely spiritual realities, such as love and freedom. This kind of analogy, it should be recalled, is reducible to a kind of univocity.

The philosophical description of what is contained in a social reality may not rely on a rigid conceptual definition, but should have recourse to an analogously flexible concept. A rigid definition does violence to social reality as the bearer of meaning and treats it as a mere fact. A philosopher who tries to obtain the clarity and manipulability of a univocal definition succeeds only in obscuring that which he intends to clarify. The definitions with which we will begin the chapters concerning right, state, work, and possession, therefore, are not scientific formulae, capable of giving a uniform character to reality, but are meant to be analogous ideal concepts. On the one hand, the meaning of the different social phenomena can be made intelligible in the light of these concepts and, on the other, spontaneous social "lived experience" can express itself as clearly as possible in these concepts.

The Analogous Phase of Social Philosophy. With the preceding remarks we have already entered the second phase of philosophical reflection. This phase is inseparably connected with the univocal phase. One who wants to understand human society in its integral givenness, i.e., one who wants to penetrate into the orientation of its meaning, must view this society as it moves from the past to the future. Reality which is the bearer of meaning is essentially historical, it is a project in which the past is taken up and projected toward the future. For this reason each of the chapters which follow contains a description of the various themes from the standpoint of a philosophy of culture. For the concrete "now" of social activity can be understood only as a taking-up of the past with an eye to the future.

The philosopher has to be on his guard against an unauthentic understanding of meaning, one that would consist in allowing the "now" of social reality to predominate in such a way that a particular historical form embodying man's ideal is absolutized in a univocal fashion. Reflection on social reality in the light of cultural philosophy helps man not to absolutize the social situation of his time in a univocal way but to place himself at a distance from that situation. At the same time such a reflection renders the social ideal more explicit by showing in what way the absolute ideal has been given a concrete form by our fellow-men in the various periods of time. All this enables man to orientate the present from the wealth of the past toward a clearer future.

Although such a philosophical-historical consideration often has to be incomplete because the sources from which its subject matter flows are not yet sufficiently developed, we did not consider it justified to omit it. Moreover, the incompleteness of the historical description flows in part also from the fact that the authentically philosophical perspective itself views the past, the present, and the future as reciprocally constituting one another. Even as the past throws light on the present, so does the present make us more sensitive to certain aspects of the past. Because philosophy always remains "on the way" and never reaches an ultimate insight into the full meaning of reality, our philosophical reflection upon the past will of necessity have the character of incompleteness. However, it is a sign of philosophical wisdom to accept this inevitable deficiency.

3. *Some Essential Characteristics of the*
   Philosophical Reflection Upon Culture

The Aim of the Philosophy of Culture. By "culture" we mean here a complex of historically situated social phenomena in which man's proper and original dimension expresses itself and becomes intelligible. The philosophy of culture wants to discover the original features of man's being in the visible picture presented by culture. In this endeavor it takes as its starting point the striking characteristics of culture in order to view from there the mystery of man's co-existence-in-the-world. The examples it uses are presented not so much as "proofs" than as expressions of human reality as the bearer and creator of meaning. In the midst of all the historical changes that have taken place, that which draws the attention of the philosophy of culture is the analogously characteristic feature and not the feature which is typically and constantly repeated. For this reason the philosophical "observation" of facts cannot strive to attain the completeness demanded of a positive science of culture. The attempt to be complete in such a fashion would be a soul-killing completeness so far as the standpoint of the philosophy of culture is concerned.

Let us clarify this point by means of an example. When philosophy speaks about the social phenomenon of work in the different cultural eras, it does not primarily intend to indicate those characteristics of work which at all times have belonged to work and which make work be work. On the contrary, the philosophy of culture wants to place work as a figure against the background of the totality of meaning proper to a particular era. It views work precisely as an incarnation of the unique spiritual reality proper to that era. When positive science, on the other hand, pays attention to the phenomenon of work in a particular culture, it will always measure and clarify the typical aspect of this phenomenon by making use of a more or less uniformly general concept of work.

Analogy and Univocity. In explicitating the proper accent and perspective of the view of man embodied in a culture, philosophy must make use again of concepts. It must endeavor to approach that which is analogously proper to a particular culture by constantly correcting the univocal concepts which it handles. It has to explain, for example, that primitive man experiences as religious something which we experience as profane, while, on the other hand, primitive religious awareness, in comparison with our religious experiences, is colored by worldly and profane features. The clarity of our contemporary view of man, univocally understood, is both the indispensable starting point of our understanding of the past and the reason which inevitably throws our picture of the past out of focus.

The subtle differences in perspective arising from an embodied view of man flow from the fact that man, precisely in his spiritual being as creative of meaning, is not merely an example representing a species, but relatively much more a species in his own right. In other words, he embodies in a unique fashion not the concept "man" but the idea "man." A conceptual expression which puts the one in opposition to the other could easily convey the suggestion that the course of history deals constantly with wholly "different" men—which would lead to naive conclusions. There is no question of wholly "different" men but of different nuances in the meaning of man which give a unique value to men of one and the same species.

The Danger of Inauthenticity. In its reflection upon the cultural phenomenon philosophy has to be on its guard even more than usual lest it become inauthentic. Because the human intellect works of necessity in an abstractive fashion, philosophy can approach and clarify culture as totality of meaning only by starting with various partial aspects of human life. Hence there is always danger that a particular partial aspect will be considered to be the whole of culture. Like man's life itself, human culture is a Gestalt, a whole of meaning, in which all aspects of life permeate and influence one another. Each aspect can be understood only in the light of the whole of meaning. Conversely, this meaning is not present merely in a partial way in the various aspects of life but totally, although in a certain perspective.

Because of the fact that philosophical reflection must begin with a particular aspect, there is danger therefore that it will absolutize this aspect and identify the entire horizon of the whole of meaning with the particular figure with which it has started. If this happens, one succumbs to explanatory theories of sociologism and scientism, which attempt to explain the whole of life by means of a particular figure as a causally determining factor. Such theories seem to be "logically" endowed with great clarity precisely because that particular aspect does indeed permeate and express the entire totality of meaning. For instance, it is not difficult to explain the whole of reality from the standpoint of economics because the economic element really permeates all values of life. However, a philosopher who succumbs to such a temptation lapses into scientistic inauthenticity. He no longer sees the figure in the light of its background, but explains the background through the figure.

The mistake of such rationalistic explanatory theories lies in their aprioristic starting point. By virtue of the limited perspective which they have accepted, the only reality that appears in their perceptive field is the one to which the thinker in question is oriented. He puts, as it were, rose-tinted spectacles on his nose, is able to see everything, but forgets that his spectacles color everything.

If the philosopher wants to reflect authentically upon culture, he has to keep in mind the bi-unity of figure and background. If he does this, then the economic aspect of culture, for instance, will be a privileged perspective only insofar as, on the one hand, it offers a good view of man's total being and, on the other, makes the totality of meaning clearly present. Philosophical reflection upon culture demands above all a constant movement from the level of analogy to that of univocity, and vice versa. This assertion applies not only to the total pattern of culture, but also to philosophical reflection upon parts of this totality, such as right, state, work, and property.

CHAPTER EIGHT
RIGHT, LAW, AND JUSTICE

1. *Introduction*

A Typical Dimension of Embodied Subjectivity. Right indicates an original way of co-existence-in-the-world. It is the typical dimension of a being endowed with an embodied subjectivity. Right is essentially concerned with a worldly order which, because of its material-bodily aspect, is characterized by a limiting and excluding individuality. What rightfully belongs to one cannot be rightfully possessed by someone else. Nevertheless, the realm of right is not merely concerned with the regulation of material possessions, but also with spiritual values, such as love, loyalty and freedom, insofar as these values assume a form in a spatio-temporal world.

On the one hand, right presupposes the isolating individuality of the material world, but on the other, it is a dimension of the personal world. It refers to relationships between subjects and constitutes an ethical reality. An animal, for example, cannot act justly or unjustly with respect to other animals. Because its content has a spiritual aspect, right cannot be seized in a univocal concept. On the contrary, it is much more an ideal concept, i.e., a concept which implies the kind of infinity proper to the idea of person and which is realized analogously in different societies. On the other hand, however, the dimension of right refers also to the bodily structure of man. For this reason right can be more easily approached in a univocal way than other values, such as love and freedom, which do not imply any imperfection. Hence, *as compared with love*, right lies more on the level of the improper analogy of attribution which is reducible to logical univocity, even though it is true that, considered in itself, right is analogous rather than univocal.

Univocal and Analogous Consideration of Right. It follows, therefore, that right can be considered in two different ways. If attention is paid to its univocity, then the primary analogate lies in those forms of justice in which the imperfect character of the material structure reveals itself most strongly. To give an example, that which is analogously prior in justice—"giving each one his due"—lies in man's relationships to things, in his rights to material goods. From the standpoint of the above-mentioned analogy of attribution, the term "right" applies in the strictest sense to the just claim on the level of material objects, which is found mostly in the realm of commutative justice. If right is approached in this univocal fashion, just titles to spiritual values are called "higher forms" of right. Freedom, for example, which is the highest spiritual good of man, refers to a higher form of "giving each one his due." By giving someone his freedom, I do him justice.

Right, however, can be considered also from the standpoint from which it transcends the level of univocity and logical analogy of attribution. It is then permeated with the proper analogous idea of value. In that case the primary analogate lies in the perfection of this value, which is intuitively intended in the ideal concept of right or rather of justice. In this way God becomes the one who is most properly just, and all human forms of right are reduced to greater or lesser participations in this Absolute Justice.

Ambivalence of Right. Like man himself, right is somewhat contradictory. The human spirit is enriched by expressing itself in bodily reality, but at the same time this spirit is also estranged from itself. The same happens with respect to right. On the one hand, right is the imparting expression of love, insofar as it means an embodiment of the ideal of personal bonds in a purposeful world. On the other hand, however, because of the limitations inherent in matter, right creates a distance and estrangement between the subjects of rights. These two aspects of the human dimension known as "right," its noble character and its poverty, totally permeate each other. Out of pure goodness, love imparts itself in right, and this is the reason why right is a manifestation of human coexistence. On the other hand, love needs to be embodied in this form in order to become fully itself; and for this reason, right remains a condition that must be fulfilled if human coexistence is to be an authentic bond with our fellow-men. By virtue of this essential ambivalence, right has a character which is both sanctifying and demanding, both inviting and obligatory.

Let us now consider this ambivalence somewhat more in detail.

2. *The Ambivalent Character of Right and Law*

Dialectics of Approaching and Remaining at a Distance. Rights confirm and reinforce the external relations between persons. By creating this respectful distance between persons, right promotes at the same time their mutual approach as persons. In this way the institution called "right" is a symbol of love. Just as any symbol reveals its content and at the same time veils it, so also does right unite persons by creating a distance between them and creates distance between them while uniting them. For this reason right implies of necessity both a negative and a positive aspect, and these two aspects cannot be separated from each other. The relationship of right consists in a dialectics of remaining at a distance from the other and approaching him, but in such a way that the negativity of remaining at a distance is part of the foundation on which the approach is based.

The laws, or rules expressing my rights, are meant to circumscribe my spatio-temporal world and to protect it against the world of my fellow-man and of society. This negative aspect, however, may not be divorced from the positive task to work together at the building of a common world, for otherwise individualism would prevail. If we would want to guarantee each one's absolute freedom to act, it would lead to such an unbridled rivalry that only tyrannical repression could keep it in bond. Man may not consider his spatio-temporal world to be exclusively his own, because it would color his relationship with his fellow-men in strongly egoistic ways. Just as man's bodily being by its very nature is a colloquy with his fellow-men, so the space circumscribed and closed by his rights must remain a living space attuned to his fellow-men.

Law as a Process of Embodiment. Laws, which express rights, are essentially a process of embodiment. On the one hand, they give expression to the personalistic ideal of community, and on the other, they take into account the raw facticity of the human world. From the univocal ascending viewpoint laws giving rights are the first step toward the humanization of society. They are indispensable because "man is a wolf for man." In this ascending dialectics, which views reality especially in its imperfect state, such laws are the first feeble embodiment of the personal community on a level of togetherness with our fellow-men which remains strongly colored by infrahuman factors. Viewed as such, these laws may be called a minimum of love.

From the descending analogous standpoint, however, laws expressing rights have an ethical and religious content. They express the mystery of love and tend to the maximum embodiment of this love. In this descending dialectics such laws reveal themselves as the terminus of love rather than its starting point.

Right and System of Laws. Because the human dimension called "right" essentially refers to the world, it possesses a functional aspect insofar as it endeavors to organize the world in order to make it suitable for man's co-existence with his fellow-men in a way that is worthy of man. Because of this purpose, right requires a system of laws, for otherwise it could not effectively lead to order and stability. Right tries to objectivize itself in law to make it possible to handle and enforce its demands. If it did not do this, it would deny its essential relationship to the world; right would no longer be right because it would lack all "objective" certainty.

Nevertheless, the reality of right may not be identified with the whole of laws expressing it. Such an identification would lose sight of its spiritual aspect, which endeavors to express love ever more profoundly. If right is narrowed down to a system of laws, it will attempt to maintain as long as possible the equilibrium existing between the various social forces and to make their present position permanent. Thus it would make "the highest right be the greatest injustice." In such a case the restless stirring of the hidden forces of life would eventually break through that juridical crust with the power of a volcano and reveal that the apparent order of the legal system actually concealed a great disorder.

According as human co-existence is more realized in a particular social group, the functional aspect of rights will become more permeated with man's spiritual character. This means that laws can now be less rigid and less strictly formulated. They become more flexible and leave more room for equity and good faith. The abstract uniform rule to which everyone must conform begins to share more in the open form of an ideal. It becomes a norm of rights inviting the members of a society in a less obligatory way, or rather on a higher level of obligation, to bring about the aim pursued by the norm in their own way rather than according to a prescribed uniform pattern.

Twofold Approach to Right. Because of its ambivalent character, right can be considered in two ways. In the approach used by the positive sciences of law, right is spoken of in the proper sense in connection with objective right or the so-called juridical order. In that case subjective right, as the subject's rightful capacity and qualification, is based on this objective order or right. Juridical science admits, in addition to right in the strict sense, a so-called right of equity. For instance, one could say that equity demands a forty hour work week for employees. Such a right is a right only in an improper sense because there is not yet question of a legally formulated demand of justice.

On the other hand, it is precisely this right in the improper juridical sense which most clearly reveals the essential and proper aspect of right in the ethical and philosophical sense of the term. In the philosophical sense something is an authentic right only if it is in harmony with the demands of justice which are expressed in and by society. Objective right in the juridical sense of the term can therefore be qualified as right from the ethical standpoint, i.e., as just, only insofar as it shares in this ethical and proper sense of right. It is the task of the virtue of justice both to bring about a condition of rightful law and to respect that condition when it is achieved.

Because we are concerned here primarily with right in the ethical-philosophical perspective, we may hereafter use the terms "right" and "justice" indiscriminately in our description of the reality of right.

Right and Its Functional Expression in Human Laws.
Because of its spiritual aspect, right has the character of a
mystery. It cannot be fully fathomed and consequently cannot be fully seized and controlled by man. Man may enter
into the mystery which right is, but he may not assume here
the sovereign cognitive attitude which characterizes the scientist's approach to reality. Man cannot appropriate right in
the same way in which he makes a scientific theory his own,
for the reality of right does not lie on the level of "having."
Man does not dispose of right, but right is a mode of man's
being arising from his co-existence with his fellow-men. Society is the guardian and servant rather than the creator and
maker of right. For this reason the legislative apparatus of
society must be above all concerned with listening to the voice
of man's spontaneous consciousness of justice. Insofar,
however, as right has also a functional aspect and there is
question of laws expressing rights, we may speak of "making"
with respect to right. This "making" is to be understood in a
diminished sense or rather in a higher sense. It refers primarily not to a labor of constructing, but to bringing right to
light. Because right becomes effective through its being given
a concrete form by man, the work implied in giving form to
right belongs to the human dimension which is called "right."
The ambivalence proper to any kind of objectivation will
inevitably exist also in the expression of human right: it will
be both an approximation to, and a deviation from the absolute aspect of man's right. It is to be noted also that several
degrees are possible in the effective or functional aspect of
right. Sometimes objectivized right is a more or less immediate expression of man's consciousness of justice. At other
times, however, the constructive element is more preponderant, so that a thing is right because it has been regulated
and organized in that way by the legitimate authorities. In
the latter case we have to do with a purely regulative function, such as traffic rules.

Right is an essential dimension of society. It would be
exaggerated, however, to say that rights are born spontaneously just as love arises as a spontaneous gift in men. Such
a claim would disregard the difference between right and love.
The regulative element, which is of necessity a human work

of construction, remains an essential aspect of man's dimension of right, alongside the spiritual aspect of this dimension. For this reason rights are not born spontaneously, but often arise only after strenuous labor and many battles. Because man's concrete shaping of right in this fashion implies elements of success and failure, the human expression of right in laws is always more or less an approximation of the ideal of right. Precisely as "human" right, it owes its real existence to this "greater or lesser" approximation of the ideal right. Human right always remains a "work of man."

Positivistic and Intellectualistic Conceptions of Right. There also exist other conceptions of the phenomenon of right. They arise from divergent views about man himself. If we abstract from certain more refined distinctions, the various opinions can be reduced to two main currents of thought, namely, the positivistic, empiricist trend and the rationalistic, intellectualistic trend. The positivistic view exaggerates the worldly character of right. It sees the world divorced from man and considers it to be an "in-itself" in the objectivistic sense. It makes the actually existing relationships in this world, the worldly facticity, the source of right. It restricts man's role to the registration of these existing relationships and to their systematization in laws. In this way the entire order of rights is reduced to being the product of material and biological forces. Such a positivistic theory does not do justice to the human aspect of right. As a result, it degrades *de facto* also the worldly character of right, for its objectivistic attitude does not make room for the human character of the world.

The subjectivistic, intellectualistic trend, on the other hand, seeks the origin of right too one-sidedly in man's interiority, divorced from the world. It loses sight of the worldly character proper to the dimension of right. Such an idealistic conception of right remains out of touch with the world. It is constantly in conflict with the reality of the world. At the same time it fails to do justice to the human aspect of right. By placing being-a-subject as a closed interiority in opposition to the world as exteriority, theories of this kind reduce interiority itself to the condition of being an object that can be manipulated.

Both the intellectualistic and the positivistic philosophies of right base themselves too much on the opposition between man and the world. They try to overcome the Cartesian split between mind and matter, between subject and object, either on the side of the subject or on that of the object. Both, however, fail to do justice to the transcendent and religious character of right, because they make man appropriate too much of the reality in question. The intellectualistic approach makes man consider right an idea produced by himself, and the positivistic approach makes him view right as the product of a procedure which he himself has devised. A balanced conception of right is possible only if the unity of man and the world, however imperfect and oppositional this unity may be, is explained through its participation in the absolute and unique religious source of being. For such a view of right, on the one hand, does not put into jeopardy the absolute and ethical character of right and, on the other, it does not neglect the relative and worldly character of this human dimension.

3. *The Relationship Between Love and Justice*

The relationship between love and right or justice has been touched repeatedly in the preceding pages. It will be useful, however, to dwell more extensively on this topic because of the great confusion which all too often surrounds this question.

The basis of all misunderstandings lies in the fact that philosophy understands all concepts in a higher and analogous sense but, at the same time, is obliged to explain what it means by starting with a kind of univocity. In its explanations philosophy is forced to remain all the time close to contradiction.

Inadequacy of the Univocal Analysis of the Distinction Between Right and Love. If we want to explain in concepts what the essence of justice is, we have to oppose justice to something else, i.e., to love. Such a conceptual thinking in terms of opposites, however, is attuned to the univocity which characterizes the material world. Love and justice are not distinct after the fashion of two things possessing a mutually exclusive individuality. Philosophy undertakes the subtle attempt to seize something lying beyond the conceptual reach without being able to dispense with reaching out toward it in terms of concepts. When analytic thinking analyzes man's integral activity in distinct acts of love and of justice, its procedure is justified to the extent that there exists indeed a "real" distinction in this matter. The reality of this distinction, however, should be understood in an analogous sense, for there is question here of imperfection and its consequent distinction within the unity of man's integral activity.

The analytic approach which puts the distinction between love and justice in the first place and their unity in the second, may never lose sight of the fact that its approach is inadequate. If it disregards this inadequacy, it will try to divide love from justice by means of strict "spatial" compartments. The result will then be a one-sided minimizing view of justice. It is in this sense that right is often described as the minimum of love. Such a description indicates that one has fallen again for the eternal temptation of every philosophical consideration to lapse into the rationalism of concepts. By unduly demarcating justice and love with respect to each other, both are one-sidedly objectivized and described through a "spatial" distinction. As a result, right or justice appears only in its lowest-ranking participation in being.

The desire for logical clarity, which is unattainable in the case of the relationship between love and justice, can easily lead one to seek the source of right too much in the occurrence of conflicts. Man then needs right because "man is a wolf for man." Such an assertion, however, is equivalent to the claim that man's bodily being serves only to impoverish him. That which this objectivizing approach considers to be constituent of right is *de facto* a degrading element. This univocally essential aspect which refers only to a quantitative limitation does not even touch the essence of right as an analogous human dimension.

The univocal approach often takes as its starting point not love but right and proceeds to describe love from that standpoint. In that case the domain of justice extends to the demands formulated by laws, and the realm of justice is considered to encompass the obligations which are left to private charity and free initiative. This view narrows right to a legal code of norms which at a given moment are in force. No jurist, and even less a philosopher, will ever consider only that which the law prescribes to be the totality of right. Moreover, such a division into separate compartments fails to give love its due. For, love wants to attain justice and is always present when justice is achieved.

The Necessity of an Analogous Approach to Right and Love. If justice and love are treated like a piece of land that is to be divided into building lots, their demarcation does harm to both and clearly reveals how artificial such a distinction is. For, one who would pursue the practice of justice would thereby diminish the realm in which he could exercise love; conversely, the pursuit of love would decrease the possibility to practise justice. The question of where justice ceases and love begins is raised in a wholly univocal "spatial" fashion. Such an approach may perhaps be valid on a scientific level and from the standpoint of a certain abstraction. However, the essence of justice and love, as human dimensions, is rendered obscure by such a "spatial" approach. One who begins by pre-establishing a conceptual distinction between love and justice and then endeavors to unify them, proceeds too much as if he were dealing with a "problem" instead of a "mystery." The relationship between these two human dimensions always remains a mystery and therefore lies primarily in the sphere of a task to be accomplished, and not in that of a scientific solution. The analytic distinction between love and justice is merely a deficient *a posteriori* explicitation of a single human activity. The univocal distinction has to be broadened and made more profound on the basis of the experience of man's integral activity. It is only in this way that we are able to arrive at an "idea" of this mysterious bi-unity.

The distinction between love and justice is not unlike the relationship between body and spirit. There is no question of an adequate distinction of two entities existing alongside each other. The duality in question presupposes man's substantial unity, in spite of the oppositional character of body and spirit.

In other words, there is question of unity through analogy and participation. Just as we speak of man as an embodied spirit or a spiritualized bodily being, so also should we speak of loving justice or just love. Love and justice are related as spirit and body are related: on the one hand, the spirit is limited by bodily being, but on the other, bodily being receives its value as a reality from the spirit. In one respect justice indicates the imperfect character of human love, but in another respect the positive value contained in being-just is already implied in love. As the personal bond of man with his fellow-men increases, one can say both that justice becomes more and more love if justice is understood in a univocal sense, and that justice becomes more and more justice if justice is understood in an analogous sense.

Like man's bodily being, right exhibits the character of both wealth and poverty. If right is considered primarily in a univocal fashion as distinct from love, i.e., in its poverty, then one has to admit that on a higher level of personal bond between man and his fellow-men right recedes and is transfigured into love. This situation is similar to that of the growth of man's personal being, in which the limiting influence of the body as matter is constantly more overcome. If, on the other hand, right is viewed primarily as analogous, insofar as it possesses its real value through intrinsic participation in love, then right becomes more right when there is a higher degree of intersubjective union. This situation is similar to that of the growth of man's personal being, in which his bodily being, as spiritualized matter, becomes more and more itself.

Undoubtedly, these explanations balance precariously on the edge of contradiction. Yet this "juggling" with concepts results from the fact that philosophical understanding is aware of itself as "learned ignorance."

Accordingly, it is not possible for us ever fully to seize the relationship between love and justice in concepts. All we can do is acquire a more profound idea of this bi-unity. Love and justice are two aspects of man's single human activity. Because of the limitations proper to human thinking, we are forced to analyze this integral human activity and distinguish it into different acts, conceived as distinct units. We may and even must say that love exercises influence on justice and vice versa, but should constantly keep in mind that such a conceptual expression is imperfect and meant to say more than it is able to express. For, if man is to acquire any understanding at all, he must endeavor to clarify the analogous distinction between justice and love in a conceptual way, no matter how precarious such an endeavor may be. It is precisely in the realization of the limitation proper to our categorical concepts that man discovers a perspective upon what lies beyond those categories. Although it is true that what he sees appears in negative colors because it is only an experience of man's conceptual limitation, nevertheless, the "positive negativity" of such limit-concepts constitute the open philosophical insight.

4. *The Relationship Between Right and Morality*

The Univocal Approach Through Genus and Specific Difference. The difference between right and morality is fundamentally the same as that between justice and love. Here again, however, recourse is often had to a kind of univocity and efforts are made to indicate a specific difference between right and morality within a common genus. For, a univocal scientific comparison of the two is interested in their partial agreement and their partial difference. The generic concept in which right and morality agree is then the concept of norm, and the specific difference in question consists in this that morality supplies the norms governing man's internal life, while right and the laws expressing right rule man's external activity.

From the standpoint of a scientific approach such a division into separate domains is justified. In such an approach right is limited through abstraction to regulations expressing right, and these regulations are viewed as having a kind of objectivized existence by themselves. Morality likewise is narrowed down to a system of norms regulating the ethical ideal. The very division of man's mode of existence into interiority and exteriority, an "inside" and an "outside," manifests the scientific and artificial character of this division. It is the task of philosophical reflection to break through this conceptual demarcation of right and morality and to confer upon these terms an analogous perspectivistic character.

Analogous Perspective on Right and Morality. Right and morality refer to two aspects of man's authentic being. In this way they are aspects of a just and loving attitude of life. Morality endeavors to bring about man's *co-existence* with his fellow-men in the world by giving it an orientation, while right, expressed in laws, attempts to assign norms to this co-existence insofar as it is a being-together *in the world.*

Human love is ethical, i.e., man's being-together with his fellow-men has to be achieved in the world. Hence there is a need to express the ethical ideal in norms. An ethical attitude will of necessity find expression in a morality. A just attitude, which wants to make the worldly order suitable for a genuinely human way of living together in society, must, in its turn, be made efficacious by means of a juridical norm.

There is a difference of accent between the juridical norm and the moral norm. The moral norm wants to be primarily an "expression" of the ethical ideal of love. The juridical norm, as compared with the moral norm, has more the character of a "means" intended to bring about social solidarity. The juridical norm tends to circumscribe its content as sharply as possible and to objectivize it, so that the members of the society know exactly what they ought to do. The moral norm, on the other hand, does not primarily want to offer a rigidly described ethical ideal, but rather to present that ideal as an invitation. For the juridical norm the important point is that its prescriptions be observed. Morality, however, does not primarily intend to prescribe rules, to be simply observed as imposed from without, but wants its norms to be ethically willed, i.e., it desires that man experience them from within as a value.

It should be evident that the moral norm as "expression" and the juridical norm as "means" intrinsically refer to each other. Indirectly the "expression norm" has also the character of a means. On the other hand, the "means norm" is already the end intended in the state of coming-to-be and, consequently, also to some extent "expression." In proportion to man's growth in his ethical dimension, the moral norm will lose its "imperative" color and acquire a more "optative" character as an inviting expression of love. In that way morality becomes *par excellence* the message of "good tiding."

Even on the high level of the ethical attitude it is undoubtedly not possible to dispense entirely with all objectivation. In other words, insofar as love is pursued and perfected in this world it will be necessary to write a "handbook" for it, no matter how poor and defective such a handbook will be. No such book, however, is necessary or possible for love as love.

What has been said above about morality applies analogously also to the juridical norm. According as man's awareness of justice grows, the juridical rules will exhibit a more "expressive" ethical character and become more flexible. Man's sense of justice will handle the juridical norm more spontaneously in the light of justice. He will interpret the juridical norm not so much in a formalistic sense but rather as guided by reasonableness and equity.

From all this it follows that right is not "entirely different" from morality. The two "realms of norms" cannot be univocally distinguished by a "specific" difference. There exists here an analogous difference within the imperfect, oppositional unity of human activity. Undoubtedly, the juridical norm possesses its own typical characteristics. The more, however, the juridical norm approaches perfection, the more it will acquire aspects of the moral norm, without ever becoming a moral norm. The juridical norm points through and beyond itself to the moral norm. If the positive content of the juridical norm were present in all its fullness and not merely in a diminished fashion, i.e., if right could be fully itself, it would become identical with morality.

Conversely, morality, as the objectivation of the ethical norm, may be called "right" in a higher, analogous sense when it is compared with the juridical norm. The virtuous man, therefore, is a just man. The more morality attains its perfection, the more also it will be concerned with making the juridical order more perfect in human society.

5. *Right as Mediator*

The Two-Sided Character of the Mediator. To clarify right further, we will try to determine its causality with respect to love. As should be clear from Section Three of this chapter, we may speak about causal relations within man if these relations are understood not in the strict sense of

efficient cause and effect, but in an analogously more profound sense. G. Madinier compares the task of justice to that
of a mediator. Justice acts as an intermediary between the
union of persons with its perfect communion and intimacy and
the material world with its impenetrability and estrangement.
Just as the mediator occupies two opposing standpoints, so
also does justice have a two-sided character. It demarcates
the exteriority existing between persons and at the same time
makes possible the intimate contact of intersubjectivity. On
the one hand, justice objectivizes the community of persons
living together in a group that is more or less colored by egoism and collectivism, but, on the other hand, it spiritualizes
this living-together by giving it a respectful solidarity.

The essence of right may be paradoxically described as
the task to make itself superfluous. For, justice endeavors to
realize the ideal of a "community of free men," in which right
will disappear and only love will remain. In this matter also
the comparison with the mediator shows itself to be very appropriate, for the best mediator is the one who knows how to
make himself superfluous in the quickest possible way and
with respect to the largest possible number of issues.

The Danger of One-Sided Spiritualism or Materialism.
The desire of right to make itself superfluous is not at all to
be identified with the one-sided spiritualism of anarchistic
idealists, who dream of abolishing right because they fail to
take the human condition into consideration. When we speak
here of right making itself superfluous, there is question of a
spiritual metamorphosis of right into love. This process of
spiritualization will never come to an end in this world; hence
right will always continue to be necessary. The desire to
neglect right and to solve all problems of society by love alone
is just as disastrous a form of one-sidedness as to think that
everything can be solved by force and laws. History shows
that freedom and the dignity of the human person find their
best defense in law and justice. As J. Lacroix points out, a
one-sided ethics of love easily leads man to impose love on the
others even against their will.[1] The result would be the
degeneration of love into tyranny. It is no surprise, therefore

---

[1]*Personne et amour,* n.d., p. 63.

that Communism, which wants to base society one-sidedly upon love, has a totalitarian tendency.

When right keeps itself aloof from life, i.e., when the juridical *order* considers itself the highest good, it becomes a principle of constant contradiction. Two possibilities present themselves in such a case. First of all, the established order may try to preserve forever the existing equilibrium between social forces and to confirm acquired rights on a permanent basis. In that case that order is fundamentally a disorder, because it prevents any kind of adaptation to new social developments. In the long run it is inevitable that the forces of spontaneous life will revolt against these vested interests. Constituted right reveals itself to be out of touch with constituting justice. The second possibility is that the juridical order will be so precariously balanced between the forces living in society that it becomes sensitive to the slightest change in these forces. In that case the juridical order will again be a principle of contradiction, because it lacks all stability and consequently is no longer an order. Constituting justice does not succeed in establishing constituted right.

It is only when justice gives love its due that a one-sided spiritualism or materialism can be avoided. In that case a satisfactory solution can be found for the problem of the stability and adaptation of the juridical order. The static aspect of this solution will be that justice confirms and renders secure what has been attained by love on the road to its self-realization. On the other hand, love will remain the source of right, and for this reason the juridical order will share in the dynamism and spontaneity of love, so that it will constantly adapt itself in a healthy way to the changing patterns of society.

Through its intrinsic participation in love, right is embodied in analogous ways in the various forms of society. In the functional society of the state there is question of right in its strictest sense. In the state objectivized right, applicable to all, can be demanded by any citizen and therefore it is the most important link connecting its members into a social union. It would be wrong, however, to use this form of right as the model *par excellence* and to apply it uniformly to other societies hav-

ing a more personal structure, such as the community formed
by the members of a church.

   Justice and Equality of Persons.   Justice aims at making
persons equal, but the equality in question is not the equality
of persons as such.   On the personal level, where love is the
dominant factor, the persons are "one," as it were, and it is
precisely this reciprocal unity which distinguishes them from
one another.   Personal equality and inequality go together here.
The equality and inequality in question do not refer to a
problem of justice but to a mystery of love.   The equality
which justice wants to attain, however, flows from the material individuality of the person.   Because this equality lies in
the spatio-temporal world, it has to be circumscribed and
demarcated.

   Nevertheless, this material equality is not something static, for every realized equality has only a provisional and
transitory character.   Just as the material aspect should be
spiritualized by the spiritual dimenson of the person, so the
equality of justice should realize in an ever more profound
way the ideal of personal union and harmony.   The equality
pursued by justice cannot be fixed in a definitive way.   Any
proclaimed complete understanding of this equality would *de
facto* make absolute the particular justice realized at a particular place and time; it would absolutize, therefore, a provisional equality.   For this reason it is not possible to determine
a priori how the tendency of justice to equality will have to
develop in the future, because justice is an embodied reality
and therefore subject to a process of evolution.

   The equality intended by justice should not be misunderstood.   It refers to an equilibrium of equality lying between radical material equality and radical material inequality.
Radical material equality would lead to the destruction of
personal freedom, just as unlimited freedom would degenerate
into an unjustified material inequality.   Both would lead to a
leveling of persons.   It is the task of justice to find the right
balance between the two tendencies.   Its equilibrium of equality always manifests a provisional character.   According as
mankind makes progress toward the ideal of a personal community, this equilibrium will have to be rediscovered and

brought to realization on a more profound level. The personal love existing in such a community is able to show an unselfish and objective understanding for the situation of the other person and to discover the genuine sense of justice underlying every social desire.

Justice regulates and co-ordinates the spatio-temporal world for the members of a society. On the level of justice the unity and plurality of persons still presents a problem of rivalry. What is a right for the one is a restriction for the other. This kind of demarcation, however, should not be pursued for its own sake, because such a closed justice would foster individualism. The demarcation of one's right must contain at the same time a rapprochement of the other. Justice should have an open structure because of its orientation to the community of persons, in which the problem of the unity and plurality of persons merges into a mysterious fusion of the one and the many.

Nevertheless, because the human community of persons has a worldly aspect, any group will continue to have its "social question" on the level of justice. The contrasts between the different rights reveal themselves most strongly in those groups in which the interrelations have a more external character. The more personal, however, the character is of a group, as for instance in the family, the more also the various demands of justice will begin to share in the heterogeneous identity of intersubjective union.

General, Particular, and Social Justice. Justice is divided into general or legal justice and particular justice. The former regulates the duties of superiors and subjects with respect to society, while the latter is concerned with the rights of individual persons or groups of persons. Particular justice itself is subdivided into commutative justice and distributive justice. Commutative justice regulates and sanctions the rights of individual persons or individual groups of persons. Distributive justice imposes on those who hold authority in a society the duty to give each member or group of members their due according to need and merit.

Alongside this classical division, the term "social justice" has become popular in the past few decades. Concerning the exact content of this concept there are several opinions. Without entering into the discussions around this term, we may remark that the expression "social justice" originated in connection with the nineteenth century origin of the "social question." Thus one can regard this term as a collective expression for legal and distributive justice because it is the task of these two forms of justice especially to solve the social question. Or also, social justice may be identified with the legal justice of the classical division. In that case social justice expresses in a more suitable way that which is the ultimate goal of legal justice.

For the modern mind the term "legal justice" is too one-sidedly associated with that which is formally established by law. For this reason modern man objects that the use of this term narrows an ethical concept to a positive juridical category. In the medieval situation, however, for which the scholastics used the term "legal justice," the law was simply everything which was traditionally considered to be in accord with justice. A thing was not right because it was established or sanctioned by authority, but because of old it had always been done in that way, and therefore had to be observed also by the authorities. The term "law" applied to both written and unwritten laws. In our time, however, legal validity requires that the rights in question be proclaimed as such directly or indirectly by the legal authorities. "Common law" as a legal right was suitable for the largely agrarian society of the Middle Ages, in which the preservation of common welfare was a static task. The task of the authorities was more a matter of preserving the existing rights than of making laws. The structural change of modern society, however, imposes a dynamic character on its legal dimension. For this reason "social justice" is a more suitable term to indicate this dynamic task. What legal justice pursued at a time when society presented a static picture, social justice endeavors to bring about in a time which demands a dynamic organization of society.

Everything which has been said in the preceding analytic explanations would, strictly speaking, need to be corrected here by means of a synthetic consideration, for philosophical reflection makes progress through such a meaningful movement from one direction to the other. Love and right are not

strictly opposites. Personal love will become constantly more
right because human love is a loving right; on the other hand,
right will identify itself more and more with love because
human right is already an embodiment of love. If in an
analytic and univocal consideration right may be called the
starting point of a human mode of being-together-with-our-
fellow-men, then one should say that right is also the terminus and perfection of love from a synthetic and analogous
standpoint. In that way right is the social aspect of love.

6. *The Natural Law as "Idea" and as "Doctrine"**

In general the concept of natural law elicits the thought
of a totality of norms that govern the actions of man and
society. The concept of natural law reflects the attempt to
protect law and morals from human arbitrariness and to give
them absolute validity. In this attempt nature is conceived
of as an absolute reality which determines man's behavior.

The Traditional Univocal Concept of Natural Law. In
traditional treatments the natural law is technically described
as the theoretical and generally valid principles deriving from
the nature of man or society. These universal principles are
considered to possess absolute, immutable, and supratemporal
value. At the same time general principles, by virtue of their
very abstractness, are considered to require embodiment in the
concrete. This means that the concrete circumstances of
place and time have to be considered when putting principles
into practice. Concrete acts must be evaluated in the enlightening intelligibility of these basic principles. The concrete
and hence variable application should remain within the orbit
of the immutable principles and may not impair them.

This traditional approach distinguishes sharply between
the immutable, supratemporal natural principles and their application to the historical situation. Modern philosophy rightfully objects to such a one-sided, conceptual mode of thought.
It is exactly man's involvement in history which forms a
central theme in modern philosophic thinking. Traditional

---

*Sections 6-9 are reprinted with some slight modifications from the
author's article in *Natural Law Forum,* Notre Dame Law School, Notre
Dame, Indiana.

natural law theory likewise assumes a historical element in
man. This element, however, is understood more as a condition, an external, though important, phenomenon which determines the person from outside. But involvement in history
goes deeper and affects the entire person in his very being.
The natural law in the traditional sense is considered far too
much as an ahistorical category.

Men have all too often propounded a univocal concept of
natural law which was closely associated with an antiquated
cultural pattern. It has been assumed that man existed in a
"given" world order of immutable and supratemporal entities,
from the appearance of which he would be able to deduce,
from without, the human norm for his actions. In addition,
human nature was largely understood as an "object," and the
norms which resulted from this "object" were placed in an
objectivistic, independent order, a "world in itself." The natural law was thus too easily used as an "object at hand."

The Analogous Personal Idea of Natural Law. A conservative influence emanated from this immutable and eternal
order to which man had to conform. This past mode of
thought makes an unnatural and unreal impression, since
man's involvement in history is increasingly emphasized by the
accelerating growth of his culture. It cannot be stressed
sufficiently that human nature is a free nature. Man, as a
person, possesses an irreplaceable originality. This originality
does not imply that as a person he confers upon the world and
upon himself an arbitrary meaning. Human freedom—a finite
and participating freedom—involves being bound by values.
It is precisely in intersubjective human relationships that
man paradoxically finds his highest freedom in being totally
bound and yet totally free.

This emphasis on personal intrinsic value does not involve a relativist subjectivism, because, no matter how contradictory this may sound, human beings are in fact equal in
their very inequality. We are here concerned with the concrete universality of absolute values such as love, faithfulness,
freedom, which can only be expressed in analogous, universal
ideas. They cannot be applied as principles of the natural law
in the sense of univocal, uniform norms. These values are

immanent in men, and by virtue of this immanence transcend man. Insofar as man has a corporal nature he can be classified as a "species," and in this regard we can speak of a certain uniform, universal "human condition." By this we mean determining factors which are biological, psychological, and sociological. It is particularly these corporal levels of personal being which can be formulated in terms of a more explicit body of uniform norms and legal regulations. But since we are dealing with a spiritualized corporal nature, we must likewise stress the existentiality of this uniform structure. Indeed the person must function within biological and psychological limitations which color his being, but he is called to make these given corporal qualities part of his personal, free existence.

The greater the spiritual content of human values, the less these values can be expressed in a univocal conceptual manner, and the more they must be expressed in an analogous ideal manner. There exists a certain inverse proportionality between nature as a concrete existential reality and nature as approached in a univocal conceptual manner. The more something belongs to the essence of personal being, i.e., to the essence of spiritual being, the less it can be considered in the light of a univocal conceptual formulation of the natural law. Rather, it is known intuitively and spontaneously, although its expression in a concept—albeit in an analogous ideal-concept—cannot be dispensed with. The more, however, something is capable of being univocally defined, the less one is dealing with those values which touch upon the essence of personal being. Then we are speaking of the biological rather than the spiritual nature of man. Thus there exists a certain inverse proportionality between nature as intuitively known and nature as univocally conceived.

Mutability and Immutability of Natural Law. The human person as an incarnate spirit is historical, that is, supratemporal in a temporal order, unchangeable in changeability. Both elements completely interpenetrate each other and cannot be separated. From this fact it follows that the distinction between natural law as an immutable law, and positive law as a changeable law, must be used with caution. We are dealing here with a tentative, conceptual, and retrospective systematization of the one historical reality; outside of this systematization the above distinction makes no sense whatsoever. The natural law as an objective totality, contained in univocal concepts and composed of rules, possesses an element of changeability; in this sense it can already be called positive law. However, insofar as the norms of the natural law tend to refer to absolute value, they also share in this value and hence are unchangeable. Positive law, on the other hand, is not purely changeable; if it were, it would be subhuman. It is only brute material reality that changes. Positive law shares, no matter how remotely, in absolute justice, and for this reason must be "respected." Thus in its turn positive law could also be called natural law, but in a restricted sense.

The idea of a natural law as an ahistorical reality, which in its supratemporality and immutability could be completely known by man in explicit concepts, is to be rejected. Man does not possess an "all-surveying" vision, a *regard survolant;* as a limited "situated" person, he can only become conscious of the absolute ideal. If natural law is conceived, according to an idealistic pattern, as a known ahistorical reality, it degenerates into an object at man's command. However, man does not have this reality at his disposal, as natural law dogmatists wrongly believe.

The advocates of such a rationalistic conception oftentimes reproach the proponents of a "historical" natural law with ethical relativism. This objection is unfounded and should rather be addressed to these dogmatists themselves. Historicity is sometimes too easily identified with pure relativism and arbitrariness. True historicity originates exactly in virtue of a transhistorical reality. The historical aspect includes an aspect of the absolute, which indeed cannot be isolated from the temporal, but from which nevertheless our total historical existence derives its ascending dynamics and meaning. It is precisely because the moral ideal possesses such a transcendent value that man can participate in it ever more fully only by his growth and searching through the centuries, so that natural law is never completed, but rather always discovered more deeply. Precisely through man's perceiving of what is relative in the natural law, he transcends relativism and touches upon moral reality in the absolute. It is the rationalist who makes his relative conception of the natural law into the "immutable natural law," and thus seals it off from any further growth. This conceptualism, which in fact identifies what is relative with the absolute, is itself the grossest form of relativism. The more the historical perspective and evolutionary nature of the natural law comes to the fore, the more profound the apprehension of transcendent truth will become.

This development does not imply that our knowledge of the natural law changes in the univocal sense of forever becoming different. Our historical consciousness implies precisely an all-pervading orientation beyond history. Knowledge of the natural law by ideal-concepts does not so much change as grow. Only insofar as we intentionally touch upon the absolute by way of conceptual structures—with their material and spatial symbols—can we speak to a certain degree of change; the concept now appears in all its poverty. Insofar, however, as the concept is the expression of that which is known intuitively—in its richness as ideal-concept—we touch upon moral reality in its absoluteness, but in a way which demands a continued growth toward truth.

Authentically Ethical Consciousness. Existential ethics emphasizes the concrete universality of the moral ideal which every person ought to fashion individually and at the same time in an analogous, universal manner. This ethics expresses itself particularly in ideal-concepts. Thus expressed, existential ethics lacks the logical, univocal lucidity of a natural law which bases itself on the nature of man and society considered in their character of "object," but this logical pseudo-lucidity is transcended in personalist ethics by the suprarational light of the authentic ethical consciousness. It is true that man, because of the determined aspect of his being, continues to need practical norms which are imposed on him from outside. Human intuition still needs to be clarified in concepts. However, a truly ethical man will not so much perceive these norms in their objective aspects as view them as existent symbolic actualizations of the concrete-universal ideal of man, which is realized in the personal union of love.

The natural law cannot be absolutely proved according to the canons of positive knowledge, since we are not dealing with a material reality. There exists, to a certain degree, the possibility of rendering a rational account according to the degrees of perfection which the natural law expresses. The more, however, we are concerned with spiritual values, the less scientific verification applies. Besides, on this higher level, the need for this verification constantly decreases. Spiritual realities are known through a believing and loving attitude; in other words, through the light of human subjectivity itself. Cognizance of the natural law is impossible without an act of faith. This form of belief belongs to a different order of things than that of knowing "objective" reality. In the case of rational scientific knowledge, faith and knowledge are indeed opposite entities. If man knows anything on the level of science, he no longer believes; and if he believes on this level, then he has not yet attained to knowledge. On this level, faith is indeed a lesser form of knowledge. However, in knowing a spiritual reality, faith and knowledge must not be understood according to the univocal manner of scientific knowledge. Here, faith and knowledge are not inversely proportionate. Whereas faith on the rational scientific level results from my knowing so very little, faith in the spiritual reality results from my knowing so very much. In this context, faith does not occupy the place of knowledge, and knowledge does not occupy the place of faith. On this level, my believing is a knowing believing; my knowing, a believing knowing. One errs if one poses the problem of "faith or knowledge" in regard to the knowing of spiritual reality.[2]

Personal Ethics and Subjectivity. The person discovers the natural law as a value from the vantage point of his freedom. In this sense, the law's values are subjective and immanent. However, the more ethically a person lives in meaningful freedom, the more he is aware that the absolute is more immanent in him than he is in himself. He experiences his freedom as a loving answer to the person of another and to the Absolute Other One. Hence, a possible reproach that a personalist ethics is subjective in the sense of being arbitrary

_____
[2] Cf. above, pp 29 ff.

appears unjustified. Many misunderstandings arise because "subjective" and "objective" are oftentimes understood ambiguously. If one puts the question whether ethical values are objective or subjective, one must carefully qualify one's answer, because the terms used should not be understood in their univocal physical sense, but in their spiritual analogous interpretation. But this analogous interpretation can, in turn, only come into being by making use of a certain univalence inherent in the external world; and this univalence, in turn, must be corrected.

If the term "objective" is understood univocally—in the same manner as the material world imposes itself upon man in a determining way as an externally given factor—then this term cannot be used in expressing moral values, since only the person himself as a free subject must fashion such values. In this sense ethics is indeed subjective. Conversely, if one understands the term "subjective" as univocally referring to a subject who can deal with a material object arbitrarily and freely, then it must be emphasized that the values are objective. The person does not create the values; rather, the values determine him. No matter how paradoxical it may sound, a well-balanced personalist ethics is subjective because it is objective, and it bears the mark of objectivity by virtue of its true "subjectivity." This paradox exists because the natural law is an analogous ideal-concept which—in the course of time and varying with the person—is realized again and again in a different, yet similar, manner. To state it once more: the natural law as an analogous ideal-concept does not change in a univocal sense, and hence the idea of an ethical relativism is definitely out of the question.

7. *The Wealth and Poverty of the Maxims of the Natural Law*

The attempt to formulate ethical reality in terms of natural law precepts remains meaningful and necessary on condition that rational understanding stays in touch with spontaneous consciousness. The implicit, intuitive moral consciousness must be rendered explicit in principles in order to take on reality. In this respect we may speak of the richness of the maxims. On the other hand, the conceptual appropriation of the principles will always remain imperfect; and seen in this light, the principles manifest a faulty character and signify impoverishment. This impoverishment can be counteracted by constantly keeping the precepts of natural law in touch with spontaneous feelings and reactions. These precepts must not be too much employed as *a priori* insights used to explain historical realities from without. Moreover, if the principles are too much separated from their historical context and from practice, they wither to the level of abstract and empty categories. Thus the norms of love and respect if divorced from every ethical experience constitute an empty formula.

The Danger of Absolutizing Historical Situations. Should the principles in their conceptual expression be severed anyhow from the experience and be taken as lucid perceptions, the result will be that the external historical actualization of the values will be particularly emphasized. Especially insofar as social principles are concerned, this result leads to a strong conservatism. Since an intuitive, absolute element is inherent in human knowledge, that which is externally perceived will be treated as absolute by such a conceptual mode of comprehension. The transcendent ethical reality will then be sealed off in a chunk of historical reality, as often happened, for example, in the case of the principle of private property. If new situations are judged on the basis of such principles, one will necessarily undershoot one's mark. This new situation will not be evaluated from the standpoint of transcendent values, but from the standpoint of norms which too largely bear the stamp of the past. How often has it not happened that in regard to social matters urgent reforms have been delayed in the name of an immutable divine law?

In every period the principles must be critically examined and constantly revised with respect to elements that are bound up with a particular era. The norms of the natural law expressing more directly the value of the person, such as those concerning matrimonial love, possess a greater measure of concrete-universal validity and have a more ideal character than the principles governing society. The latter contain more elements bearing the stamp of time and are more pragmatic. Nevertheless, even the principles of natural law which are concerned with society, in spite of all their situational aspects, try to make the absolute the norm in the organization of the world. A principle lies more in the sphere of the ideal and of man's task to reach the ideal than in the sphere of an intelligibility that is based on a scientific and rational foundation. Nevertheless, both the ideal and the scientific basis play a role in the way the principle is formulated and applied.

Necessity of a Dialogue Between Principles and Reality. Neither should we make too rational a distinction between the principles on the one hand and their application to reality on the other, especially if such a distinction then implies primarily a one-way direction from the principles to the applications. The relationship between the principle and a particular case should be understood as that of background and figure. Just as the background appears behind the figure as present but also absent, so one recognizes the principle behind the factual circumstances. On the other hand, as the figure stands out against the background, so the factual circumstances appear meaningful only in the light of the principle. An enriching dynamic relation must persist continuously between both.

If the natural law is grasped in a purely univocal concept, this will easily lead to a minimizing of its values. The abstractive method seeks what is uniformly common. The criterion is: what is not present in all subjects should not be included in the description of their essence. In this way what is valid for everyone at the level of a common denominator is taken as essential natural law. In the existentialist vision, however, the natural law grows with the increase of the moral sense.

A Rationalist Pseudo-Problem. By continually visualizing the principles as ideal-values, one can avoid also the rationalist pseudo-problem as to how one elementary principle can come into conflict with another. The conceptual method has a divisive character and contrasts the various precepts of the natural law with one another as distinctly separate entities which then must be brought into harmony. In a conflicting situation it is supposed that one principle dispenses a person from adherence to another. According to this approach, for instance, the doctrine of private property is modified by the correction that numerous social obligations are attached to private property.

When, however, the concrete-intuitive experience also plays its role actively and participates in conceptualization, concept and experience converge, and a retroactive modification need not be made. The integration takes place from within. The distinct principles then represent the many-sided features of the *one* moral ideal, which is ultimately expressed in the formulation—which is at once conceptually meaningless, and hence intuitively in all respects meaningful—: do what is right for the other person in this world for the sake of the Absolute Other One. When a principle is conceived as an ideal-value, all integrating tendencies towards the other ideal-norms automatically come to the fore.

It is precisely this integrating tendency towards identity with the moral ideal, towards total union in love, which invests the norms with moral values. Thus it is not necessary, for instance, that a possible theory of private property based on the natural law be modified in retrospect by the principle of social responsibility. The proprietary right in its ideal-value visualizes property against the background of human relations. The owner's subjective right is then seen as an intersubjective one.

8. *The Natural Law in Its Shifting Historical Interpretations*

The Concept of Nature and the History of Culture. The various interpretations of the natural law are intimately bound up with the various shades of meaning attached to the term "nature" during different cultural periods. Nature is not an immutable and fixed entity. The concept of it undergoes changes which are contingent upon man's attitude toward it. This evolving concept emerges in historical perspective. There exists an interconnection between man and nature: nature is related to man, and man is always related to nature. Nature and man constitute correlative entities that are mutually explanatory. The different meanings of "nature" result from the fact that man is called to cultivate nature. On the one hand, man employs nature as an "object"; on the other, he realizes that he is immersed in nature and participates in it.

The relationship between nature as object and nature as origin is characterized by the dialectics of background and figure. Nature as a horizon is not the external framework of nature as an object, but causes nature as an object to come to the fore. Conversely, only from the viewpoint of nature as an object does nature as a horizon become clearly visible. Between these two mutually complementary polarities, nature as origin and nature as object, the different interpretations of nature oscillate. Man becomes aware of nature as origin to the extent that he succeeds in bringing nature as object to the front; yet this delimitation of nature as object always possesses only tentative validity, because it is achieved within the horizon of nature as origin whose boundaries can never be completely objectified. The manifold interpretations of the concept of nature are thus closely bound up with man's changing attitude with regard to nature. In other words, the concept of nature varies with the history of culture.

The natural law, which considers nature as the origin and fountainhead of ethical standards and legal norms, shows in its historical development a constant shifting of perspective which is contingent upon man's changing attitude toward nature as an object. In the following presentation of some of these shifts in interpretation we should never lose sight of the unchanging identity of natural law exactly insofar as it is the expression of the absolute ethical ideal.

The Concept of Nature in Primitive Culture. Nature in the primitive world-view possesses a more sacred and normative character than in our cultural climate. Primitive man experiences nature as an absolute, mysterious reality which eludes man's controlling power. Despite the differences in mentality existing among the primitives, a number of general characteristics can be noted.

The primitive mentality is characterized by a nondifferentiating experiencing of all aspects of life. The sacred and the profane, the personal and the social, the inner and the exterior worlds are most intimately and indistinguishably blended. The primitive mind does not at all—or at most, very vaguely—distinguish between the various categories of life such as space and time, the part and the whole, objects and their properties. It is difficult to imagine such a primitive world-view from the standpoint of modern man's world of sharply distinct categories. Nature, which to the technical man has become an object that can be controlled and put to use, is to the primitive man a mysterious sacred power. To him it is the Origin, Being, and Becoming of everything, of himself as well as the universe. It reveals itself in man and in the realities around him as a numinous force. The many-faceted dependence on nature is experienced as a dependence on mysterious divine powers. Even the soul which belongs to man appears as an inscrutable divine force which dominates man. This all-embracing nature bears for the primitive always an essentially sacred character. That is why every striking aspect of nature is surrounded with a religious ritual. All the cosmic happenings, such as the lunar phases, the solstices, light and darkness, the succession of the seasons, are observed and celebrated. Also the human physiological functions, such as feeding, eating, sleeping, defecating, copulating, constitute a participation in a sacred natural order. Nature virtually possesses a supernatural quality; yet, the supernatural is still completely situated in the world, the here and now, the *diesseits*. The primitive's religious approach is not as yet purely spiritual and supernatural because nature is not yet material and profane.

In primitive mentality this mysterious nature from which everything takes its being, is "prior" to man, but this "prior" does not mean a past time in our sense of the word. It is a mythical time—to our conception an atemporal one—in which past, present, and future intermingle in undifferentiated fashion. Its *"in illo tempore"* cannot be described in terms of our time categories. Primitive man continually longs to participate in the constant rejuvenation of nature. The principal events of his life are therefore encompassed by initiation rites. In these rites he dies in order to be born anew, and in so doing he becomes one with nature.

The primitive's entire life is determined in religiously normative fashion by this "supernatural" nature. The traditional customs and habits possess a profoundly religious meaning and are accepted without question, so that they need no rational proof. Since this nature embraces and guides everything, all of society is ruled by its "demonic" authority. In this primitive acceptance of life, the natural, ethical, and religious dimensions constitute one and the same reality.

The Greek View of Nature and Natural Law. Vestiges of such a mythical mentality can still be found in early Greek man. The Greek epic teaches us that the sacred and the profane spheres of life were experienced in an undifferentiated way. However, the culture of Hellas gradually outgrew the realm of myth and magic. The Greek thinkers embarked upon explaining the universe rationally and they attempted to penetrate into the natural order. These philosophers began to express their thoughts on the universe in logical instead of mythological terms. Through this first attempt at objectivation man gradually began to place nature opposite to himself, and the religious aspect was pushed into the background. This objectivation of nature also entailed an objectivation of man, who still belonged to nature. More and more, nature came to be understood as a reality that existed independently and in itself. Pre-Socratic philosophy searched for the first principle that would encompass the many entities and at the same time was their very origin and essence. Behind the multiplicity of the phenomena the philosophers attempted to discover a unifying eternal principle which they called nature. One thinker saw this eternal principle as water, another as light, and again another as number.

Greek thought kept pace with the general progress of society. Because man began to interfere more and more actively in the existing world order, the traditional ethos began to lose its mythical character. When, through the development of crafts the city-state came into being and the citizens started making their own laws, a crisis occurred in the realm of the commonly accepted certainties. The existing worldview lost its self-evident religious character and became secularized: the new polis with its own government and laws was felt to be a purely human concern. Moreover, the contact with nations that held different views and customs caused a notion of relativeness to gain ever-wide acceptance. Typical of the changed outlook of this period was the Sophists' distinction between laws that were valid *physei*, "by nature," and laws that were valid *nomooi*, "by agreement." The age compelled man to begin contemplating the origin and the content of the norms that were to sustain order among men and in society. The philosophers searched for the eternal and immutable in the multiplicity of phenomena and believed that the universe was governed by law and not by chance.

Man proved himself capable of gaining insight into the harmonious inner order prevailing in nature and within himself. The ancient mythological world-view was based on the capricious and arbitrary power of the gods, which, in turn, reflected primitive man's defenseless and dependent position in nature. Although this archaic "cosmology" was replaced by the concept of a rational and beautifully ordered cosmos, nature itself remained of a higher order. Life was based upon a nature that was no longer divine in itself but was nevertheless visualized as a higher law of life. Through the philosophies of Socrates, Plato, and Aristotle the divine logos became more and more a cosmic rationality and necessity which permeated nature as well as human consciousness. Thus there arose in antiquity the doctrine of the natural law as the expression of this rational cosmic order. The Greek and subsequently the Roman world continued to express great diffidence and respect for this natural law as a norm for man's actions. According to the Stoa, leading one's life in accordance with the laws of nature remained an absolute ethical norm safeguarded from every human whim. In antiquity logos, cosmos, nature, and law were intimately bound up with one another.

The Medieval View of Natural Law. The medieval outlook bore great resemblance to the Greco-Roman world-view. Yet during this period man succeeded in putting himself at a certain distance from nature by overcoming somewhat his dependence upon it. In this way he was able to gain for himself a margin of freedom. But even at this time man did not advance in his technical ability beyond the application of those laws in which nature revealed itself. He was able to use only those forces which were volunteered, so to speak, by nature. Some harnessing of nature occurred, but its extent remained quite limited and insignificant. The feudal relationships had naturally grown out of the ancient tribal associations, and urban society was founded on a natural division of labor. Life took place according to a familiar, stable pattern which was therefore looked upon as natural.

Yet here too arose the need for renewed reflection on the norms of life which man needed in order to control and keep pace with his increasing involvement in the secular. Medieval philosophy fell back on Greek cosmic philosophy and on the concept of the natural law inspired by it. At the same time Christianity placed the task imposed on man in a more meaningful light. Greek culture envisioned the human ideal too much in the perspective of earthly existence; the religious aspect was still too closely identified with the profane. It should be remembered that virtue in the stoic sense consisted in the imitation and affirmation of the cosmic necessity and rationality to which all things, including man, were subject. Belief in a personal, transcendent God, who freely created man and the world, increased the value of both world and man. The Christian religion attributed to man a unique value, because he was called to serve God in a personal relationship. A supernatural dimension was bestowed upon human dignity. The universe, being God's creation, was also designated as good; and to man was assigned the task of bringing this goodness to completion. In this manner the world shared in the Christian eschatology.[3]

During the Middle Ages the mythical attitude towards life was supplanted by a philosophical-contemplative worldview. The universe, again understood in terms of a reality governed by immutable laws, was at the same time envisioned by theocentric medieval thinkers as a static reflection of the eternal divine order. It was conceived as a unified hierarchy within the framework of which man and society were assigned a pre-established position. Everything inside as well as outside man was traced back to a given nature as an objective order of things. By means of logical reasoning man attempted to infer the immanent divine order. In contrast with contem-

---

[3]Cf. A. van Melsen, *Science and Technology*, Pittsburgh, 1961, pp. 206f.

porary views, nature in this period was conceived of in a strongly objectivist vein. This given nature was the revelation of being, the norm of knowledge, and the code of conduct. In this world-view based on the physical, the natural order was considered to be the prototype of all order. Even God Himself, being the primordial cause of this order, was preferably named the prime ruler, the unmoved mover and the eternal law.

The revival of Roman law, through the efforts of jurists and theologians, particularly brought out the dual nature of the medieval position. On the one hand, linking up with the past, it attempted to create a suitable foundation for the mythical-religious conception of life; on the other, it attempted to take hold of the newly arisen situations in a normative way. The more conservative current of thought, based on Ulpian's formulation of the natural law, sought to found life on an objectively given natural law which pertained to all living beings in common, animals as well as human beings. The other trend stemmed from human attempts to render nature subservient to man's designs; it understood the natural law as a typically human order which as such was known solely by man. Both views continued to recognize the *lex aeterna* as the supreme normative principle and the archetype of all natural law.

With the growth of the cities through the expansion of crafts and commerce, new social structures arose for which neither the criteria and guiding principles of the family relationship nor the traditions of the feudal system could provide the philosophical and spiritual foundation. There grew a need for a legislating and organizing authority which was in a position to impose norms upon the members of the community, although the law during this period was not yet a sovereign law imposed from above. The Middle Ages were still engaged in solving the juridical problem from the vantage point of an objectively given order. The mythical spirit developed into the more rational, logical principle of the common weal. The common weal gave suitable natural legitimation from the viewpoint of natural law to the social relationships which had come into being through crafts and commerce. Legislative authority still concerned itself primarily with the social justification of situations which had naturally developed. The stress on tranquility of order as the highest social principle of natural law resulted from the still predominantly static character of medieval society. The desire for order did not go beyond sanctioning that which already contained an element of order. Law was more customary law than legislative law. It was not so much oriented toward the unique intrinsic value of the person himself as towards the protection of socially acquired privileges. We can speak of a corporative rather than of a personal law, since human interrelationships bore an intercorporative rather than an interpersonal character. One still perceives below the surface even during this period the cosmic substructure of life. In the Middle Ages, man still felt himself bound by the immutable laws of the cosmos which in its harmonious order referred to God.

The View of Nature and Natural Law in the Seventeenth and Eighteenth Centuries. The Greek and medieval attitude towards life which derived its security from a natural order embracing all men and all things was increasingly shaken when in the modern era man made nature more and more subservient to himself. Through the natural sciences of the sixteenth and seventeenth centuries, logical, systematizing reason developed into calculating, measuring reason. With Descartes, Copernicus, Pascal, and others, the concept of infinity invaded the closed sphere of human life. With the rise of the natural sciences man's attitude towards nature assumed a dynamic, creative character. From the feudal relationships arose, in the postmedieval period, the national states which came to concern themselves more and more with technical and economic problems. The idea of the welfare state grew and with a greater centralization of government became necessary.

The medieval concept of organic unity, according to which the several corporate units were interrelated "by nature," increasingly ceased to correspond to the developing situation. The corporative and feudal relationships lost their strength. In the place of an organic concept of state and society arose the idea of a rational order promoted by the central authority of the state. The Greco-Roman and the medieval world tended to view man as a nature among many natures, at one with the cosmos. Their emphasis was on the universe as a totality of which man is a part. In modern times, man emerged from the familiar cosmic shell and attempted to design his own universe. He viewed himself in opposition to nature, which as an "object" was capable of being manipulated at will. Undoubtedly man had always looked upon nature as an object of exploration. But whereas formerly only those aspects of nature were cultivated that invited use, man now abandoned his passive attitude and dauntlessly attempted to appropriate to himself all of nature as an object. This led, on the one hand, to a greater awakening of the "self" and a confrontation with nature as a "non-self." On the other hand, every further objectivation of nature came to signify also an objectivation of human nature itself within the scope of scientific investigation.

Because the man of this new era became conscious of his own self by viewing himself and nature as opposites, the human image acquired a curious schizoid character. On the one hand, in his natural strivings man felt himself to be in harmony with nature and became himself the object of the sciences. This tendency led to empiricism. On the other hand, in the capacity of an organizing, ordering being, he felt himself to be distinct from, and elevated above, this reality which he could master. This view led to a greater emphasis on human subjectivity. Since man's awakening took place as to nature and not as to his fellow man, as is happening in our time, this "subjectivity" was characterized by an individualistic rationalism. Already with Descartes the schizoid image of man began to come into prominence, as in his philosophy spirit and matter were understood as two dualistically opposed realities.

The natural law concepts mirrored the changes described above. While the Middle Ages had visualized the natural law as a reflection of the eternal law, God as nature's lawgiver was now pushed into the background. As man's abilities increased, the natural order increasingly lost its sacred character. To be sure, philosophers such as Hugo Grotius still recognized God as the origin of the laws that governed the universe, but after the divine act of creation the natural order was considered to lead an independent existence. Thus the natural law was reduced to a purely immanent order of the universe, and hence was secularized. Whereas the Middle Ages recognized a natural law which man could rationally derive from an objectively given world-order, such realism and objectivism lost its appeal in the face of the new conditions. The nominalism of the Middle Ages began to replace this "realistic" natural law with the subjectivist principle of the human will which in time adopted social expedience as its lodestar. This rationalistic principle of volition was better suited to the changed circumstances that forced Western man to build up the world according to his own image.

The medieval harmony of the spheres was upset, and the individual parts gravitated towards their own sovereignty. Natural law nominalism led, therefore, to the exaggerated individualism of the citizen and to an absolute and unlimited sovereignty of the state. There no longer existed a stable objective order which united both. The only way in which the two could be balanced was by the principle of contract, and in time this principle was degraded to a purely arbitrary and formalistic device.

The natural law theory of the seventeenth and eighteenth centuries was characterized by the conflict between these two spheres. The growing national states found their justification in Machiavelli's theory of *Staatsraison* as the formulative principle of the power-state and in Bodin's theory of sovereignty which placed the authority of the state above the law. The new natural law principles of government became more and more formal constructions and increasingly lost their material content. They often served the purpose of logical justification of the absolute power of the rulers whose tasks became less static, less the administration of justice, and more legislative and dynamic. Meanwhile natural law nominalism still attempted to safeguard the citizen's inalienable liberties. This attempt evolved into a drawing of lines "against" the state, as the idea of a harmonious given order between the spheres of private law and public law steadily lost its value. This led to an individualistic conception of natural law, as with Locke, Wolff, and others, in which there was hardly room for genuine communal law.

The nominalist conceptions of natural law were developed in a rationalistic as well as in an empirical direction by philosophies in these centuries. The flourishing natural sciences, based on the interplay between mathematical rationality and empirical observation, furthered the development in both directions. In this manner, de Groot, Pufendorff, and Thomasius undertook to construct a system of eternal, immutable rules of natural law which could be derived from the ultimate axioms of human nature by the mathematical deductive method. The empirical tendency was found in Locke, Hume, and others. Yet both currents initially showed a good deal of similarity, especially in method. The more concrete rules in the detailed natural law system of de Groot were not derived from human nature according to the a priori method, but according to the empirical method, and hence a posteriori. Conversely, Hobbes forced the empirically observed phenomena into a deductively derived system which he had constructed along geometric lines.

Postmedieval empiricism and rationalism in the concepts of natural law corresponded typically to man's dualistic attitude with respect to nature. Man still experienced nature as a reality withdrawn from man's controlling power, whose laws he could merely discover. But it was soon realized that a knowledge of these laws would enable man to start dominating nature. Through these developments natural law in its secularized form began to flourish during the seventeenth and eighteenth centuries. The writers of this time were less mindful of God as lawgiver and author of the natural law; but they continued to adhere to the conviction that an immutable order prevailed in the universe. Still basing themselves on this latter notion, they thus attempted to invest the evolving social conditions with a stable foundation. Man's technical ability was still in its infancy. With the progression of its development nature lost its normative character and became in the nineteenth century a matter of an empirically determined regularity.

The Nineteenth Century. When the scientific development which had started in the sixteenth century reached a flourishing stage in the nineteenth, the law was interpreted pretty well from the standpoint of man's control over the world. Now that the one-sided mathematical apriorism of Descartes had been adapted to experimental observation, the aprioristic systems of law lost ground to the empirical modes of thought. Positivism began to prevail. One only needs to think of the theories of law inspired by sociological, utilitarian, and materialistic doctrines. Legal positivism reduced natural law to the level of a logical, technical category which virtually could be associated with any material content. The magical element which formerly had been frequently attributed to the order of nature was now attributed to the scientific concept of law, and this in turn led to the ideology of progress.

Although man himself now undertook to create order and to render the world of nature more and more artificial, he still lived under the illusion that there existed a permanent order which could be gradually and scientifically discovered and put to use. However, this order was no longer experienced as possessing a normative character, but as an empirically observable fact. These speculations began already to anticipate the later development of decreasingly viewing nature as a given reality which man was expected to obey. Only in retrospect did philosophical thinkers discover the transformations which already had been brought into practice in man's technical actions. During the twentieth century, the realization was born that man himself creates order by means of his technical power and that a permanent order as an objectivistic independent world, a *monde-en-soi*, is nonexistent.

The Contemporary View. Contemporary thought, becoming aware of the metalogical and metarational, takes a stand against the distorted rational and logical attitude of the preceding centuries. The natural sciences particularly emphasize this change. Classical physics was founded on the idea that the laws of nature, which man discovered, were objective realities. Contemporary physics realizes that man is not an objective observer, but that he himself remains present in the concepts whenever he approaches nature. The goal of the natural sciences is no longer "nature in itself," but nature as approached by man, in which approach the natural scientist himself also plays his part. Even in the most exact science the word "nature" assumes a less objective and given character. Von Weizäcker writes: "Perhaps the most important intellectual contribution of contemporary physics is the discovery of the necessity to consider the interrelation of matter and consciousness, of object and subject, in a different light than it was conceived of in the philosophical tradition of the last century."[4] Bacon's idea that man must first observe nature as a neutral onlooker in order to be able to subsequently utilize it, is closely bound up with the concept of a given objectivistic independent world, a *monde-en-soi*, which is not tenable. Science is less the progression from one certainty to the next, as the reflection of an immutable natural order, than the revealing of a reality in the construction of which man has always played his part, a reality which recedes like a horizon with every objectivation.

According to the rationalistic conception of the preceding centuries, scientific knowledge constitutes the thesis, and the as yet unknown factor X the hypothesis. Strictly speaking, modern science now poses the thesis that reality will always transcend human reason and that all scientific endeavor is merely hypothetical, i.e., it bears a tentative character, and its results will have to be continually altered. There is no given natural order existing from eternity, whose laws science attempts to trace. Nature begins to assume the character of an object to be employed in the service of man creating order. That which is natural in the sense of the orderly now becomes that which is artificial. Planning supplants the naturalistic principle of laissez faire. But with this rising power grows a new impotence. Man becomes aware that he may fall victim to the impersonal powers and organizations which he himself has created. Powerlessness against the technical world has replaced powerlessness against the world of nature. It is being more and more realized that the essentially human qualities cannot be made by man, but are received as a gift. The ideologies which believed in an economic and technical order that creates happiness have lost favor. The law of life does not lie in the power motif, but in the surrender to and the

---

[4]*Physik der Gegenwart*, 1953, p. 11. See A. Kockelmans, "Eenheid en Verscheidenheid in de Wetenschap volgens het Standpunt der Phaenomenologie," *Tijdschrift voor Philosophie*, vol. 22 (1960), p. 343.

respecting of the other person. The new security will be found in interhuman relationships which are not purely the result of human achievement.

Against the background of these revolutionary changes in the technical, natural world-view the shifts in emphasis regarding the natural law as a normative criterion of human actions can now be understood. We are not any longer primarily concerned with a natural order, but rather with a personal one. The norms are not vested in the immutable laws of a world-order seen through the eyes of physicists, but they are vested in the immutable value of the human person. This means a shift in ideas from a static morality of duty to an ethics of the ideal. When the natural law was still the reflection of a stable social pattern, the meaning of human life was, so to speak, made objective and circumscribed in social morality and customs. Ethics then placed a strong stress on man's dutiful and conforming adaptation to the given social ethos. Personalist ethics today shows a greater awareness of the intrinsic value of the person in the capacity of designer of his own life, and does not envision natural law primarily as a series of set tasks, but as a charge and a calling. Contemporary ethical consciousness appeals much more to the responsible self-commitment of each human being. Self-development means first of all the creative surrender of self to one's fellow men. The ethical élan is not directed towards adaptation to a static natural community, but towards the dynamic construction of the ideal personal community. The new task then is to make my fellow man—and, by implication, myself— "be" in the fullest ideal capacity, within the framework of a supraindividual community of persons.

The world of technocracy is permeated with brotherhood and companionship. Man no longer encounters his fellow men indirectly in a commonly owned and understood nature, but he virtually must rely on the other person for the very development and cultivation of this world. One cannot deny that the values of love, respect, admiration, and loyalty are acquiring a more profound significance in our time. Whereas primitive men were captivated by the spell of the unknown, mythical forces of nature, and man during the rationalistic period manifested a magical admiration for a rational world-order, it

is now man's personal dignity which constitutes a new source
of ethical inspiration.

Love and respect for the irreplaceable and eternal values
inherent in every person invest contemporary natural law with
a greater spiritual content.   Natural law is no longer one-
sidedly understood as a given factual order, but rather as a
spiritual entity, which is not imposed from the outside as an
object, but which reveals itself in sincere intrapersonal contacts.   In the personalist conception this "supernatural" ethics
of natural law is preferably called the ethics of values.   In
this personalist ethics the biological and psychic aspects of
the person remain as a given natural aggregate which sets its
own normative standards.   But this given aggregate is absorbed in the totality of the person whose being is not a given
entity, but rather a charge.   It is exactly each person's primary task to spiritualize these corporal aspects and make them
part of his personal, free existence.   The personalist vision
does not see man's corporal nature in the first place in its
character of object, but rather as a concrete expression and
actualization of an all-pervading love.

The traditional natural law theory was implicitly founded
on the idea that man lived in a world of immutable and
supratemporal entities, from which the ethical norms could
supposedly be deduced.   This undoubtedly fitted into the
cultural vision of those days, but this pattern of society has
been outlived.   Within the framework of the contemporary
cultural development, with its acute awareness of man's involvement in history, such a concept of the natural law makes
a conservative and unrealistic impression.   It formalizes the
ethical consciousness, particularly in its external phases, and
applies the rules of the natural law too much in terms of
theoretical axioms.   Every objectivation, including the objectivation of morality in the law, is abstract-universal.   That is
why the ethical ideal, through a one-sided objectivating approach, easily fades into a colorless uniformity of a minimized
set of norms valid for the average man.   If concrete ethical
living is too largely a practicing of a scientifically developed
theory of the normal, then the sense of personal responsibility
weakens and easily leads to an unauthentic performance morality.   Undoubtedly objectivation in terms of standards and

norms remains a valuable facet of ethical conduct, but this aspect must not be exaggerated. Personalist morality speaks in terms of value rather than of natural law. It emphasizes that the ethical reality must not be employed as an "object at hand." We are concerned here with an existential reality. The ethical values pertain to persons. Ultimately, moral truth is not an object, but a subject. It is for this reason that sacred scripture states: "I am the Way, the Truth, and the Life."

Now that ethics has developed from a social *ethos* to a personal morality, the legal order also possesses a more creative content. It endeavors to establish ethical personalism on the level of man's life with his fellow-men in society and to offer the necessary margin and means for this purpose. The legal order shows itself less physicalistic and traditional and more humanistic and creative. Since the beginning of the new time the legal order and morality have become more profoundly distinct from each other precisely in their orientation. There has been important shifts in accents. The following section will discuss these shifts more in detail.

9. *The Natural Law in Juridical and Ethical Perspectives*

The Distinction Between Juridical and Ethical Perspectives. As is the case with human life itself, the cultural pattern of a society constitutes a totality of meaning in which the various aspects of life interpenetrate and mutually influence one another. Contemporary personalist society manifests the tendency towards an ever-richer differentiation of the different levels of life within the framework of an ever-growing unity and integration. Thus, the realms of law, ethics, and religion, for instance, in their increasing independence are actually growing more mutually dependent upon one another. Here unity and distinction, integration and differentiation go hand in hand. Between the various levels of life one cannot make univocal specific distinctions. Jurisprudence is not something totally different from ethics. We are dealing here with an analogous distinction within the unity of the structural totality. Jurisprudence has its own sphere; but the more the legal order achieves its own perfection, the more it transcends itself in pointing to the realm of ethics, without ever becoming ethics. The same situation prevails with respect to the ethical dimension. To the extent that the ethical attitude assumes its own perfection, the more it transcends itself, without ever becoming religion. When a certain phase becomes mature, it then truly is a "phase," i.e., it particularly points to the next higher one.

Two important conclusions result from this mysterious simultaneity of unity and differentiation, insofar as the ethical and the legal dimensions are concerned. If the legal sphere ignores its élan towards ethics, it cannot itself flourish. Law then involuntarily draws ethics into its own sphere, with the result that the legal order will be absolutized ethically. Conversely, if the ethical order does not respect the inherent value of the sphere of law, this will lead to a degeneration of ethics. Ethics then will in turn identify itself easily with law, and the ethical consciousness will assume the appearance of what is outwardly and socially proper and enforceable.

The Univocal Preindustrial View. When during the preindustrial era man was still familiar with a stable pattern of life, the legal and ethical dimensions were far less distinct. The same categories of natural law and positive law were employed for both aspects of life. This mutual identification was possible because the natural law was understood as a totality of general normative rules, founded on a traditionally given natural order. In this static society the norm was characterized by regularity, and what was regular assumed a normative character. Thus the concepts of the natural law could be quite univocally understood and applied in ethics as well as in law.

The Growth of the Analogous View. In our dynamic society this traditional pattern of existence has been outlived. In ethics as well as in law the natural law must be interpreted less univocally and more analogously. This has not always been done. The result for the realm of law was that an established social situation frequently was considered as ethically absolute. Let us remember, for instance, how difficult it was to accept changing relations in regard to ownership or questions of social security. Social progress was often arrested in the name of the immutable natural law. Ethics, which in turn incorporated a strong legal strain, came to be at the service of what was socially proper, and ethical precepts were far too unauthentically lived.

In the present period of growth the natural law is distinguished analogously in the realms of ethics and law. In an ethic oriented towards the person the natural law becomes a more existential reality, which can be expressed only in ideal-concepts. It appeals to the authentic choice of man, who, from his very being as a person, must fashion a concrete universal image of man, more in the manner of a creator than of a conformist. It is precisely this spiritual, ideal nature that deepens the laws of physical nature, since it is man's corporal nature which makes its demands exactly as an incarnate spiritual reality. Natural law interpreted in terms of persons emphasizes more the normative and less the ruling character of law. It poses the personalist ideal as being normative, the ideal which man should fashion individually out of his unique and, hence, concrete-universal, intrinsic personal value. It does not take as its point of departure a set of fixed rules; that is to say, it does not pose first and foremost a general and uniform image of man, although this image has its place because of the quality of "species" which belongs to man as an incarnate being.

The sphere of law, on the contrary, places greater emphasis upon the uniformly fixed rules of the natural law and attempts to effect the personalist ideal in the world of space and time. Because of this element of practical application, the natural law of this legal dimension possesses another, although not totally different, color. The personalist strain of ethics renders law itself more functional. Law's content of rules is seen not so much as dependent on a natural static order but as possessing a dynamic, functional character because of its active orientation towards the ideal personal community. Law, then, originates less from an observed natural regularity; it is not so much customary law. On the contrary, it attempts to create regularity, and through this becomes law-creating law. It is in this way that the basic rights formulated constitutionally—being natural law in legal perspective—render the personal values applicable in terms of

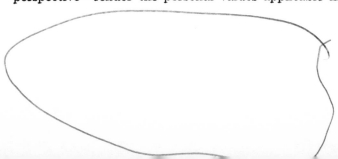

generally valid rules.   By virtue of its essence this natural law
requires elaboration in specialized legal regulations in order
to create for the moral ideal a frame of reference which
is at once as enlargeable and as ingeniously structured as
possible.

However, in distinguishing between the natural law in
terms of ethics and law, the unity of human existence must be
adhered to.   One must continue to visualize ethics and law as
an inseparable dual unity.   The ethical and the legal must
continue to be regarded as an inseparable bi-unity.   The natural law endeavors to make the ethical absolute and the su-
pra-arbitrary the basis and the starting point of morality and
law.   In modern society, however, the natural law possesses a
more profound expressive character in the ethical perspective
and presents itself as a value.   In the legal perspective, on the
other hand, the natural law is more immediately orientated to
the space and time within which values are posited and for
this reason tries to attain a greater flexibility, as is manifested, for example, in the United Nations declaration of human
rights.

CHAPTER NINE
THE STATE

1. *Introduction*

Philosophy has always been very interested in the state. There is hardly any philosopher who has not reflected upon the phenomenon called "the state." The reason is not far to seek. The state is a society without which human life is not possible. The state constitutes a bond which man encounters in practically every realm of life. Especially when it has reached a relatively high degree of perfection in a particular group, the state is able actively to promote the welfare of its members. Sometimes, however, too much is expected from the state, so much even that the state is, as it were, deified. Hegel, for example, viewed the state as the embodiment of the absolute spirit, in which man's freedom would ultimately be realized. Despite all his exaggerations, however, Hegel should be credited with having recognized the importance of the state for the realization of man's ideal.

The state is a historical datum of culture which, like human life itself, always continues to develop. For this reason philosophical reflection upon the state is never finished. Constant attention is needed to recognize political development for what it is and to lead it into the correct channels. In trying to understand the reality of the state, one should be especially on guard against an erroneous form of conceptualism. Too rigid and too univocal a definition of the state could easily absolutize a particular historical situation and block the possibilities of its further development. The concept of the state must constantly be confronted with actually existing political progress. The state should be conceived in an analogous idea, which, on the one hand, is understood in the light of reality, but, on the other, functions as an illuminating horizon, capable of clarifying the actually existing developments. "The state" may not degenerate into a formula which is indiscriminately applied to all situations. On the other hand, however, we cannot simply reject every conceptual determination of the state, because such a rejection would

191

mean that man's power of understanding is not given its due value. Man's thinking must give orientation to political developments in the light of a correct idea of the state. For this reason we want to arrive first at an analogous determination of the state's essence and then, against the background of this idea of state, try to understand the historical growth of this form of human society. The reasons for this methodical procedure have been explained in the preceding chapter.

2. *The Essence of the State*

As a spiritual-corporeal being, man is directed to the other. On the basis of this bi-unity, we have made a distinction between the personal community and the functional society. The personal community is the sphere of co-existence with our fellow-men, in which especially man's spiritual orientation to the other grows and develops. The functional society contains the various group organizations which are primarily concerned with the material and bodily aspect of man's being.

Man is an embodied spirit. That means that his bodily being is not a purely biological unit, but a spiritualized reality. Man's social orientation therefore pertains to him primarily as a spiritual being. Man as a person is not given his due by any social philosophy which bases his social dimension primarily on his biological and psychological needs and conceives his social orientation as a spiritual being merely as a reflex of his bodily sociability.

Man's Biological Need of a Closed Group. In spite of man's spiritual orientation to the other, it would be wrong to disregard his biological characteristics. In a certain respect man is also a being belonging to a species, which, because of its imperfect realization of the specific perfection, stands in need of the active collaboration of others belonging to the same species. As a biological being, man needs the bond of a group within which all his biological needs are protected and can be filled. At the same time, however, by virtue of his spiritual principle, man will spiritualize this "specific group life" and develop it into a human form of sociability. The union of individuals into a group is based on man's bodily mode of being, which, consequently, is a "specific" mode of being. Because of the compelling way in which the primary needs of this specific mode of being impose themselves upon man, the group has a necessary, unconditional and closed character. In this sense the group must be a complete, "total" society, for it must encompass all vital needs and conditions of man, precisely as a being which is specifically oriented to living in a group. If this union into a group did not have a "total" character, it would not be able to exercise its essential function of protecting its members against internal and external dangers.

The undeniable datum which the enclosing society is can be explained by means of both an ascending and a descending dialectics. If this group alliance is considered in an ascending dialectics, it will take its starting point, as we have just done, in man's biological nature. In that case the group appears as a quasi-instinctive society. We say "quasi-instinctive" because in man the instinctive forces are from the very beginning integrated by virtue of his higher life. In the descending dialectics, which takes man's co-existence with his fellow-men as its starting point, the enclosing society manifests itself as a rational functional society destined to make man's life with others possible and to promote its development. Because of man's bodily being, his togetherness with others runs its course in the world and creates also in the world a society which takes care of and promotes the total worldly dimension of its members.

The "Original" Character of the Closed Society. The need for such a protective and encompassing society is implied in the embodied character of man and his being-in-the-world. Men will always build their actual life together on the basis of this social frame. The enclosing society, which makes the world a livable milieu for man, is a datum pertaining to the "human condition." In this sense it should be called a "natural" and "necessary" society. Thus it belongs to the "original" or "primordial" content of being-man and has its place in the reflection of philosophers and their endeavors to indicate its meaning.

The "original" character proper to the enclosing, physico-rational society does not imply that this social alliance will always be seen clearly in a form of its own throughout history. If we speak here about this self-sufficient bond of living to-gether in the world as an original phenomenon given to-gether with man's nature, we are not primarily concerned with any particular organizational structure, but with a necessary worldly implication of man's being. This necessary implica-tion refers to an analogous reality, an idea of an enclosing society, which has been developed in a manifold analogous way in the course of history. Because any analogous idea can be interpreted only in the light of a certain univocal embodi-ment, the idea of an all-encompassing protective society mani-fests itself most clearly to us in the form of the state, in which this analogous reality has assumed a social structure of its own. The state itself, however, is a particular historical form in which this analogous reality appears, it is the contem-porary civilized embodiment of the analogously necessary en-closing society.

Accordingly, on the one hand, the state is merely a historical form in which the reality in question was given form. In this sense the state is not a datum that is by necessity of nature included in our original experience. On the other hand, the original datum of the enclosing society will assume the form of the state when there is question of civilized man. In this sense the state is an imperative de-mand when man's living together with his fellow-men reaches a certain level of development. In such a historical constella-tion, the state may be said to be a datum given by necessity of nature.

The Origin and Development of the Political Society. Man's essential need to live within the protective cover of an authority possessing certain sovereign claims, has in the course of history appeared under various forms. These forms were often connected with social relations of a different kind. At first, the primitive bond of family or tribe exercised that essential function. Later, the enclosing society appeared in the form of the city, the seigniory, the earldom, the duchy, the nation, and other similar forms. It was only slowly that the state made its appearance.

Because it appeared so late in history, the term "state" is less suitable as a collective term for all the various group alliances which put into practice the original datum of the enclosing society. The term "political society," which is derived from the Greek *polis*, is more suitable to indicate the typical essential feature common to all the above-mentioned group alliances. In other words, the political society belongs to all times, but was given its historical structure as a state in modern times only.

Machiavelli was the first political philosopher to use the term "state" in its specific sense. The term referred at first to the court, the royal estate, but from there was gradually transferred to the political society headed by the king. Thus the term can be understood in a narrow and in a broad sense. In its narrow sense it refers to the government apparatus which guides the political society and is at the service of this society. In its broader sense the term is used for the political society itself, of which the state, in its narrow sense, is a part.

In the following pages we will use the term "political society" to refer in an ideal and typical fashion to the analogous enclosing social alliance. More than any other group, the political society has aspects under which it is changeable and relative. Since this society is based on man's being-in-the-world, it is in a constant process of development. Unlike the historicity of the spirit, which may increase or decrease in self-identity, the action of the historical dimension on the worldly level produces a continuous change, a constantly becoming different. In a continuous ascent the universal openness of the spirit endeavors to overcome the limitations of the material world.

When the level of civilization is still low and man is still under the tyranny of the physical world, political society has only a limited purpose and scope. However, according as civilization develops and conquers the limitations of the physical world, the political society becomes much clearer in purpose and structure. In the course of history it manifests with increasing clarity the proper sphere of the enclosing social

group.   This sphere is the efficient building of a suitable
milieu for man's earthly life.   Thus the modern national state
is the end product of a long historical development, in which
the political dimension of man has given birth to an autonomous structure of its own.   The general welfare of this political society increases all the time because the possibilities of
satisfying man's needs become constantly greater.   The modern state has become a welfare state which, thanks to man's
economic and technical progress, has the means to guarantee
an existence worthy of man.

Relativity of the State.   The state, which has taken over
the former prerogatives of self-sufficiency and sovereignty of
the city-state and the region, is not itself something definitive.   The necessity of its structure is likewise historically
relative.   Although in our society the state is a necessary
form of the political society, it becomes more and more evident that the state cannot be the definitive embodiment of
the enclosing society.   The increasing world-wide dependence
in the realm of technology and economics, the reduction of
geographic distances by modern means of communication, and
the enormous destructive power of nuclear arms, all these
factors drive the national states toward a league of states
possessing supranational authority.

It is difficult to predict how fast and in what direction
this development will go.   Nevertheless, it is already evident
that in the long run the relations between the national states
cannot be regulated by agreements based on the sovereignty
of these states.   As long, however, as there does not yet exist
an enclosing league of states or as long as the existing organization of nations cannot display sufficient power, the individual states are in a situation in which they have to take the
demands of general world conditions into consideration with
respect to the pursuit of their national welfare.   The unsatis-
factory aspect of that situation is that national states have to
interpret the supranational welfare at a time when their own
structure is still the embodiment of national interests.   As
long, however, as this growth toward more-encompassing supranational units and a world-wide political society has not
yet reached maturity, there is no other possibility than that

the individual states assume this responsibility to the best of their abilities. In doing this, they should keep in mind that this task is not definitively theirs and that, therefore, they should be willing to transfer this old prerogative of sovereignty to a world-wide political organization when the appropriate time arrives. Because the human spirit has a universal orientation to be united with all in love, a world-wide political organization represents a higher form of the analogous enclosing society.

Many philosophers identify the state too much with the political society and fail to consider it as a historical form in which this society has appeared. For this reason they find it difficult to assign a place to a supranational or even world-wide political society. Arguing that the state is part of man's original experience, they try to hold fast to its sovereignty, even though the new historical development has made them realize that the individual states must ultimately transfer a part of their sovereign status to an organization of states. For this reason some of them emphasize that the individual states belonging to an organization of states must continue to retain their autonomy, be it a relative one, and must remain perfect societies in their own order.[1] Others argue that an organization of states must of necessity assume a federal structure.[2] They claim that the organization of states may not assume the character of a unitary state because that would make its members lose their character as states. On the other hand, the organization of states must possess state-like authority, so that it is not possible to maintain the absolute autonomy of the individual states. In this matter the principle of federal union offers a solution, making it possible to recognize the undeniable political evolution toward an organization of states as well as to maintain the sovereignty of the individual states as much as possible.

Undoubtedly, such considerations about the organization of states are meaningful, as long as they are not vested in a proclaimed philosophical necessity. The state itself is a histo-

---

[1] Cf. A. F. van Leeuwen, "De staat en zijn taak," *Annalen v.h. Thijmgenootschap,* vol. 42 (1954), pp. 237-287.

[2] Cf. O. von Nell-Breuning, "Zur christliche Staatslehre," *Beiträge zu einen Wörterbuch der Politik,* Heft 2, 1948, pp. 101-106.

rical form of the political society. Only this political society itself belongs to man's being in an analogously essential way and is, in this sense, an absolute datum of original experience. The question of how this political society will historically develop is a matter of scientific research. This research may try to deduce from the univocal essential structure of the modern state the univocally essential aspects that the federation of states will possess. Its conclusions may have scientific value, but should not be presented as essential demands imposed by social philosophy. Even in the philosophy of the state, it remains necessary to distinguish between the scientific approach and the philosophical approach.

3. *The Classical Definition of the State as a Perfect Society*

In this section we will examine the scholastic definition of the state, which many Catholic philosophers continue to hold, in order to see whether or not it is in harmony with reality. Our purpose is not so much to argue about terminology as to use the opportunity presented by the term "perfect society" for a more detailed discussion of certain essential characteristics of the political society which were only briefly mentioned in the preceding section.

The Classical Definition. Traditional social theory speaks about the state as the "perfect society in the natural order." A society is called "perfect" if it is complete both internally and externally. By internal completeness the classical theory means that the society in question pursues all human values. If a society does not aim at the total development of man but pursues only a partial development, then that society is said to be internally incomplete. External completeness implies that the society has at its disposal all the necessary means to attain its goal and therefore does not have to become a part of a higher social organization. In case a society is subordinated to a greater whole, then it is characterized by external incompleteness.

In this division the state appears as the only society possessing the character of both internal and external completeness. Accordingly, there exists only one perfect society in the natural order, namely, the state.

The Medieval Background of the Classical Definition.
When one considers this classical definition, it becomes evident that several restrictions need to be made. One can
hardly escape the impression that this scholastic determination of a perfect society may have been suitable for the
medieval situation, but no longer corresponds fully to the
modern developments of the political society since the time of
Machiavelli. Before the transition from the Middle Ages to
the Modern Period, the various social spheres in which man
spontaneously embodied his social orientation were not yet
sharply distinguished and arranged according to their levels of
mutual competition. The family circle, the trade organization, the religious society, and the political alliance merged
without much differentiation. Man's political dimension was
interwoven with all kinds of non-political elements arising
from religion, ethics, and a *mystique* of the family.

The political society was preferably described as a super-
family, in which the ruler's paternalistic authority educated
his subjects in virtue. The political society differed only
quantitatively, and not qualitatively, from the family. Its
boundaries coincided with those of the locality in which people were in familiar contact with one another because they
dwelled closely together and had the same pattern of work.
Against this historical background, the political society of
that time could be called a "perfect society" without giving
rise to any serious objection. Its structure was still that of a
simple community (*Gemeinschaft*) rather than a society (*Gesellschaft*).

The scientific-philosophical world view of the Middle
Ages played an important role in this description of the political society. Medieval scholasticism sought God's greatness
especially in the hierarchical order of the universe and
thought in terms of structural units in which the lower was
harmonically ordered to the higher. The theory of the state
also was dominated by this idea of order. The state constituted the all-encompassing society extending over all other
groups as imperfect, partial societies. The state's general
welfare was the synthesis of the "particular goods" which the
other groups tried to attain. The political society constituted
the apex of man's entire life with his fellow-men; it was the

edifice within which all other groups dwelled. The desire to see God's greatness everywhere in the order of creation was so strong that they often were interested in the hierarchical order for its own sake to the neglect of reality itself. An example to the point is St. Thomas' detailed description of the hierarchy of the angels.

This exaggerated idea of entelechy, borrowed from Aristotle, failed also to indicate clearly which reality exactly was supposed to correspond to the perfect society. Sometimes the thinkers of that time referred to the city, sometimes to regional alliances, and then again they meant the unity of Christendom, symbolized by the emperorship.

Modern Development of the State. In the sixteenth century the state began to become qualitatively different from other social groups. It developed into a specific category of its own, governed by its own laws and principles. From being a simple community (*Gemeinschaft*), the political group-alliance progressed to being a society (*Gesellschaft*). It became a functional organization which provided the basis and the legal framework for man's life with his fellow-men. In its modern form the state ceased to be the universal community within which all social groups could find their ultimate completion. The political society was no longer the summit of a hierarchical pyramid of social alliances, but rather the foundation upon which man's social life could develop in its manifold forms. It became an institutional magnitude, constituting the necessary condition for all other social forms of life.

The modern national state can hardly continue to be described as a perfect society against the background of this new development. The political dimension, which has received its own differentiated structure in the state, lacks the element of internal completeness. For Thomas Aquinas, following Aristotle, education to virtue could still be the principal purpose of the state. Because in the medieval situation the state was conceived as a super-family, its purpose, like that of the family, was to orient man to his eternal happiness. Today, however, no one will consider the state with its authoritarian and compelling power to be the one to train its citizen in morality.

The Danger of Totalitarianism. If man's integral perfection is considered to be the task of the state, one easily lapses into collectivistic thinking. Classical Catholic philosophy of society, however, has managed to evade this danger, despite the fact that it continued to call the modern state a perfect society and therefore to regard it as internally complete. It succeeded in avoiding that danger by emphasizing the principle of subsidiarity when the power of the state began to increase and the administrative apparatus continued to grow. However, this principle was too much handled in a negative way as a necessary correction on a theory of the state which could be interpreted in a totalitarian fashion because of the changed historical situation. Thus the principle often unduly restrained action in realms pertaining to the proper function and the task of the state. A certain conservatism in social matters found protection behind this principle. We will speak more in detail about this point in the next section.

In a certain respect the state does indeed possess an all-embracing character. The state is a society of men in the world which is externally organized as completely as possible. It bears the character of a certain completeness, because all of man's actions and his entire living-by-certain-values occur in a spatio-temporal world and are, therefore, subject to being regulated by law. For this reason the task of the state is not restricted to safeguarding public peace and security, but extends in principle to all realms of life, including even the realms of culture, morality and religion. However, in this matter it is of the utmost importance to keep in mind that the state may consider only one aspect of man's living-by-certain-values to belong to its competence. That aspect is the one in which man's living-by-values enters into the order of the external world. The all-embracing character of the political society is concerned only with that partial aspect of man's living-by-values which is based on the worldly dimension of man's being.

There is constant danger that this partial aspect will be expanded and made to encompass the whole of human values. As an external organization, the state has to have the power to enforce its decision in order to accomplish the task which pertains to it. Having the "power of the sword," it is in a position to impose its legal order by force if necessary. As history shows, the state can become an absolute power exercising tyrannical control over all human values. Because the modern state has a strong power of enforcement at its disposal, it demands a political democracy to control the authorities in the exercise of their functions. Because democracy now is a historical necessity, we will devote a special section to this matter.

The Open, Analogous Concept of the State. The description of the state as an external enclosing society expresses its reality in an open, analogous concept and does not terminate its development by describing it in a univocal formula. For, what exactly is contained in the "exteriority" of a human society cannot be fixed for once and for all, but remains always open to historical growth. Moreover, the term "exteriority" correctly expresss the "total" dimension that is involved here. Man cannot be schematically divided into interiority and exteriority. His exteriority is permeated with the dynamism of his spiritual interiority, and conversely his spiritual interiority is embodied and assumes a form in the exteriority of the spatio-temporal world. In other words, the terms "external" and "exteriority" indicate the whole of human life, but only under one particular aspect.

According as man develops as a cultural being, the task of the political society will be differently determined on the basis of his culture. The task remains always the same insofar as it is always concerned with man's external aspects, i.e., his being in a spatio-temporal world. This same natural task, however, constantly evolves, precisely because man, as a natural being, is a cultural being. The state remains an undivided bi-unity of a natural and cultural society.

It is not possible to determine *a priori* the extent of the state's power and authority on the basis of its external function. It is difficult also to state with respect to a particular step of the state's authority that it goes beyond its competence. The important point here is not so much the particular step as the entire political line followed by the state. In a general way, one may say that the state's political competence with respect to more material values, such as economic matters, is greater than with respect to higher cultural values. With respect to moral and religious values, we must say that these, by virtue of their own nature, demand special social forms. The state should give its support to them, but respect their proper character.

The moral ideal, which constantly endeavors to make the political society more human, continually changes the domain in which the state is active. The boundaries of this domain are shifted according to the degree of emancipation attained by the political society in question. On the one hand, the modern state, because of its growing technical ability, receives constantly more functions. In this way it develops into the welfare state, which makes itself socially responsible for a satisfactory economic security of its members and safeguards for them a life worthy of man. It liberates man *from* the most urgent worries of life. On the other hand, the personalistic ideal demands that the citizens have the opportunity to develop into full and independent persons within the framework of the state. For this reason the modern state must leave more room than ever for a *freedom to* self-development on the level on which man tries to attain the values constituting his own happiness in life. Alongside its increasing functional authority, the modern state demands that society have a pluralistic structure. We will revert to this point in a later section when we will discuss the principle of subsidiarity.

Summary. The classical definition of the state as a perfect society can hardly be maintained in the present situation. The political society, however, should possess an external completeness; it should be able to make its authority felt both within the society and outside it. Even with respect to external completeness, contemporary political life is in a transitional stage toward larger supranational units. The atomic era has removed the security which was formerly proper to the territorial state. Internal completeness is not a characteristic of the state. The political society merely endeavors to create in the external order the framework and the conditions which are necessary for man's being together with his fellowmen. It aims to organize man's being-in-the-world, and therefore is, as a functional society, a condition as well as a deficient form of man's personal union with his fellow-men. One should be on guard against any mystification of the "common good." The state's common welfare does not extend intensively to all human values, but is merely the milieu within which all values can flourish because of the element of a worldly structure contained in all of them.

4. *The Origin of the Modern Idea of the State*

Pre-State Forms of the Political Society. The state is a phase in the development of the political society which becomes possible only when a high stage of culture is reached. The "pre-state" forms, which could be indicated by an analogous concept of the state, but for which we prefer to use the broader concept "political society," usually consist of alliances protecting a number of families. In a primitive stage of culture the function now exercised by the state was fulfilled in an analogous fashion by the patriarchal family, the sib, clan, or tribe. These primitive communities were based on birth, descent and tradition and therefore exhibited a strongly communal character. The mythical world in which their people lived united them also by a kind of cultural bond.

When it is claimed that the bond uniting people in such primitive groups was more personal than the one encountered in modern political unions, care should be taken not to misunderstand that claim. In our time man's personal life is much more clearly distinct from his political life than was the case in those primitive phases. Moreover, political life now has a more functional character. In the primitive stage of culture the personal aspect of political togetherness had a strongly biological accent. Political relations were not yet businesslike matters because the relations between men were not yet personal. In its further evolution, however, the closed political society constantly increased its elements of businesslike relationships.

The "Polis" and the "Res Publica." In the Greek *polis* and the Roman *imperium* or *res publica* the political dimension received a structure of its own, at least to a certain extent. Nevertheless, this structure cannot be equated with that of the modern state, which gradually began to emerge in the transition from the Middle Ages to the Modern Era. The process of political growth of the Greeks and Romans took place in a world still dominated by mysteries and oracles. Especially in Greece, political authorities hardly ever undertook anything without first consulting the oracles. True, with the establishment of the Roman Empire there was a progressive secularization and the state began to be seen increasingly more as a human affair. However, even though for Cicero the state was no longer immediately a religious matter but a question of human interest to which justice had to be done, religion and magic continued to play a role. As Rome extended its power, an appeal was made precisely to religious and magic elements to keep the Empire intact. Caesar Augustus, for example, considered himself a divine ruler. Emphasis was laid on the mythical aspect of the ruling authority because the ancient Romans had great difficulty in finding a suitable political form of rule for their Empire. They continued to think in terms of the city-state; the Senate was not geared to the task of governing a huge empire; hence the divine authority of the *Pontifex Maximus* had to supplement for the lack of ruling power.

The Old Germanic Tribal Community. The European system of states, as it developed in the sixteenth and seventeenth centuries in a process of individualization and secularization, is a typical European phenomenon. Before considering its origin and development into the modern state, we must first consider the forms of the political society which lie between the Roman Empire and the modern state.

Regarding the old Germanic tribes, although they considered themselves originally a single people, they did not possess a political organization encompassing them as a whole. The people consisted of a large number of small clans and a few more numerous tribes. Clan and tribe originally were not territorial but personal bonds. Although they would assign themselves a certain region or area, this region would not be essential to the existence and continuity of the clan or tribe. The important points were the personal bond and blood relationship. Any member of a clan or tribe who went among "outsiders" continued to share in the rights of his old clan or tribe and did not share in the rights proper to the place in which he settled.

The clan was the first rudimentary beginning of a political alliance, but its realm of activity remained very restricted. Feuds within the clan were usually decided by family fights. Against dangers threatening from without, the clans pertaining to the same tribe formed a league. Such leagues were a loose form of "federation of states." In times of war the tribe gathered to choose a leader. When the chosen leader happened to be a strong personality, he often managed to establish his rule for a shorter or longer time over a domain extending beyond the limits of his tribe. When, however, this leader or king did not succeed in becoming the sole ruler of his tribe, there would be as many kinglets as there were clans in the tribe.

Kingship and Nobility. The term "king" originally indicated "someone of quality," that is, someone belonging to a prominent family. The royal sib was the most noble family of the clan. It possessed a mythical value and embodied the happiness and security of the clan. No matter how high the cultural esteem enjoyed by the king, his position of power was accurately circumscribed by ritual and sacral rules. He was, moreover, chosen by acclaim in the assembly of the clan. For a strong personality, however, the magic power by which the king ruled could become the lever enabling him to capture control over the clan or tribe. We find here the origin on which the hereditary monarchies of the Frankish Empire were based. In Germany, however, the right of election was always maintained.

Alongside the royal sibs, there were also noble sibs. They shared in the magic power of the king, but also possessed a charismatic authority of their own. This distinct cultural mandate of the nobility was a source of constant conflict with the kingship.

The foundation of the Frankish Empire by Clovis became the basis on which the position of the king grew to greater strength. Royal right began to develop alongside the people's right. The authority of the king, and later also that of powerful lords, was not based on a function given to them in that mythical and sacral world. Authority was not yet a functional category, of which man could dispose and which he could delegate. The king ruled by virtue of a heavenly mandate. He represented the realm of the sacred and derived his authority from it. Under the influence of Christianity this mythical idea of authority was gradually replaced by a theocratic concept, according to which the king, even if elected, received his power directly from God Himself. Kings and princes were not representatives of the people, but embodied the people. We may even say: they were the people. For this reason people owed obedience to the king, not on the basis of any kind of contract, but on that of faithfulness. They were still living in a mythical world in which the king was visibly present as mediator between heaven and earth.

The government apparatus consisted of the king's trusted men. Counts, as local rulers, did not so much fulfill the functions of officials with clearly circumscribed tasks, but rather made the king present in the locality as his loyal lieutenants. They also did not derive their authority from their function, but rather their function had its authority from the magic power of the king which irradiated them. Faithfulness to the sacral power remained the strongest bond in the kingdom. The entire people could be conceived as the retinue of the king, in whom the sacral power had been embodied on earth. Still at the mercy of nature's secret powers, man experienced the state as the bond of a cult which had replaced the old clan or tribal ties.

The Feudal System. The Frankish Empire, which replaced the old German clan and tribal bond, in the long run proved unable to protect its subjects and give them security. Moreover, the invasions of the Normans, the Saracens, and the Hungarians, against which the central authority was powerless, promoted the rise of regional powers. New social structures came into existence around castles and fortified manors for the purpose of protecting the lives and possessions of the people. The sense of security, which formerly had centered on the clan and the tribe, now found its focus in the feudal system.

Feodality derived its origin from typically Roman and Germanic sources. Vassalage constituted the oldest element of feudal relationship. The ancient Romans already knew the *commenditas*, the subjection of the poor, unable to feed and clothe themselves, to a powerful lord. Such a subject was called a *vassus*. By being mixed with the Germanic relationship of loyalty on a reciprocal and more personal basis, the Roman vassalage gradually rose to a higher level.

Another element of feodality was the benefice. Kings rewarded the services of their officials by granting them a benefice in the form of landed property. In the later part of the Merovingian Period this kind of royal munificence led to the disintegration of the kingdom, because the landed lords demanded for their domains also the sovereign rights which the Roman system of domains recognized. In their turn, these landed lords took vassals in their service and compensated them by according them the usufruct of certain grounds. In this way the feudal society arose from a combination of vassalage and benefice.

Charlemagne tried to integrate the feudal system into his empire by organizing the fealty in such a way that all vassals owed the highest allegiance to the king as the supreme feodal lord. This attempted centralization did not meet with much lasting success. After his death the centrifugal tendency of feodality regained the upperhand. When their kingdoms were invaded by barbarians, the kings often had great difficulty in recruiting the necessary armies, because the rulers of unthreatened regions refused to contribute troops. There was constant tension between the idea of fealty and that of the kingdom or empire. Moreover, grave conflicts of conscience sometimes arose from the vassal's oath of fidelity. A low-ranking vassal often had to solve the question of whether he had to support his immediate overlord or resist him in the name of a higher fidelity to an upperlord. At the end of the tenth century, the immediate sphere of royal influence in France was limited to the crown domains. Nevertheless, the emperorship continued to be surrounded by a sacral nimbus because it symbolized the idea of a universal Christian empire. For this reason it experienced periods of bloom when the times were favorable, as happened, for example, under the rule of the House of Saxon.

The old German alliance of clans and tribes had lost its power to the kingship and the new nobility endowed with domains or in the service of the king. Nevertheless, many aspects of the old alliance continued to survive in the new social structures. The changing relationship of power between clan and tribe existed in an analogous way between kings and the new nobility. To speak in modern terminology, the king's authority did not yet have the character of public law and that of the landed lords was not yet private. The spheres of public and private competence still remained undifferentiated.

The feudal system took over also the Germanic concept of group solidarity. The new feudal relationships were characterized by bonds of personal fidelity. These relationships of fidelity were not directly affected by the fact that later, when Roman lands were conquered, the dominion structure was taken over as an undifferentiated right on the land and its inhabitants. Landed domains were considered to be benefices given as rewards for fidelity. In the long run, however, feudal right became less personal and more real, so that the relations were reversed. In the Late Middle Ages the vassal did not hold a fief because of his service, but served because he held a fief.

The Rise of Cities. From the eleventh century on, development toward the modern state made further progress because of the rise of town and city communities. The old feudal situation had been characterized by vertical relationships and had been based primarily on the desire for enclosure and protection against the surrounding world. With the rise of towns and cities, however, there came into existence communities possessing horizontal relationships, characterized by greater openness and an orientation to mutual collaboration in making the world a more suitable dwelling of man. Through the revival of commerce and crafts, man began to assume a more active attitude toward nature. The new economic needs drove people together in centers of commerce and industry.

The movement toward this kind of community originated in Italy, where especially the bishops developed their cities into industrial and military centers. From Italy the communal movement spread to France, especially in the North, where it manifested itself in the centers of handicraft. In Germany the movement toward autonomous towns began especially in the great centers of commerce along the Rhine.

At first, these new communities did not desire to cause the collapse of the feudal system, but to find a place within the system which would politically guarantee their special economic interests. They wanted to form a collective seigniory, which would have a vassal relationship to the lord or king and acquit itself of its feudal obligations. They did not aim at a city-state, but wanted to be a privileged legal domain within a greater whole. For this reason the policy of kings and princes toward these communal centers was marked by opportunism. Sometimes they favored the burghers to secure the support of the cities against recalcitrant feudal lords, but in other cases they hampered the movement toward these communal centers.

The city entered a period of bloom in the High and Late Middle Ages. It became the bearer of culture and witnessed the first beginning of early capitalism. The most important point for us, however, is that the city became the cradle of the democratic freedoms prevailing in the modern state. This fact indicates that the development of the medieval city differed from that of the ancient Greeks. The old *polis* flourished mainly through its noble families and possessed primarily a political character. Insofar as there was any question of the people being sovereign, civil rights belonged only to a small group. Slaves and *perioikoi* had no such rights, even though the latter were free men. Prominent citizens of the ancient *polis* looked with scorn on economic activity. The medieval city, on the other hand, arose precisely through the need for collaboration in economic matters. Its citizens were craftsmen and merchants. Even later when patricians began to play an important role in the medieval city, they belonged to the class of wealthy merchants.

A medieval proverb used to say that "the air of the city gives freedom." Nevertheless, this civil freedom remained restricted. It was a freedom from serfhood and villenage with respect to the lord. This civil freedom itself, however, was limited by guilds and other fraternities. These organizations encompassed their members with their families in every realm of life. In the Middle Ages the burgher could make his rights or freedom prevail only if he was supported by the power of the group to which he belonged. Nevertheless, the collaboration of equals on the basis of mutual trust was an important step in the right direction, even though individual civil freedom would not become a universal political right before the French Revolution. The importance of the medieval development lies in the evolution from the closed forms of sociability known in the feudal system to the open alliance of a group with common interests. It was a development from a system of protection against men and nature to a system of collaboration in organizing the world. In this way the early cities prepared the road for the more dynamic function of the state.

The Beginnings of the Modern State. After 1300 the contours of the modern state slowly began to appear more clearly. A need arose for an autonomous and centralized organization of authority, endowed with sovereign power over other social alliances. The merchants especially and the industrial trades needed the power of the kings and influential rulers to overcome the economic barriers of feudalism. Commercial cities wanted a larger international market, without paying the toll duties levied by local feudal lords. The burghers were inclined to be loyal to the king, provided the king took care to create a single nation with a toll-free market out of the mosaic of counties and duchies. On his side, the king saw great possibilities in the wealth of the merchants. He could ask them money instead of crops and services. The alliance between the cities and the kings played an important role in the rise of national states and absolute monarchies. The strength of the absolute monarch lay mainly in the struggle of interest between his opponents. In such conditions, the only possible way of bringing about the structural demand for a powerful central authority was the absolute monarchy.

Another characteristic of the modern state in the New Age was the secularization and depersonalization of the power structure. The struggle between the pope and the king or emperor concerning investiture, which resulted in a separation of spiritual and secular authority, was the beginning of this process. The sacral significance of the kingship began to diminish. The sacred patriarchal authority of the king and his court began to be replaced by a functional authority. The state no longer identified itself with the king as its physical bearer, but appeared in an abstract concept of a juridical person, in whose service the king and officials with a fixed remuneration exercised their authority. The territorial state with its organization of functionaries took the place of the state based on personal bonds.

The state based on feudalism and its successor, the state composed of the "three estates," were founded on the past, while the modern state aimed at the future. The latter no longer represented a "natural" community, as had been the case with the sib, the clan, and the tribe. It was also unlike the community formed by feudal bonds, which arose from, and was kept together by the need for a protective form of sociability. The new European state was the product of culture and technique. It did not call to mind a "natural" condition, passed on from generation to generation, but a planned and planning organization, which in an open orientation adapted itself to the aims of society. The new political structure bore witness to man's tendency to conquer, to make history out of nature.

Absolutism. The preceding characterization should not make us forget that this political development took many centuries and that many residues of the feudal period continued to play a role. The new state structure with its centralized government apparatus and professional bureaucracy arose first in England and South-Italy under the influence of the Normans. From there the system spread over all of Europe after the investiture struggle. Until the French Revolution, the royal houses ruling most European states managed to monopolize the growing political power. Progressive thinkers and practical political reformers supported them in their efforts.

The political theories and philosophies of the sixteenth and seventeenth centuries tried to justify the changes that were taking place in the realm of political government. Numerous works were written to give a foundation to the sovereignty of the state and royal absolutism. The most important problem was the justification of the king's legislative authority. In the Middle Ages rulers and subjects had been equally bound by laws which had arisen largely from customs and unwritten privileges. At that time rulers did not have the power to make laws which would derive their binding force from the simple fact that they had been proclaimed by the government. The task of rulers had remained largely restricted to jurisdictional matters.

Thus "peace and justice" had been the device of the medieval rulers. The laws valid in the Middle Ages had been mainly the unwritten laws of custom. In the mind of the people this law had been recognized as being at the same time divine, natural, positive, and moral. All the ruler had to do was to remain faithful to this system of law, which constituted the medieval concept of "justice." Such a source of law had been sufficient for the limited situations of medieval life, but was not adapted to the increasing task facing the government of later ages in the economic and social realms. Thus the first characteristic of the modern state with its sovereign authority became its legislative power. The accent of the ruler's task shifted from jurisdictional and static matters to legislative and dynamic functions.

Machiavelli. Among the defenders of state absolutism in the sixteenth and seventeenth centuries a prominent place is occupied by Machiavelli, Bodin, and Hobbes. Machiavelli defended the value of the power state. He was the first writer to analyze the political category as an phenomenon *sui generis.* In his attempt to secularize the reality of the state, he showed himself a true representative of the Renaissance. This Italian wrote a political treatise on a rational basis and dropped all kinds of irrational ideas about divine intervention and imperial or papal supremacy. He regarded politics as an independent category, having its own laws and principles. According to him, the state had a morality of its own, adapted to the purposes of government, viz., the establishment of order and welfare. Machiavelli the revolutionist was theoretically in

favor of the republic as the most ideal form of the state, but
from the practical standpoint he realized that in the given
situation Italy could be unified only through kingly power.
However, the absolute power of the monarch was to be at
the service of the state and not vice versa.

Bodin. In France, Bodin became the spokesman for the
new political ideas. Toward the end of the sixteenth century
the need for recovery and order had become so great in
France that Bodin and many others saw no other solution
than giving the state unlimited and indivisible power. The
originality of Bodin's theory of sovereignty lies in this that he
did not connect this sovereign power with the will of God, but
derived it as a necessary demand from the aims and character
of human society. Although he admitted that the idea of
sovereignty could be realized also in an aristocracy or a
democracy, Bodin opted for the absolute monarchy.

Thomas Hobbes. The third classical defender of state
absolutism was Hobbes. On reading the works of this En-
glishman, one can feel the influence of the new physical
science. Hobbes started with physical conformity with law
and transferred it to the biological, psychological, and political
levels. He reduced the phenomenon of the state to movements
of hatred and aversion. To escape from the natural condition
which knew only the struggle of all against all, people conclud-
ed a social contract and transferred all their rights to a sovereign, who did not have to account for his actions to anyone
and was himself a source of right. Hobbes preferred the absolute monarchy, but accepted also other forms of government,
provided they possessed an absolute and undivided power. Even
religion should remain subject to the state.

The essence of the "social contract" theory did not consist so much in the reality of such a contract as in the fact
that the relations of the parties should be as they would have
been if there had been a contract. The natural organic idea
of society of the Middle Ages was replaced here by a planned
and mechanistic concept of state.

Absolute Power and the "Natural Order." Hobbes' view
of the state was criticized as being atheistic and for a long

time met with great opposition, especially in England. Many of his contemporaries continued to view the monarch's absolute power as an immediate gift of God. There was a difference, however. In the Middle Ages the theory of the ruler's divine power was used to escape from papal supremacy, while in the seventeenth century it served to defend the interest of the monarchy against its subjects. In this sense Bossuet also still endeavored to give a theological justification for the absolute monarchy.

Nevertheless, the divine character of the monarch's right was more a relic of a traditional and uncritical popular belief than the product resulting from the thinking of the contemporary minds. Prominent thinkers considered the state to be a worldly dimension, even if, like Bodin, they recognized the existence of divine laws behind this dimension. The theory of sovereignty with its idea of the power state emphasized for the first time in history that the political relationships had an original and functional character. Thus they abandoned the personal and religious-like political bonds of former ages.

The state absolutism, which began to flourish during the Renaissance when there was a general conviction that the world lay within the reach of man's power, soon met with resistance. The burghers, who had sought the support of the kings in their struggle against the privileges of the nobility, wanted to see their freedom realized and respected in the new system of state. Although Machiavelli defended the unrestricted power of the state, nevertheless, among the people and even among such thinkers as Bodin and Hobbes, there remained a conviction that there existed a natural order which even the absolute monarch had to respect.

The idea of a natural law received new life in the struggle for safeguarding human freedom. Hugo Grotius, Spinoza, Thomasius, Pufendorff, and others defended the view that the sovereignty of the state and consequently also the monarch's power remained subject to the higher norms of the natural law. They went back to the medieval idea of a natural law, but gave it an entirely new interpretation by secularizing the natural law. For them, the basis of the natural law lay in man's reason. Thus the question of whether this law came from God or not, became a matter of secondary importance.

Here, too, the influence of the new physical science made itself manifest. The existence of a natural order was accepted, but this order could be fully explained on the basis of human reason. However, the theories of Grotius and his followers revealed themselves unable to guarantee man's freedom against absolutism. For there was no longer any institution capable of defending the natural law. In the Middle Ages the Church had undertaken this task, but the secular power of the Church had greatly diminished.

Constitutionalism. When the appeal to the natural law revealed itself unable to break the absolutism of the theory of sovereignty, efforts were made to safeguard human freedom effectively by changing the power state into a constitutional state. Constitutionalism formulated two demands: 1) the executive power must be limited by a legislative power in which there is parliamentary representation; 2) the executive power must be controlled by an independent judiciary power. The main foundation of constitutionalism lies in the mutual check and balance of these three powers, the legislative, the executive, and the judiciary power. Together they constitute the mechanism of the state. In England the first constitutional form of government arose from the Bill of Right of 1689 and the Act of Settlement of 1701. John Locke became the first defender of the constitutional monarchy, which was born in England. Montesquieu, Hume, Kant, and Rousseau gave further developments to the idea of the constitutional state.

Although the constitutional idea and the recognition of a fundamental organic law above the unwritten common law meant a greater legal certainty, there were still very few guarantees preventing this legal certainty from becoming a certainty of injustice. The power state had been changed into a legal state, but the latter had too much the character of being a purely empirical construction. There was question only of a formal constitutional state, but not of material rights. The influence of the Illumination made itself felt in this matter. Its state did not go beyond the rationalistic idea of a technical apparatus. The political philosophers of the time were intent on the creation of internal organizational safeguards for man's formal freedom and equality before the law. Because of this functionalistic standpoint, democracy was seen solely as a technical political affair. As a matter of fact, democracy was limited to the mere acceptance or rejection of the king by the people of the state.

The thinkers of the Illumination saw the world as an interplay of forces and relations which would produce its own order if true nature were given an opportunity. They believed in the constant progress of this "natural order." Montesquieu's theory about the separation of the three powers attempted to make the state into an ingenious mechanism in which justice would automatically come about through the mutual check and balance of the three powers. This positivistic view of law and justice deprived the idea of right of every normative content transcending the arbitrary, so that the law could easily become an arbitrary power of compulsion.

Nevertheless, it was to the credit of the philosophers of the Illumination that they worked at the constructive development of the state. The state was seen as the most important instrument of progress by all trends of thought, by the illuminated despotism of Voltaire as well as the republican ideal of Rousseau, and the limited monarchism of Montesquieu.

Although influence of the people and democracy were the ideals of the Illumination in political matters, most philosophers did not dare to put them into practice. They tried to realize their ideas within the framework of the monarchic system. Most rulers were quite willing to listen to them. The illuminated despotism which originated in the eighteenth century differed from the older absolutism in this that it showed a greater interest in making social reforms and in bringing about a more radical secularization. It no longer appealed to a kind of sacred mandate to rule, but justified itself in the light of reason through its social usefulness. The old idea that the state belonged to the monarch by a kind of sacred right of property changed into the newer idea of the impersonal autonomous state, in whose service the government was taken care of by officials under the guidance of the king.

Frederick the Great, for example, used to call himself the first servant of the state.

As a matter of fact, however, the system of absolute or limited monarchy was an antiquated structure of sociability, which had long ago ceased to be in harmony with the growing democratic tendencies. Illuminated despotism, which wanted to promote the equality of all, actually undermined its own foundation, viz., hereditary and absolute kingship. The tension between the existing desires and the antiquated structure finally erupted in the French Revolution. This revolt against the monarchy, which had its repercussions in nearly all countries of Europe, revealed how much the monarchic form of government had really outlived itself. It had become an institution with its eyes fixed upon the past and was unable to adapt itself to the new spirit of the time.

The Rise of Modern Democracy. In its declaration of the rights of man the French Revolution formulated in principle the program of the new constitutional state with concrete rights for its citizens. The road of democracy, however, appeared still difficult to follow in the nineteenth century because at first all energy remained concentrated upon the safeguarding of the individual's fundamental rights against possible inroads of the state. The state's task was one-sidedly restricted to the organization and protection of civil law and neglected the domain of public law. The liberal attitude with respect to this domain threatened to make the new-born democracy a willing tool in the conflict of interest between the capitalist group of property holders and the propertyless class of laborers. In the long run, however, the new constitutional state could not remain aloof from the social question of the nineteenth century if the sphere of its competence was to extend to social matters.

Because the class struggle forced the interested parties to organize themselves into groups, the state had, on the one hand, to provide guidance in social matters, and on the other, to add social divisions to its government apparatus. If the political democracy wanted to be in harmony with its own inner tendencies, it had to take the road toward social democracy. As a consequence, state and society began to restore their mutual connections, which had been lost in the preceding phases of development of the political community.

The modern state with its creative possibilities is able to make an important contribution to the free development of society and, on its side, society can provide the building blocks of a democratic government. Unlike what was the case in Rousseau's time, the modern idea of democracy is no longer exclusively a state affair, but has become a question of importance for the whole of society. The formal constitutional state has been placed at the service of the "material" constitutional state, i.e., it is made to help the state's subjects to acquire and retain human rights. The formal constitutional state embodies moral values.

The two main foundations of modern democracy are the personalistic principle and the positive constitutional structure of the state. The state is actively implicated in the building of the personal order. For this reason the fundamental social rights of the citizen are not merely a restriction of too individualistic a sphere of freedom, but also emphasize the responsibility which state and society have in their respective realms for the realization of the citizen's personal rights. This contemporary idea of the state is expressed in the term "the welfare state."

The formal structure of the state tries both to embody the ideal of the community of persons and to be a means toward making this ideal a reality. It demands a pluralistic social structure, characterized by a differentiation and integration of the economic, sociological, and political structures. In other words, it demands a subsidiary development. We will revert to this point later. Other elements of this democratic structure are universal suffrage, a party system, a constitutional order, parliamentary responsibility, freedom of opinion and expression, and other similar rights. It is the task of juridical and sociological sciences to determine how the formal democracy can be strengthened. In Section Six of this chapter we will make a special socio-ethical study of the democratic ideal, which derives its origin from the personalistic view of man.

5. *The Progressive Character of the Principle of Subsidiarity*

The Origin of the Principle of Subsidiarity. Man's increasing control of nature had the result that constantly more functions were assigned to the political community. In the Middle Ages the political situation was still of a static nature. The existing order was then viewed as inviolable and willed by God. One who wanted to rise above his appointed station desired to revolt against the order established by God. The emphasis upon the "tranquillity of order" as the main political principle flowed from the character of the medieval society, which was based on tradition and privileges. Customs rather than laws provided the source of rights.

The increase in the task and the power of the state in the long run demanded a new reflection upon its nature and purpose. There was a constantly growing distinction between society as a community of life and the state as the organized apparatus of government. In the transition period of the eighteenth and nineteenth centuries the increasing centralization of state authority had abolished other social bonds. Historically speaking, this was not surprising. The guilds, cities and the feudal system had become veritable states within the state. If the state wanted to exercise its legitimate authority, it had first to limit the authority and privileges of these groups. Moreover, the citizens themselves desired the abolition of these privileged caste-like structures. The initial effect, however, of the state's action in this matter was that all intermediary bonds were abolished which existed in between the individual and the organization of the state.

Thus group organizations no longer existed between state and individual. With this situation were connected the conflict between liberal and totalitarian theories of state as well as the position taken by Catholic thinkers against both these one-sided concepts of state. Pope Leo XIII, in his encyclical *Rerum Novarum* (*The Condition of Labor*), had taken issue with the liberal theory of state. Pius XI, in *Quadragesimo Anno*, (*Reconstructing the Social Order*), combated especially the authoritarian and totalitarian regimes. The state had become inclined to exercise control over man's entire life and thus to deny its own character as a political community. The idea of subsidiarity arose as a weapon to combat that dangerous misconception of the state. It was formulated as a principle of Catholic social philosophy.

The social encyclical *Quadragesimo Anno* of 1931 clearly emphasizes the idea of subsidiarity. It says literally: "Nonetheless, just as it is wrong to withdraw from the individual and to commit to the community at large what private enterprise and industry can accomplish, so, too, it is a disturbance of right order for a larger and higher organization to arrogate to itself functions which can be performed efficiently by smaller and lower bodies. This is a fundamental principle of social philosophy, unshaken and unchangeable, and it retains its full truth today. Of its very nature the true aim of all social activity should be to help individual members of the social body, but never to destroy or absorb them."[3]

At first it may seem strange that the principle of subsidiarity is described here as an age-old truth, although it had never been explicitly formulated before the social encyclical in question. Yet this is not as strange as it may seem. The subsidiary function is essentially implied in the character of the political community as the all-encompassing and external bond of its members. In the Middle Ages, however, there was a kind of symbiosis between the various social groups, and the political community was not yet distinguished from but interwoven with the bonds of family, profession, and religious community. Thus the existence of the principle remained still hidden.

From that diffused plurality of social groups, however, there arose gradually a concentration of power in an all-encompassing organism, which assumed charge of guiding the subordinate groups and of assigning to each its proper place. In this way the political community became a reality insofar as its qualitatively distinct character was concerned. As soon as this happened, we find also its characteristic subsidiary function. This function flowed from the very nature of the political community, even though at first there was not yet any need to formulate that characteristic in an explicit way. When, however, the power of the state began to grow and

---

[3]*Five Great Encyclicals*, Pius XI on "Reconstructing the Social Order," ed. by Gerald C. Treacy, New York, 1939, p. 147.

showed a tendency to regulate everything by law and ordinances, emphasis began to be placed on the subsidiary function of the state, its task of serving society.

Positive and Negative Aspects of the Principle. Because of the danger threatening man through all kinds of authoritarian systems which considered the state to be the highest embodiment of man's social bonds, the principle of subsidiarity has often been handled in a reactionary fashion to restrain government influence as much as possible. The principle was often expressed mainly in a negative fashion. The state, so it was said, should abstain from activities which lower groups themselves can perform, and lower groups should not attempt to do what the individual himself could do. A secondary formulation, containing its so-called positive content, stated that only when individuals or lower groups are unable to do what is needed, higher groups and ultimately even the state may help them or, if necessary, take the initiative. This positive content, therefore, came only in the second place and actually was nothing but a limitation of the primary formula with its negative orientation.

If we keep in mind that the state has the "power of the sword" and therefore can easily extend its sphere of influence in an excessive way, we must admit that the preceding formulation of the principle shows a sober appreciation of the facts of life. Nevertheless, it lacks constructive vision. Here also one can notice the one-sided background of classical solidarism, which because of its historical opposition to individualism and collectivism often revealed itself as a kind of compromise and was not yet able to reflect from within upon social reality. With respect to the principle of subsidiarity, for example, emphasis was laid on the individual's own initiative in opposition to collectivism, but, on the other hand, the state's authority to intervene in private matters was stressed in opposition to individualism.

Private Initiative and the State. Because of this historical approach, it was difficult at first to unite the two aspects into a constructive synthesis. The state was regarded too much as a necessary evil and permitted to become active only when individuals and lower-ranking organizations were unable to overcome their difficulties. For this reason it could easily happen that the principle of subsidiarity would become its own enemy. For, if so-called private initiative may address itself for aid to the state only when it is in a difficult position, then it has to negotiate from a disadvantageous situation. By virtue of the somewhat one-sidedly formulated idea of subsidiarity, the government will then feel obliged to take over certain tasks from the lower organizations and individuals since they confess that they are no longer able to cope with the situation. Even when this extreme is not reached, the government will easily go too far in its interference, because it has to deal with private groups which have already become totally dependent on the government.

The negative formulation of the principle of subsidiarity, in which the emphasis falls primarily on the limitation of governmental authority, is closely connected also with the classical description of the state as a perfect society in both the external and the internal order. To counteract that description of the state's aim with its totalitarian undertone, it is then supplemented by the thesis that a higher and more general organization should not take over tasks which a lower and less general organization can perform just as well or even better.

The idea of subsidiarity has often been given a conservative context because of the fact that its formulation placed the function of the state in the second place and permitted government action only when it became necessary to supplement the failure of private initiative. No attention was paid to the fact that often it is precisely the state which is in a position to let new historial developments prevail against a wrong conservatism of groups and individuals. For example, all kind of social security benefits, such as old age pensions, at first met with opposition on the basis of the individual's private initiative and self-sufficiency. A particular form of the person's self-sufficiency was again made absolute in a univocal way.

As an analogous dimension of man, the development of his personality is a process which runs its course in harmony with the form of society in which the individual lives. The person needs also, and even especially, the political community, whose function it is to safeguard the primary needs of its members, in order to make them free for higher forms of activity on a higher level of personal culture. One of the aims of technology is precisely to liberate man from being totally immersed in labor for a bare subsistence and to offer him the means for a higher and more spiritual life.

The Positive Contribution of the State to Material Welfare. The state as a political community must make a positive contribution to material progress. When a higher level of personal culture is reached, its task will become correspondingly greater because an increasing number of human needs are experienced as necessities of life. The growing number of government-provided services will mean that man's personal activities can now be directed to higher levels in other forms of social existence. However, care should be taken not to lapse into a false form of spiritualism and to forget that spiritual values have to be embodied in all kind of spatio-temporal activities. In other words, man must remain on guard against an exaggerated kind of state "worship," which would expect the state to assume responsibility for all material activities in order to make man free for spiritual endeavors.

Such a state, taking care of everything, would appropriate to itself that which belongs to the realm of the personal community. It would be the greatest mistake which the state as a functional society could commit. This mistake would lead to bureaucratic procedures of regulating everything without consultation with the citizens. If those whom the state serves show a lack of concern for the interests of the community, they undermine the very foundations on which the community is built.

On the other hand, it remains true that the state has a positive function to fulfill with respect to man's progress. The principle of the individual's self-sufficiency has to be understood on the basis of the historical situation. For example, in the present situation no one will refuse to endorse social security on the ground of the principle of self-sufficiency, claiming that it is very formative for the individual to take personal care of those responsibilities. In the realm of political matters that principle should not be handled in a conservative and individualistic way. If the political community manages to relieve anxiety about man's primary needs through social provisions which provide for the consequences of death, illness, old age and similar disadvantages, then it is our duty to show a positive appreciation for this broadening of society's task instead of viewing it as an inevitable concession to an irresistible social development.

Man needs a certain freedom *from* worry about abnormal situations and biologically inevitable events if he is to be free *for* devoting himself to more normal and less compelling tasks. For this reason it is not right to address to employees and laborers the reproach that they take all kinds of social provisions for granted. A paternalistic attitude, which would demand gratitude for social provisions as if they were a kind of charity, would frustrate their awareness of responsible citizenship. On the contrary, we should consider it rather abnormal that in the liberal era man could not have a sense of security in the political community, for the very reason for the existence of that community is precisely its function of protecting and taking care of its members. True, the state may not claim to be the only organization which can make human coexistence possible, but on the other hand, we should beware of claiming that the state is a necessary evil and simply the result of man's sinfulness.

We should beware of representing matters as if the state would be permitted to act subsidiarily only when the citizens themselves are no longer able to perform all kinds of subsidiary activities for the benefit of properly human existence. Such an idea would make the principle of subsidiarity too conservative. On the contrary, it pertains precisely to the competence of the political community to undertake those subsidiary activities.

Although there is a certain hierarchical order of individuals, free associations and the state, this order does not mean a sequence to be followed in becoming active. The functions of all three are equally primary. The order indicates a division of functions, in which each group has its own distinct task in relation to the other groups. The idea that this order indicates a sequence, in which private initiative is supposed to be primary and government initiative secondary or "subsidiary," leads to a reactionary policy in social matters. The civil authorities may not assume an attitude of waiting but have from the very start a task of their own. This task is subsidiary in the sense that it should support, promote, co-ordinate, and guide the efforts of individuals and free associations, taking into account the various interests of each group. The vocation of the state is all-encompassing but also of a delicate nature. It is all-encompassing because all human interests, even the most spiritual, have material aspects and, therefore, lie within the state's jurisdiction in some respect. It is of a delicate nature because the government must support but not kill the free initiatives manifesting themselves in society.

With respect to man's view of life, therefore, the task of the government remains very limited. Its main function here is to respect human freedom and to guarantee that freedom will have the necessary room for development. In the realm of culture and science the state should stimulate and prudently co-ordinate without trying to assume the direct management of man's activities. With respect to economic matters, however, it belongs to the competence of civil authorities to provide direct guidance. The government may not limit itself here to being an impartial arbitrator between the economic interests of individuals or of private corporate bodies, but should also give directives to these interests in the light of the perspective in which it wants to guide the development of society.

The task of the state in the realm of its sphere of activity is primarily of an educational nature. An educator can do too much if he tries excessively to impose his ideas and decisions on others. He can also fall short of his duty if he leaves the person to be educated too much to his own devices and fails to guide his development. Like the educator, the state has to be constantly alert to preserve the right balance. Sometimes it has to allow more liberty, sometimes it must take the initiative into its own hands. The principle of subsidiarity is a formal principle of structure, describing the hierarchical competence of the various social bodies in relation to one another. As a formal principle, it does not indicate materially in an absolute way what exactly belongs to the competence of each. Concretely speaking, this competence is subject to much diversity according to the particular situation in any given state.

The Principle of Subsidiarity and the Principle of Sovereignty. The principle of subsidiarity is often called a Catholic principle. For this reason we want to compare it here with the principle of the group's sovereignty within its own realm, which is of a more Protestant origin. The proponents of the idea of sovereignty point out that the various sovereign organizations possess inalienable divine rights. Each organization has its own structure of individuality and is essentially distinguished from the other organizations by reason of that structure. One cannot attribute any hierarchical eminence to the state organization over the other social organizations. The lower groups are not hierarchically ordered to the higher. Each of them is sovereign in its own field by virtue of a divine ordinance. The state organization has its place alongside, not above, the other organizations; but the state should see to it that every organization remains within its own field. In other words, there is question, not of subordination, but of co-ordination on the basis of equality. The state organization is surpassed by the others in age and value. The sovereignty of the state became necessary only after mankind's fall into sin, while the other organizations are in line with sinless tendencies of man's nature. The state organization must try to keep on the right track the life of the different organization which sin has disturbed.

The defenders of a group's sovereignty within its own organization do not admit that other organizations possessing a different individual structure have a subsidiary function to fulfill. They do, however, accept a hierarchical order in so-called "autonomy." In the case of "autonomy" there is question of the relationship between higher and lower, more general and less general, societies which possess one and the same structure of individuality. For example, there exists a hierarchical order of part and whole in the case of town, county, and state and in that of department, division or branch, and the whole company.

If we compare the principle of subsidiarity with that of the above-mentioned sovereignty, it becomes evident that, despite the difference in theoretical approach, there is very little diversity in practice.   The points of difference which used to be stressed in the past were based on the classical Catholic definition of the state.   In that definition there was question of a hierarchical structure of all organizations within the state as the all-encompassing association, possessing both internal and external completeness.   This definition, however, is increasingly abandoned by Catholic political philosophers. They now stress more the proper purpose of the state, the family and other associations of man, as is done by the principle of sovereignty.   The hierarchical idea, however, may be used with respect to the realm of external order.   The various associations existing within a state are more subject to the state's control in the external order in proportion to their increasing grade of exteriority.   However, the proponents of the principle of the group's sovereignty within its own realm also admit this point, for they speak of the hierarchical autonomy of associations or groups having the same structure of individuality.

The only difference between the defenders of the two principles lies in this that those who argue in favor of the principle of sovereignty think it possible to make a rather sharp distinction between the various structures of individuality, while our explanation emphasizes the unity of the internal and external order.   The essential differences between the groups are seen in a less univocal-definitive and more analogous way by those who base themselves on the idea of subsidiarity.   To this we must add that the theory of the state is affected also by the difference in the view which the two groups have regarding the relationship between nature and supernature.   The followers of "Calvinistic philosophy" view the state as a result of man's fall into sin and the idea of sovereignty goes precisely against any accumulation of power, especially that of the all-powerful state, to which man's corrupt nature always threatens to lead.   Catholic social philosophy ascribes a greater value of its own to natural life in the relationship between nature and supernature.   Thus the state, which is conceived as given together with man's nature, receives also a positive orientation independently of man's sinfulness.

The Principle of Subsidiarity and Functional Decentralization. In conclusion of this section, we will now compare the principle of subsidiarity with the idea of functional decentralization favored by certain socialistic groups. These groups point out that this decentralization is not a principle but a method. In other words, one can be a defender of subsidiarity or of sovereignty and still have recourse to functional decentralization as a method in concrete cases. Hence one cannot say that the method of functional decentralization is in principle in favor of the more central organ. The aim pursued by functional decentralization is to bring government affairs as close as possible to the citizens. Dr. Jitta, who in 1933 first spoke about functional decentralization, declared that it is concerned with certain functions which the government has taken over. It wants to withdraw these functions to a large extent from the existing representative organs of government and entrust them to new organs in which experts and those whose interests are at stake in these functions can make their voice heard. In other words, the new organs are not to be purely governmental organs, although, on the other hand, the government will continue to exercise control.

Sometimes the socialist view is represented as being in favor of governmental centralization and of wanting to proceed to functional decentralization by having recourse to lower organs or creating them only when such a course is judged to be desirable. The principle of subsidiarity, on the other hand, so it is claimed, wants to have recourse to higher organs only when the lower organ is no longer able to fulfill its function properly. Such a way of representing things fails to do justice to both views. It places too much emphasis on the opposition between government and governed and seeks a synthesis only after starting from that opposition. In reality, both the defenders of the principle of subsidiarity and of personalistic socialism are primarily concerned with a constructive approach. The difference between the two is only a matter of emphasis. Socialism expects more from government intervention than do the defenders of subsidiarity. The former hopes to promote social solidarity by governmental regulations, while the latter prefers to create favorable conditions, through which free social life will spontaneously develop from within toward a more profound social solidarity.

Both ideas have their disadvantages. The danger run by socialism is that it may prematurely have recourse to governmental power, thereby imposing a welfare state on citizens who have not yet developed a real social solidarity. The danger in the idea of subsidiarity is that its defenders may rely too much on the spontaneous development of the necessary solidarity, which would actually mean that their social policy remains conservative.

In practice, the two views have gradually come closer to each other because they approach the state as a political society less from the standpoint of dogmatic foundations than from that of practical considerations. This convergence, however, does not mean that the political life of society is not connected with man's view of life. Socio-political life possesses, on the one hand, a kind of autonomy as a reality within the world but, on the other, that reality has to be integrated into man's project of being wholly human. The reality in question presents itself also as a moral task. It always assumes from within the perspective of man's integral humanity. A political life which is neutral with respect to man's view of life is not merely a fiction but would also impoverish man. Man's religious-ethical sense of values is precisely that which provides him with internal reasons for his political activity within the world. On the other hand, it would not be permissible to disregard the autonomy of worldly reality by imposing dogmatic solutions on it from without.

6. The Democratic State

Democracy or Totalitarian Regime. The political community with its quasi-instinctive type of sociability developed in the late Middle Ages, by way of feudalism and city, into the historical form of the national state. The rise and development of the state was an important step in the development of human existence. A further evolution of the reality of state led to the rise of democracy. Personalism with its respect for man's dignity continues to penetrate ever more profoundly into the government of the state and embodies itself in the political community as a democratic ideal. However, the factors stimulating the democratic trend are not all of an ideal nature. The state with its centralized form of government can easily resort to oppressive totalitarianism because it has all kinds of modern sources of power under its control. Hence, the democratic idea of the state is now the only alternative to a totalitarian regime. As a matter of fact, if we look at the history of Europe after 1800, we notice that the choice between these two kinds of government is constantly present. Whenever democracy fails to accomplish its task, there is always a movement toward totalitarianism. Examples of this trend are the Hegelian deification of the state, as well as fascism, national-socialism, and communism. It is to be noted, however, that this totalitarian absolutism can no longer base its legitimacy on the traditional power "by the grace of God" but in one way or another has to find its foundation in "the will of the people."

Democracy as an Ethical Value. In the past, democracy used to be considered as one of the many forms of political government. Following Aristotle and Thomas Aquinas, philosophers viewed democracy as a morally indifferent form of government and on a par with other forms of government such as the monarchy and aristocracy. Our contemporary personalistic mentality, however, has broadened the idea of democracy and made it more profound.

The idea has been broadened. We no longer speak about democracy only in matters political but also with respect to any other dimension of life. Examples of this broadening of the idea are: democracy in industry, the democratic type of family, democratic education, and democracy in the church.

At the same time, the idea of democracy has become more profound. It is no longer a form of government which is morally neutral and free of value and which people select arbitrarily in preference to other forms. In modern civilization democracy is viewed as the most suitable form of government to bring about the realization of the ideal of a personal community. Democracy has a positive moral content and

refers to a moral ideal which man wants to realize also on the
level of government. Democracy implies a positive value
judgment, as appears from the very fact that no one likes to
be called undemocratic. To be undemocratic is felt to be an
unfavorable epithet. To appeal to modern man, any aim, no
matter in what realm, has to be marked with the qualifier
"democratic." Even the communist regime with their rigorously absolutistic form of government like to refer to themselves as the ideal of a "people's democracy."

Formal and Material Democracy. The progress of the
democratic ideal may be clarified by means of the distinction
between "formal" and "material" democracy, which is used in
the technical literature about this topic. The term "formal
democracy" refers to the form of government, and "material
democracy" indicates a moral value which may be best described as respect for everyone's human dignity. Formal democracy has value only insofar as it can serve to bring about
the realization of the idea implied in material democracy.

This distinction correctly expressed the development of
modern democracy. The democracy of our time is sometimes
compared with that of ancient Greece, but that comparison is
not quite correct. The Greek city democracy had a historical
background which differs from our contemporary democratic
awareness. In the time of Pericles all citizens still shared in
the government of the city, so that there was literally question of government by and for the people. The city state still
had the character of an undifferentiated "community" (*Gemeinschaft*), so that formal and material democracy still coincided.

The modern state, however, has a much more rationalized functional structure and, therefore, it is proper now to
distinguish between formal and material democracy. Democracy is now first and foremost the ideal of human equality,
the equal dignity of every human being, which is expressed in
the concept of material democracy. In this way formal democracy is the functional structure which endeavors to realize
the democratic ideals. One could say that among the Greeks
there was a measure of personal democracy based on democracy of government, while in our time the recognition of the

democratic ideal of personal equality is the basis of democratic government. The essential characteristic of democracy lies no longer primarily, as was the case with the Greeks, in the fact that everyone actively and in person participates in government, but in the democratic spirit of government, i.e., in the fact that the government is guided by the principle that all men have the same dignity. On the other hand, it remains undoubtedly true that this personal solidarity must find its appropriate institutional form also with respect to the governmental functions of society.

Democracy could also be described as the embodiment of the personal community in the functional society or of the functional society as orientated to the personal community. These descriptions imply that the functional character of society may not be disregarded. In other words, there is always question of government. On the other hand, the functional society is already the beginning of a personal community, i.e., the personal responsibility of the citizens ought to find expression in the form of government. Material democracy is the driving force of formal democracy and for this reason formal democracy, as a structure, is not morally indifferent in itself.

The Analogous Idea of Democracy. Democracy is an analogous idea expressing an ideal which cannot be realized according to a fixed pattern or univocally. This analogous character implies that one must take into account the historical situation of a society and also that democracy has to be realized in different ways in different forms of society. The form which democracy assumes will exhibit other characteristics in a society in which personal relationships are more emphasized than in a society whose structure is preponderantly functional. Democracy assumes one form in the economic realm of an industry and another in that of politics, one form in the family and another in the church community. Nevertheless, all these "different" forms of democracy resemble one another because they are approximate participations of the ideal democracy. That ideal tends to the superdemocracy of the pure community of persons. As a transcendent value, that pure community lies beyond every concrete form of community and, at the same time, is immanent in each of these forms.

In a very general way we may say that in a group whose members are united by a personal bond man's actions are primarily an "expression" of that personal solidarity, while in a society whose bond is functional man's functional actions are primarily a "means" to attain a personal bond. We speak about the "expressive" character of action if an action primarily tends to let the person express his presence in it. An action which as a means is directed to an end places more emphasis on the functional aspect of the activity. Both these aspects, however, imply each other to a certain extent. Expression has indirectly also the character of a means, and the means is already the end-on-the-road-to-fulfillment; consequently, it is already to some extent expression.

Authority in the Personal Community. When a group is united by a personal bond, the authority within the group is based on the existential position of the person rather than on his function. For example, in the family the father does not have authority because he fulfills the function of father but because he is the father. When the bond is personal, obedience also has more the character of an active dialog. In such a community the authority is based upon values by which the community lives and of which the persons are not makers but only interpreters. Obedience here means primarily being-bound by values and does not aim first and foremost at making the community function properly. In such a community genuine obedience manifests itself in simple love. It is even dangerous to speak too much about obedience in a personal community, such as a religious community, because obedience is already endangered when it is excessively praised or defended.

In the personal community the "government" is primarily an "expression" and only indirectly a means to arrive at material democracy. There is question of "government" only in an analogous sense, for that which is involved here is the common acceptance of a common vocation to be attained especially through the intensive communication of all its members.

Authority in a Functional Society. In typical functional societies, such as the state or a business enterprise, authority and government assume an entirely different position. Everything here belongs to the sphere of the means. Authority is derived from the function, and obedience is practiced primarily for the sake of making the society in question function properly, as is required by the very essence of the functional society. Direct democracy, i.e., self-government of the society, is not possible in this type of social union. There is question here of government in the strict sense and of maintaining the relationship governor—governed or ruler—ruled. To the extent that the means is also already the goal, i.e., insofar as this formal type of government is already the beginning of a material democracy, it must contain democratic features. The authorities have to exercise their functions in a sphere which permits the consultation of their subordinates and leaves the latter a certain share of responsibility. To a certain extent the authorities should even render an account of their actions to those whom they govern or direct. Those, however, who are governed can never be at the same time bearers of authority to govern.

It stands to reason that the above-mentioned distinction between personal community and functional society does not mean a separation. Both aspects which we have called "expression" and "means" are always present, but in the personal community the emphasis lies more on the expressive aspect and in the functional society it lies more on the aspect of means. It should be obvious also that all kinds of grades and variations in that emphasis are possible in different types of social groups.

Democracy in the Political Realm. The characteristics of the formal democracy as a functional and efficient form of government manifest themselves especially in the political realm. Sometimes democracy in this realm is represented as the broadest possible form of self-government. However, direct democracy, involving everyone's active participation and even his bodily presence in bringing about decisions in governmental matters, is no longer possible when there is question of large national units. The idea that democracy consists in the self-government of many reveals ignorance of political reality. It fails to do justice to the character of formal democracy in the political realm. Precisely in our time, when the state has become a functional society which actively pursues the creation of general welfare, there is a need for a strong form of government.

The Middle Ages conceived the state in the perspective of the solidarity proper to a family. An echo of this medieval idea can still be heard in the declaration of the Holy Alliance of 1815, which stated that the participating monarchs would consider themselves as fathers of a family in their relationship to their subjects. Even at that time, however, such a declaration could hardly have been more than empty words when we consider it in the light of the increasing functionalization of the political order.

Now, more than ever, government is based on the position of authority which its officials occupy, and not on persons who are invested with authority by virtue of their birth or tradition. Many modern democracies fail to realize the democratic ideal because their form of government is weak or inefficient. This assertion, however, should not be understood as if we wish to plead for a dictatorial form of government, for we have sufficiently stressed that man's human dignity must be respected. On the political level formal democracy is a means to attain material democracy, but even in its institutional form this means should try to be a reflex of the aim which it pursues. Differently expressed, formal democracy, as means, should contain the necessary safeguards to secure a democratic spirit of government. Among these safeguards we may name general suffrage and representation of the people.

The historical realization of democracy on the political level demands that the spiritual and material components of this ideal be constantly re-integrated. If one of the two aspects is neglected, the resulting ideals of life and society would assume a utopian character. An example of such a one-sided utopian approach would be to expect that the democratic ideal can be realized by brotherly love alone. Even if everyone lived by the gospel of pure brotherly love, man's bodily being would still leave us with the problem of how that brotherly love can be realized externally on the organizational level. However, the organizational form of government on the political level is not primarily an expression of an already existing spirit of fraternity but a means to promote democratic solidarity and equality. A democratic form of government is an essential characteristic needed for the realization of this moral ideal.

The opposite extreme would be reached if one would try to attain man's universal fraternity too much by means of the powers possessed by the government. Such a perfectionism would also fail to reach the goal of the democratic ideal and lead to dictatorial collectivism. It would forget that democratic respect and solidarity consist primarily in a free and deliberate relationship of man, which cannot be obtained by force but merely promoted by proper stimulation. It would be wrong, therefore, to introduce a particular formally democratic type of government, proper to a higher level of social development, into a society in which the true democratic spirit has not yet reached maturity. The result could only be chaos. But, at a later stage of that society's social development, such a government structure could perhaps be suitable.

Moreover, in its formal and material components, state democracy lies on the political level, i.e., in the sphere of the rational society (*Gesellschaft*). Democracy as the embodiment of the personal community finds its most profound realization in the relations of man to his fellow-man. The state as the political society merely offers the framework and the necessary conditions for a richly variegated social life of the group. We do not mean to say that the political dimension is solely a question of relations that are concerned with government and power, but that these relations are directed toward a certain communal framework of society—namely, the state. The state, however, is not the highest form of personal bond. Anyone who tries to make the state heaven on earth will succeed only in making it hell.

Freedom in the Political Democracy. We want to add a few remarks concerning liberty, equality and fraternity in connection with political democracy. In its reaction against the abuse of power by the *Ancien Régime*, the French Revolution at first interpreted liberty in an individualistic sense. The revolutionary movement therefore guaranteed a negative sphere of freedom to the individual. As an embodied being, man needs room in which he can freely move and act. If he does not have enough freedom to act, his more immanent spiritual freedom to give meaning to the world will be asphyxiated. The French Revolution, however, brought to light only this one aspect of human freedom and, as a consequence, this aspect was unduly emphasized. If personal freedom is to flourish in man's spatio-temporal situation, it is not sufficient that governmental interference is negatively restricted. What is also needed is that the development of this freedom is positively made possible in man's concrete situation. An individual freedom without situational possibilities makes an illusion of human freedom.

The liberal thinkers of the nineteenth century viewed human freedom as something absolute and failed to realize that this freedom is situated and consequently only relative. This relativity means not only that the individual's right to freedom is limited by the rights of his fellow-men and of society, but also that man's human rights have to be established by their mutual support. It is an illusion to declare that man has freedom to possess property and freedom to work if the concretely existing situation does not provide him with any possibility to possess property or to work. The rugged individualism of the *laissez faire* era gave a one-sided advantage to the bourgeoisie and its expansive tendencies. They used it in their struggle against the restrictions imposed by royal absolutism and the privileges of feudal lords and guilds. But their victory led to a new kind of feudalism, the feudalism of industrialists and merchants, which one-sidedly seized the economic power.

Democratic Equality. The formal ideal of freedom making all persons equal before the law needed to be given a more material and more real content through the principle that all men are of equal dignity. The political democracy, which had its first beginning in a juridical concept of freedom, had to be developed through a social democracy. This social democracy tried to make freedom and equality socially meaningful also for those who were economically weak. At first, it emphasized work as a title to social rights, but later the accent was placed on the equal dignity of all human beings.

Democratic equality can be viewed from several standpoints. The person has an irreplaceable and unique value. As a spiritual being, a man is neither quantitatively nor qualitatively more or less than the others, but he is something original. This unique value of every person finds its expression in the statement that all are of equal dignity before the law. However, insofar as the person is also a bodily being and situated in a spatio-temporal world, his unique character manifests itself externally in a rich variety of talents and qualities. Each person, therefore, should have every possible opportunity to attain full development in accordance with his personal abilities.

Some people think that democratic equality leads immediately to the conclusion that the possessions of all should be equal. However, democracy as the realization of the equal dignity of all men in a material world does not demand that kind of uniformity. Human beings are not similar to a series of equal numbers but original subjects endowed with different gifts and abilities. To reduce them all to the same level would endanger the person's unique character and his freedom. On the other hand, democracy may not resign itself to the constant increase of material inequality flowing from an acquired position of power. Otherwise it would fail to do justice to the equal dignity of all human persons. Man's personal being remains the fundamental title of all rights to the material world; all other titles, such as work, property, birth and inheritance are secondary. The latter have value only insofar as they tend to confirm the fundamental title of being-a-person. "Having" should not determine the sphere of being-a-person, but being-a-person should determine the sphere of "having."

A society which wants to give equal amounts to everyone and in which all want to have the same amount is not yet a genuinely democratic society. It seeks man's happiness too much in the individualistic sphere of having and too little in that of communicative love. A society which simply accepts material inequality as a given starting point also remains below the democratic standard. It does not take the equal dignity of all persons seriously since it does not offer equal opportunities for the development of each one's abilities. The realization of the democratic ideal in the external world demands a relative or proportional equality, i.e., the equality must be proportionally adapted as much as possible to the genuine personal needs which are based on each one's task and mission within society. Irrelevant privileges, such as birth, sex, wealth, or religion, are no reason for creating or maintaining inequality.

Democratic Fraternity The tension between equality and inequality can be relaxed only through understanding love. It is through brotherly love alone that man acquires a genuine objectivity and becomes able to enter empathically into the other person's needs. We do not mean that genuine democracy will not know any struggles, misunderstandings and factional interests. If, however, the persons involved are animated with a genuinely unselfish spirit of brotherly love, then the conflict of interest will spark in them the light of understanding the other's position.

Love is ultimately the inspiring dynamic force of every democracy. Transcending all qualitative and quantitative differences, personal love goes out to the other person in his innermost being. Democratic fraternity endeavors to be an approximating participation in this pure love. However, the ideal of a personal community uniting all human beings cannot be reached because of man's earthly condition. Hence democracy remains essentially a being "on the way." It tries to permeate man's functional societies with personal solidarity and thereby give them more content. Passing through the stages of the political democracy, in which the accent was placed on the equality of all before the law, and the social democracy, in which emphasis was given to equalizing the social opportunities and possibilities for all, the democratic idea has developed into a personal democracy, in which responsibility and respect for the human dignity of every person is stressed.

True democracy is an approximation, a participation in the community of love. Genuine democracy is an embodiment of the personal community but is not identical with that community. For this reason democracy will always imply worry, labor, danger and trouble. Democracy is an analogous concept containing an imperfection. The primary analogate is the most imperfect form of democracy, viz., democracy in the realm of the political community, in which the aspects of rivalry and functionalism are still most striking. Starting from this primary concept of democracy, one can call other societies, such as family and church, democratic in an analogous sense. Nevertheless, even the democratic political community is an adumbration of the personal community of love, although it would be a false utopianism to identify democracy with the personal community.

Marxism absolutizes the personal element in democracy and makes it the whole of democracy. It simply identifies the people's democracy with the personal community. For this reason, it thinks that in the final stage the state as the organ of compelling authority can disappear because people will make the necessary decisions after fraternal consultation and mutual conviction. In the eyes of the Marxist, the dictatorship of the state is merely an inevitable intermediary stage. The dictatorship of capitalism has to be overcome in the higher stage of state dictatorship, but the latter will ultimately be dissolved in a democratic personal community.

It is in this light also that one should view the critique and self-accusations occurring in Marxist countries. In the final stage society will be ruled not by force but by persuasion. The Marxists endeavor even now to hasten that democratic solidarity and resoluteness by means of brain-washing education and self-critique. It should be obvious, however, that there is question here of imposing certain ideas rather than of convincing people of their truth. Marxism overshoots its goal. Democracy, and especially political democracy, remains tied to man's earthly condition. It is therefore essentially an imperfect participation in the personal community, a participation which may begin in this world but can never reach here the state of perfection.

CHAPTER TEN

WORLD AND WORK

1. *Introduction*

The realization that work belongs to the fundamental structure of man's project of life is rapidly gaining ground. Sociology and social psychology long ago began to emphasize that work is a meaningful way of human existence. Under the inspiration of Hegel, Marx, and the philosophy of existence, work has now become one of the central categories of philosophical thought. The underestimation of work in the philosophical literature of the past has disappeared and has been replaced sometimes by a corresponding overestimation. It is the task of philosophy to reflect upon the meaning of man's labor by starting with its situation in the culture to which it is temporally attached. This temporal bond means that the proper meaning of work can be understood only if we take into consideration the historical totality of human behavior. However, before sketching the main lines of human meaning which work has assumed in the course of history, we will first endeavor to present a philosophical description of this reality in order to prevent it from being confused with other human activities. The reason for this procedure has been explained in Chapter Seven.

In the description of the human dimension called "work," care should be taken to avoid two extremes, viz., to indulge in either excessive univocation or excessive analogy.

The Danger of Excessive Univocity. Too conceptual a philosophy has often compared work with the activity of the animal and considered the specifically human element of work too much as an extrinsic differentiation of the same kind of activity. In such an abstract view, work is defined as an intelligent way of acting to satisfy the biological needs which man has in common with animals. This logical view, which adds rationality as a further extrinsic determination to a univocal generic concept (animal), has often obscured man's philosophical insight. It induced him very easily to regard

242

work as a purely physical necessity flowing from the fact that human nature has a biological aspect. Whatever human value was to be ascribed to this physical occupation was one-sidedly sought in the inner intention with which work was done and in the external result to which it was directed.

If, however, the meaning of work is sought solely in man's interior disposition, for instance, by declaring that he should labor for the sake of brotherly love or the honor of God, one lapses into a one-sided morality of intentions. One forgets then that the external act itself ought to be an embodiment of that internal disposition. A good intention which cannot be embodied in man's work itself cannot last and terminates in the spiritual estrangement of work as such. On the other hand, if work is one-sidedly drawn into the realm of the external world, it can be esteemed solely as a means, in the sense that man simply has to work in order to live for values to be pursued outside his working hours. In that case morality will be concerned only with the just remuneration of work, but not with other aspects pertaining to human labor. Thus there would again be a material estrangement because no attention would be devoted to the human character of man's laboring activity.

The Danger of Too Much Analogy. The opposite of this conceptual view is the phenomenological way of speaking about work. It calls work an encounter, a dialogue, an involvement. Some authors, such as J. Lacroix,[1] manage in this way to give a very broad content to the concept "work." Although the original meaning of the term expresses the idea of making the world serviceable for man, these authors speak of work even in reference to man's strictly ethical and religious acts because these acts are performed in the world. For example, they call human love a working love because it has of necessity an expressive bodily character. Such a philosophical terminology deviates too much from the normal and current acceptance of the word "work."

If expressions such as dialogue and encounter are too readily identified with work, it can easily happen that the goal is missed again. There is then a possibility that work

---

[1]"La notion du travail," *La vie intellectuelle,* Juin 1952, pp. 4-31.

becomes too much idealized because of the vagueness attached to its concept. The result would be so-called *"travaillisme,"* which elevates work to an integral kind of humanism and makes it the sole source of truth and morality.

The phenomenological way of speaking about work as an encounter, a dialogue, or a dialectic relationship is undoubtedly a valuable contribution. For these terms are strongly referential and make it clear that man's work also must share in the structural aspects of being-man which they express. They rectify the one-sidedness of the abstract view, which sees the essence of work too much in man's physical limitation and places its spiritual aspect too much in the background. If, however, phenomenology neglects to explain the various forms which the encounter or dialogue can assume, i.e., if it does not show exactly in what sense work is an encounter or a dialogue, then it exaggerates in the opposite direction. It idealizes work and neglects to pay attention to the physical aspect of this human activity.

A Univocal—Analogous View of Work. To understand work as a human mode of existence, we have to keep in mind what has been explained above regarding philosophical forms of knowledge. Because work is a human act, it shares in the analogous ideal value of the person. Since, however, work implies also the physical condition of man, it is less permeated with this analogous ideal value than are other human acts, such as knowing and loving, which refer solely to spiritual aspects of being-man. For this reason the concept of work remains in the stage of the logical analogy of attribution, in which the primary analogate is the activity most strikingly characterized by its physical structure. Hence work refers primarily to manual labor and intellectual work is a higher form of work.

Because of its ambiguity of univocity and analogy, the concept of work can be considered in two ways. If emphasis is placed on the concept's univocity, one could not say that God works, for the physical structure that is now emphasized is absent in God. From the standpoint of the analogous view, however, we should say that God works most of all. Moreover, we encounter here the phenomenon that the concept of work, as expressing the lower levels of human activities, undergoes a modification and enlargement of its meaning, so that gradually higher forms of activity can also be simply indicated by the term "work." The reason for this enlargement of content lies in the technical development of the concept "work" corresponding to the increasing value of modern work as the creator of culture.

2. *Some Characteristics of the Human Dimension Called "Work"*

Orientation to the Production of an External Good. Work is a typically human activity. Neither animals nor pure spirits work. Work occupies the mean between purely organic functions and purely spiritual activity. Work means both impoverishment and enrichment for man and is therefore accompanied by different moods. While organic functions give pleasure and spiritual activities provide happiness, work is accompanied by feelings of joy and trouble. The joy results from the "plus value" of the spirit with respect to matter; the trouble and effort flow from the opposition offered by nature, which I try to overcome in my work. To work is not the same as to enjoy nature, for instance, by gazing at a beautiful landscape.

Work is an activity directed to "outside," it does not find its terminus in the worker himself but comes to completion in the production of an external good, a thing or a service. No matter how much work itself may be the source of man's humanization, it remains essentially directed to the production of a useful result. Hence work appears to be primarily an economic category and to belong to the "giving in exchange" sphere of justice. The specialized service of the worker is changed into all kinds of counter-services through the economic exchange of its financial remuneration. On the other hand, it is not necessary that every type of work be directly taken up into the strict exchange of an economic order. For example, the work done by a housewife remains work because within the family there is also question of a division of functions.

Work and the Classical Distinction Between Immanent and Transient Action. Thomistic thinkers characterize work as a transient action in opposition to immanent action, such as acts of knowing and loving. This distinction is enlightening insofar as both actions are seen primarily as an inseparable bi-unity, as a structural whole. A unity by reciprocal implication is involved here. Transient action embodies an immanent act, and the immanent act manifests itself in a transient action. It is only on the basis of this structural whole that one can distinguish transient and immanent actions according as either one or the other aspect predominates.

In the light of these remarks we may say that work is that activity in which the body appears in its quasi-objectivity as an instrument to change and humanize the material world. Man's bodily being in its quasi-subjectivity, on the other hand, is the person in his immediate expressive self-revelation to the other. In this revelation there is no longer question of purposive actions, but we have here *inter alia* the immanent acts of knowing and loving, which transcend the sphere of the "giving in exchange" relationship and therefore are no longer work. In proportion to their spiritual value these acts have less the spatio-temporal character of an "event." To know and to love, for example, are permanent fundamental attitudes rather than actions occurring at a particular place and time. Work, on the other hand, refers to that activity whose emphasis lies in acting on something else in its physical distinction from the worker. For this reason work is a transient action.

Because of this transient element, work, in spite of all its positive value, implies an imperfection. For, if a being has to attain its perfection at least to some extent through a transient action upon something physically distinct from itself, i.e., through changing material things and self-estrangement, then such a being is also subject to the blind laws governing the material world. Thus work has the character of a means, it serves to attain something else and always retains an aspect referring to conditions. Man works in the service of life. To work means also to create conditions for a properly human existence. Work implies a self-loss. If it were pure self-development it would cease to be work and become contemplation. Even with respect to its power to form man socially, work continues to have this aspect of self-loss. The solidarity of man in work arises in part also from a material need and, because of this need and the scarcity of goods to fill it, will always be accompanied by rivalry and competition.

Work Versus Contemplation. As a transient activity, work is usually opposed to contemplation as an immanent activity. Contemplation refers to the ideal of total immanence, in which understanding and loving have become one and in which there is no longer any acting on something else in self-estrangement. This contemplation should not be confused with the Greek contemplative ideal, which aimed too one-sidedly at an intellectual gazing at eternal truths. Contemplation, as we consider it here, is rather the total mutual self-revelation and self-surrender of persons. We are referring here to pure intersubjectivity, in which persons become immanent in each other. This contemplation appears to man as a kind of rest because it transcends the busy world of purposive activities. On the other hand, it is also dynamic because it is the highest form of man's personal unfolding.

People living in certain religious communities are said to live a contemplative life. Their life is called contemplative because these persons leave the busy activities of the world, draw apart in a community, and devote themselves to God. This kind of life, however, is merely a certain form of contemplation. Contemplation is an ideal concept, which can be embodied in different ways in different persons. This ideal should not be charged too much with a cloistral connotation, for ultimately there is a contemplative orientation in every man's life. Contemplation is the loving dwelling with the other, it is a structural aspect of the interpersonal "we." Contemplation, as thoughtful togetherness with the other in love, sets the we-community apart as a home from which man goes forth to the world of work and to which he returns when his labor is finished. By working, man tries to overcome the infrahuman level; but while working, he does not produce that which is properly human, viz., the persons' contemplative mutual revelation of their being.

Immanent Aspect of Work. The preceding paragraphs showed work primarily as a necessary condition for man's proper life of the spirit. All this, however, demands to be made more precise by the consideration of work from other viewpoints. Work is not only an impoverishment of the spirit but also its enrichment. We do not merely work to live, but work itself is life. These two aspects of work are inseparably united. Work is essentially more than procuring the necessary sustenance of life. As a human action, it possesses a certain degree of immanence and therefore itself represents a value. Work is formative of man. By working, man not only becomes estranged from himself by adapting himself to its object, but he also creates himself by making the humanized object serve the subject. In the product of his work man faces himself and thereby recognizes himself. The spirit gives itself away in work to find itself again. It becomes involved in the physical world in order to disengage itself, enriched from the world. Man experiences his "plus value" with respect to the product of his work.

Work and Man's Social Formation. In man's humanizing interaction with the physical world work is particularly formative from the social viewpoint. Because human beings inevitably need one another and have to work for one another, man acquires a spirit of solidarity. Even his utilitarian activities are to some extent permeated with this idea of co-existence.

Especially in the contemporary rationalization of labor, man depends in his work on the collaboration of many. Today's work can be experienced as meaningful only if it is performed in the spirit of solidarity. Work is constructive of society. True, man's work community with its tendency toward human relations should not be idealized. It is not the central form of co-existence *par excellence*, but a solidarity of interests. It is not possible for man to find in work the fulfillment of his entire life. The ambiguity of work, which implies both self-development and self-loss, can never be integrated into a meaningful whole within the limits of work itself. That integration demands the broader perspective of intersubjectivity, in which the man who loves becomes himself by losing himself totally to the other. If, then, a man lets his whole being be encompassed by work, his life loses its orientation. The functional world of work always remains a condition of, and a demand for something else. If life is fully dominated by work, then it remains a purposeless and restless pursuit of something else. Work is then unable to find its completion in the contemplative rest of suprafunctional co-existence.

If work is to remain human, it must at the same time be socially formative. The human value of modern work does not lie so much in the making of products or the rendering of services as in making or rendering these things together with our fellow-men. The growth of intersubjectivity in work does not depend solely on good intentions, for otherwise one would again make a dualistic division between an inner world and an outer world. Man's participation in work must be the first beginning, no matter how imperfect it be, of a genuine personal community. Because work is essentially directed to the production of goods or the rendering of services, man's sharing in the common task of work must be reflected also in his sharing in common in the results produced by his labor.

As Marx correctly remarks, when man is estranged from the product of his work, this alienation leads to the destruction of human sociality. The product of his labor becomes not only the property of someone else but also turns against the worker who produced it. For this product is changed into capital and, by its own inner logic, capital tries to grow by making the laborer work for even smaller wages. Man is deprived of the results produced by his work through the egoistic desire for profit of someone else who exploits him. For this reason work should belong to all even with respect to the results which it produces. We mean that the division of those results into mine and thine should not be the effect of an individualistic striving for power, but should be arrived at in common concert in such a way that everyone receives as much as possible what is due to him.

Technical Growth and the Appreciation of Work. According as work is done more with the mind and less with the body, i.e., according as work is more rationalized, it offers greater possibilities for man's moral and social growth. In a primitive phase man tries to make use of tools in his work; next, he has recourse to instruments. In a following stage the machine takes over man's work and man runs the machine.

Finally, the machine is made to run and service itself. The acceleration of technique in modern time finds its explanation in the fact that man's scientific reason has been geared to practical concerns. Man has made his scientific knowledge subservient to the control of nature. This technical growth is accompanied by an increasing appreciation of work.

Among primitives the whole of life is still marked with care for mere subsistence. All other dimensions of life are undifferentiatedly interwoven with work. As soon as there is a first beginning of cultural development, a split occurs as a rule between those who live to work and those who live on the work of the others. In the Greco-Roman civilization we notice that work and life still remained divorced. Work there still meant the labor performed by slaves and "unfree" men. The only people leading an authentically human existence were those who devoted themselves to the disinterested pursuit of science and art, which are not directed to useful aims. They alone were "free" men. In the Middle Ages work was viewed as an honorable mode of being on a par with other modes of being. Finally, in the contemporary view of society work is regarded as a meaningful task for everyone. Contemporary man feels himself successful only when he knows that the work which he does is socially appreciated.

This development of the situation of work is accompanied by a shift in the structure of society. In the Greco-Roman period society was divided into groups of free men and groups of unfree men. The Middle Ages had different classes based on privileges flowing from one's birth. Next, came class distinctions based on the possession of property. In our era work makes men increasingly feel themselves to be of equal dignity and less inclined to recognize privileges based on ancestry or property.

Broadening of the Concept of Work. The concept of work itself was broadened through the development of man's technical powers because they demanded not only greater intellectual abilities but also that higher-ranking human activities be integrated into the realm of work. When the level of culture rises, man's primary needs, to which work is primarily oriented, assume higher forms, so that even the correction of insociability is regarded as a necessary social work. Moreover, the expressions of cultural interests, such as art, learning and sport, which in former times were "free" pursuits, can now be regarded also as a kind of work and thus enter into the sphere of a "giving and receiving" relationship. In this way work offers more opportunities for the formation of man and society. The more univocal content of the concept "physical manual labor" now becomes permeated with a higher analogous content because man's working occupation itself rises to increasingly higher levels. The result of all this is that man's work constantly acquires a more ideal value, as is manifested by the fact that we have now both civil and religious celebrations of labor days.

Nevertheless, work retains its own ambiguous character. One must even say that the more work gains in value as creative of culture, the more it also becomes a means toward man's proper goal of life, which transcends the realm of work. It is necessary to remain critical with respect to an ideology which endows work with the central position and makes its value encompass the whole of man. Anyone who expects that the cultivation of work will unconditionally result in man's full bloom can be sure that he will be disappointed. While it is true that the human values made available in and through work have increased, it is equally true that the possibilities of man's self-estrangement in and through a one-sided order of labor have been multiplied. The functional aspect of work increases, and this ultimately means that work should be placed in function of man's personal self-development.

The Tendency to Differentiation and Integration of Distinct Levels of Life. For many centuries the whole of life was dominated by work, not only for the employer, who devoted himself wholly to his enterprise, but also for the laborer, who together with his entire family had to work to earn a bare living. Our contemporary society, however, slowly abandons that exaggerated attachment to work, which had neither time nor patience for anything else than work.

We find here again that remarkable tendency to differentiation between different levels of life and to their integration which we have noted in a preceding chapter when we spoke

about ethics and right.   A relative autonomy with respect to
each other manifests itself in the personal and the functional
sphere, the sphere of life and the sphere of work.   Work
becomes more functional and life becomes more personal.   As
is the case with every dimension of life, the functionalization
of the modern world can go in a positive and in a negative
direction.   It goes in the wrong direction if the modern community of work degenerates, threatens to level the whole
person and to make him nothing but a functionary.   It goes in
the right direction if, as a community of interests, it also
takes care of its material aims in a positive businesslike way
and lets the person be a functionary within these limits.
Strange as it may seem, the human dignity of modern labor
consists to a large extent in the realization that work is, after
all, only work and not the whole task of man.   Today's work
increases in human value also because of the fact that it
offers man the time and the opportunity to pursue higher
activities than those of the economic level.   In this respect
modern work manifests again the tendency to the integration
of the various levels of life.

The community of interests which work is should never
be regarded too much as a community in the personal sense,
for otherwise we would let the whole person be absorbed by
his function.   The building of a world worthy of man through
work must be put in the service of man's personal self-
surrender to the other.   Conversely, the person may not identify himself with his work and must respect his fellow-workers
in their personal life.   Yet the mature person will devote
himself loyally to his work because he realizes that he labors
for those with whom he is united by a personal bond outside
his working hours.

3.   *The Marxist Conception of Work*

Marxist and Christian Analogy of Work.   The Marxist
view praises work as the highest value.   Through his work
man begins to dominate nature, he "humanizes" nature.   On
the other hand, nature activates the forces and potentialities
dormant in man.   As Marx expresses it, nature "naturalizes"
man.   Because in the Marxist view work is the activity in

which man is self-creative *par excellence,* work possesses the highest value. In Marxist ideology work appears to be an analogous idea without any imperfection. All forms of being busy with work in man's ascent to the final stage of the classless society are viewed as imperfect approximations to the absolute ideal of work. The Marxist view of work differs in this respect from the Christian view. The Christian also regards the concept of work as an analogous concept, but he does not consider it to have the transcendental value which the Marxist ascribes to it.

For the Christian the value of work always implies an imperfection and for this reason needs to be orientated toward the transcendental values of love, which in its perfection transcends work. One could express the difference between the appreciation of work by Marxism and by Christianity in the following way, making use of scholastic terminology. For Marx, work, as a transcendental value, is known through a philosophical analogy whose primary analogate lies in the fullness of an absolutely posited ideal of work. For the Christian, work always remains also to some extent a predicamental value and therefore stays in the realm of logical analogy, so that the primary analogate refers to those forms of work which are most clearly marked by imperfection.

According to the Christian view, work never fully transcends the sphere of the useful. However, one would commit an essential injustice against Marx by asserting, on the basis of the Christian view of work, that his ideology of work makes the useful and the technical the highest values of man. Marx' concept of work can hardly be identified with its Christian counterpart. His concept has an entirely different analogous background and for this reason is scarcely comparable with the Christian concept of work. For, comparison is, strictly speaking, possible only when something that is univocally "the same" is attributed to several and can be abstracted from the difference existing between them. In the analogous order, however, there is no question of a partial sameness and a partial difference, as is the case with a predicamental plurality, but there is a total sameness and a total diversity in such a way that this sameness and this difference can hardly be separated from each other through abstraction.

According to Marx, in the final stage of society everyone will work according to his capacities because of his unselfish orientation to the universal community of men. In that stage man will find his happiness in his love for his work, which he performs in genuine brotherly love. The problem of property will also be solved in that stage. Everyone will be rewarded according to his needs. If one receives more than the other, it will not cause any jealousy since man will no longer work to earn monetary rewards. Work as service rendered to the community carries happiness within its bosom and therefore is self-rewarding. Considering Marx' elevated utopian view of the final stage, no one is entitled to reproach him for presenting a materialistic view of life.

The difference between the concept of work in the Marxist and the Christian views of life may be compared to the way in which one and the same term may be understood differently according to the connotations which the term carries for persons living in different worlds. In the nineteenth century, for example, liberalism meant freedom from undue government interference for the capitalist, but in the eyes of the laborer it meant unrestricted oppression of the working class. If the two worlds of connotation are not taken into consideration, so that the other's view is interpreted wholly according to the meaning which a term conveys in one's own view, one obviously fails to understand the other and does him an injustice. For this reason it is imperative that any attempt to compare and evaluate the Marxist and Christian ethics of work should pay attention to the differences of meaning involved in the terms. There may be verbal agreement but real contradiction in what is meant by the same terms.

Love and Work. In a certain respect the Marxist concept of work has a more profound background than its Christian counterpart. It has a stronger aspect of love. Marx often speaks about work in terms of pure love. One could say that for Marx work, understood in its univocal sense, contains more than it implies in the Christian view of work. On the other hand, Christianity regards human love as a participation in the supraworldly divine love. For this reason work, as a condition and orientation to that love, has also a more profound meaning in the Christian view than in the Marxist view of life. In other words, work, considered in its value as an analogous idea, goes beyond the Marxist ideal. If absolute love is wholly sought in man's worldly existence and if the aspect of usefulness is essentially inherent in this world, the Marxist ideal of universal brotherhood is bound to acquire a strongly technical and egoistic utilitarian overtone, in spite of all efforts to prevent it. The strong identification of this brotherhood with the myth of mankind as a community of labor is a confirmation of this assertion.

In the Christian view also work is an essential category of human existence, but it takes the term "essential" in another sense than that of Marxism. Its meaning lies more on the level of univocity than on that of analogy, as is the case with the Marxist meaning. Marx deviates from Christianity not so much by the fact that he makes work an essential category of human existence as by the fact that he makes human love self-sufficient. For him, the community of work is not a still-deficient form of co-existence and contemplation, a being-on-the-road to the ideal, but he regards that community as belonging to the ideal in a univocally essential sense.

The final ideal of Marxism ultimately remains a working love because of its atheistic perspective, while for Christianity work is ultimately absorbed in love. The ideal value of work in the Christian sense lies in the supraworldly divine love, which no longer knows work. However, the Christian recognizes that this personal love has to assume in this world also the form of work, but this work finds its ultimate completion and reward in a workless co-existence. Because its horizon is limited to intraworldly reality, the Marxist system, despite its glorification of love, ultimately places truth and human love too much in the sphere of that which is useful and subject to technical operations. It is inevitable that this restriction results in unfavorable consequences.

The Christian Reply to the Marxist View of Life. In connection with these ideas, one may ask whether the institution of a Christian feast of work[2] has been an excellent idea or too much inspired by the ideology of the Marxist view of

---

[2]May 1, the Feast of St. Joseph, the Worker.

work. Shouldn't the Christian view rather have led to a feast celebrating the equality and brotherhood of all men on the basis of their personal dignity? It is man's personal value which ultimately makes all men equal in dignity in spite of the differences in social position which flow of necessity from the mutual relations of human workers.

Marxism is a philosophy of life characterized by extremes. On the one hand, its ideal for man in the world is more idealistic than that of Christianity; on the other, its system is extremely rigorous, for love which is imposed creates servile dependence. Marxism remains an enigmatic mixture of utopian idealism and technical materialism. One who does not go to extremes but wants to preserve moderation will never feel at home in its philosophy of life.

The Christian reply to the Marxist paradox will have to be greatly differentiated. Some Christians favor an idealistic optimism, going so far as to claim that Marxism ought to be met solely on the basis of Christian love, i.e., without protective self-defense. They forget that the Marxist system with its totalitarian claims makes it very difficult to meet it with Christian love. On the other hand, it is a sign of short-sightedness if one wants solely to combat Marxism without regard for the spiritual background on which its philosophy of life is based and which give it its utopian and forced character. The system demands a reply that is neither naively optimistic nor narrowly pessimistic. It is possible that in Christian circles too much attention has been paid to the materialistic aspect of Marxism so that the accent has fallen too one-sidedly on combating it. At any rate, certain realistic aspects of the system, despite its general utopian character, need to be given more consideration. The truth of this assertion will manifest itself more clearly in the next chapter, devoted to the value of human property.

4. *Historical Sketch of the Appreciation of Work*

Work in the Primitive World of Myth and Magic. Our time with its tendency to specialization knows different relatively independent realms of life. The primitive mind, however, lived and thought in an undifferentiated fashion. Although in some respects the primitive patterns of life and thought in different areas were widely divergent, the modern anthropologist notices a few general characteristics, which determine the background of the primitive world view. Among these we find that for primitive man work was not a special activity which in a spatio-temporal sense was clearly distinct from other activities. His entire life was still marked with care for his bare existence. Moreover, in the primitive world view work was not yet a profane activity inspired by norms of usefulness and efficiency. The primitive did not yet view the world as something to be changed and manipulated.

The activity which we now call "work" also had the character of a cult in this stage of civilization. It implied especially a dedication to, and care for sacred nature. Work at that time was not merely a profane and economic occupation but possessed also a religious and contemplative meaning. The economic motive remained undifferentiatedly interwoven with other motives. Economic rationality, as an autonomous category with its own laws, lay beyond the primitive's horizon. Barter, for instance, no matter how much it was inspired by biological need, was more than a relationship of "giving and receiving." It was also a symbolic event. The primitive did not barter merely to make an economic exchange of goods but also to give himself by means of the exchanged object. The mythical bond of the group found its visible expression especially in the ritual of that exchange.

According as the primitive became more familiar with this everday religious world of rites and sacred institutions, material motives could manifest themselves more explicitly. The ritual force itself helped primitive man to go beyond the stage of instinctive action and become sensitive to rational motives. This view is confirmed by the efforts of Europeans who try to teach agriculture to primitive tribes. When the grounds are divided among the members of a tribe, the latter will as a rule fail to cultivate them because they do not feel bound to do so through a sacred ritual. Purely rational motives do not yet appeal to them. Even if supervision induces them to sow, they will often eat the crop before it is ripe and reserve nothing for next year's sowing.

When, however, a tribe made the transition from the stage of hunting and gathering fruit to that of cattle breeding and agriculture, its primitive existence underwent one of the most important cultural changes. Instead of being forced to live where food could be found, man now became able to supply food wherever he lived. That transition usually meant a great step forward on the road to civilization.

To abandon the former irrational way of life, characterized by a never-ending search for food, would appear to be particularly rational to our eyes. However, the primitives did not switch to cattle breeding and agriculture on the basis of utilitarian considerations and calculations alone. The religious aspect of their cult also exercised much influence in that decision. By taming and breeding animals, by sowing and reaping wheat and barley, they wanted to offer the gods a more worthy sacrifice of firstlings. This cultic zeal contained as a secondary motive the tendency to arrive at a greater security of life. Gradually, however, this secondary motive gained in strength.

Historians of religion point out that the growing mastery over nature occurring at the transition from nomadic life to agriculture and cattle breeding often is reflected in primitive mythology. The old cosmic or uranic gods slip into the background and their place is taken by a large number of gods of a lower rank and lesser importance. Thus we find gods of the hunt, of agriculture, of forests and rivers, and dwelling places. They were less powerful than the old gods, but more in harmony with the new practical needs of daily life. They were demigods, often the offspring of a cosmic god and a mortal. Even man's own ancestors were frequently raised to the rank of the demigods. Such gods were closer to man than the old gods, they were less powerful and less sacred. In this way the old mythologies pointed to man's increasing appreciation of the earth and his growing power over numinous nature.

Irrational magic also was a concealed attempt to master nature in a rational way. Magic was a kind of supernatural technique born from man's desire to bring security in his life. He wanted to safeguard the natural rhythm of events by means of magic. Man's urge to acquire control over nature manifested itself even more strongly in the magic phase than in the mythical phase.

Work in Greek Life and Thought. The thinkers of Greece gradually broke through the primitive world of myth and magic. They were known for their great confidence in the powers of reason. Their philosophy was based upon the conviction that the world is governed by *logos* and that the universe constitutes a harmonious whole. We do not mean to say that science and technique had already joined hands, but only that the Greek mind made an effort to discover order in the universe. This attempt divested the cosmos of its inviolable sacred character and opened the way toward the principle that "science is power."

For this reason it is less correct to claim, as is sometimes done, that Greek culture with its dichotomy of disinterested pursuit of knowledge by free men and utilitarian work by unfree men formed an obstacle to the encounter between science and technique. Such a view evaluates the Greeks from the standpoint of a later stage in the history of civilization and therefore leads inevitably to an incorrect evaluation. For the Greeks knowing and doing were not yet as closely connected as was the case later for Descartes. That stage of development had not yet been reached by them. Nevertheless, the Greek thinkers, who broke through the mythological attitude of life and made an effort to understand the world in terms of laws, opened the road to man's will to dominate the world.

Strictly speaking, we may even say that Greek philosophy was already a science with a practical orientation. Even Plato's theory of ideas, which still exhibited a strongly mythical trend, attempted to obtain power over the world through knowledge. True, Plato conceived all knowledge as contemplation of eternal ideas and essences. Nevertheless, by means of this knowledge man was to be lord and master over himself and the world because the whole of earthly reality was a shadowy image of the world of ideas. Thus man had in principle the possibility to plan his world and the actual course of history could not bring him anything new which he had not already contemplated *a priori*. Moreover, Plato's

doctrine in fact also emphasized the power of scientific understanding and the importance of theory with respect to
practice, although this emphasis was still placed by means of
a mythical representation.   Philosophy and science were not
yet rigorously distinguished at that time.   The philosophical
reflection of the Greeks was at the same time a rudimentary
practical knowledge of science.   Only later were these two to
become more differentiated.   Philosophy would then become
more   disinterested   wisdom   and   science   more   functional
knowledge giving power to man.

Despite the fact that the Greeks made the world profane,
there remained many mythical elements, especially in the first
period.   The Greek evaluation of work illustrates this point.
Their tendency to *autarky*, or self-sufficiency, which had its
beginning in their agricultural existence, had a mythical background.   Man should try to live independently from others in
close contact with Mother Earth and the other gods, just like
all other beings in nature.   For the primitive Greek, agriculture was still a genuine cult.   The farmer accepted responsibility for the care of sacred nature and this care was rewarded
with fruitfulness.   The farmer did not yet work with the
purpose of purely economic rationality to adapt nature to
human aims.   That kind of mentality was still foreign to the
Greeks in their earliest history.   They would have viewed
such an idea as impious.   One who tilled the land acquired his
skill automatically in his contact with nature.   If someone
was an inefficient farmer, the reason was not so much that he
lacked sufficient technical skills as the fact that he showed
too little dedication to the service of mythical nature.

Agriculture constituted a kind of religious service, but a
trade or craft was regarded as "work" and often demanded
the possession of secret, unnatural and therefore areligious
knowledge.   The craft of the smith, for example, had an
almost sacrilegious character, for he changed matter, as it
were, against its very nature.   The smith, whose first job was
to manufacture weapons and tools, was considered to be really
an "outsider."   His craft was looked upon as an illicit occult
occupation, no matter how much the products of his skill were
appreciated.   Hephaestus, the god of the art of forging, was
represented as a cripple, for whom the gods of nature had

little regard, although they were happy to use his services in their internal strife.

The bloom of crafts and trades and the city culture connected with them caused the transfer of the ideal of *autarky* with its religious overtones from agriculture to the *polis*, the city. That ideal was now to be an independent citizen, taking part in all activities in the political, cultural, religious, and even economic realm. This participation in all these activities constituted also the content of the Greeks *aretē*. The meaning of this term was not purely moral but had a much wider range and aimed at the harmonic development of all human activities. The norm of *aretē*, which is best translated by "excellence," was the harmony of the whole man and not one or the other special ability. For specialization created dependence and was therefore something to be pursued by slaves. To work, however, insofar as one still remained one's own master and could participate in the assemblies of the people and in other cultural activities was something that could go together with this Homeric conception of *aretē* as excellence in every realm. For this reason the growth and bloom of the Greek cities arose from the industriousness of their citizens themselves rather than from the labor of slaves. The latter, moreover, remained relatively small in number.

Gradually, however, the development of the city began to demand so much expert knowledge and specialization that the individual citizen was no longer able to devote himself to all tasks. In a later period we see, therefore, a growing division between the occupations of the free citizen and those of the unfree citizen. The ideal of autarky now became a privilege of the free citizen, who began to live on the work of the others. Many gradually came to be occupied so much with economic affairs that they had neither the time nor the necessary knowledge to devote themselves to cultural and political pursuits. In addition, they became dependent upon jobs assigned to them by others. In this way these people slowly became part of the lower social class of the "unfree." This term referred not only to slaves but also to all citizens whose work left them no time and possibility to pursue activities fully worthy of man.

The ideal of *aretē*, which now became the goal of a small elite, still possessed a mythical background. That background revealed itself in the public games, which occupied such an important place in the life of the free citizen. The contests, which included both sports and other cultural activities, were held not only to show man's *aretē* but also to honor the gods. They remained a part of a religious ritual. During important international games, such as the Olympic games in honor of Zeus or the Pythian games in honor of Apollo, a religious truce was proclaimed so that contestants and spectators could undisturbedly travel through enemy territory toward the site of the sacred games.

The autarkic way of life, however, gradually lost its validity not only for the craftsmen of the city but also for the agricultural population. Cities grew in size and introduced a greater division of labor, so that agriculture also became part of commercial traffic. The farmer became dependent upon others in his work. In this way agriculture became, like the technical crafts, a rational use of physical forces for human purposes. It began to lose its original sacred and natural character. The transition reveals itself clearly in the writings of Aristotle. He sometimes describes agriculture as a cultic activity devoted to nature and calls it *aretē* in opposition to the work of the craftsman, but sometimes he also puts agriculture on the same line as crafts and regards it as a servile, non-free task.

Unlike the rationalization of labor which at the time of the Illumination gave an important impetus to technical development, the first form of that rationalization in the Greek city culture still possessed a natural character. The technical rationalization of the modern era flowed from a systematic and purposive plan. It was used and made more perfect as a method in its own right. The Greeks' division of work, however, was much more "natural" because it was concerned with the plurality of human needs and the natural limitation of human capacities. Hence the Greeks compared the division of tasks among men with the natural division of work existing in the animal world.

Greek *technē* was nothing else but the development of man's natural abilities and did not know the artificial purposiveness which characterizes the modern industrial revolution. Agriculture and crafts were still pursued within the framework of nature. They made use of the possibilities which material things presented, as it were, spontaneously, in contrast to the technological era of modern times, which seems to force the material world to disclose all kinds of artificial possibilities. Greek industry was determined by naturally arisen needs which demanded to be satisfied. The craftsman worked to produce the means to satisfy those desires. For instance, the shipwright was told by the boatman what kind of a boat he should build. This economy geared to the satisfaction of needs is the opposite of the contemporary productive system, which is typically a culture of *means*. Today's manufacturers often first produce the goods and then try to stimulate demand for them in an artificial way by means of advertizing. The economy of Greek antiquity was still largely a "natural economy" based on the exchange of goods between consumers. To the old Greeks trading in money and goods did not seem natural and such commerce was at first regarded with suspicion.

As we have seen, in the Greek city culture the ideal of autarky shifted from an agrarian existence to cultural and political activities. This shift resulted in a decrease of esteem for work because work now began to imply a great lack of independence in the socio-economic realm. The Greeks began to view work as a necessary means for most people to provide a living. Undoubtedly, the lack of esteem which especially the Greek philosophers showed for work should not be made too absolute. For it remains true that ultimately Greek civilization, driven by a philosophical instinct, tried to explain the world and in this way prepared the way for experiments in later times. Under the influence of the Greco-Roman civilization, the West has followed the road of man's embodiment in the world, in contrast to several civilizations of the East, which went the road of disembodiment by restricting man's natural needs and denying his worldly dimension. On the other hand, it remains typical that the philosophical writings of that time did not yet see work as an important factor in the development of man and society.

The Medieval Situation of Work. Before indicating the central position of work in modern society, we want to present a brief characterization of the medieval situation of work because in the Middle Ages work acquired a higher moral value thanks to the predominance of Christianity.

Starting from the fourth century and the fall of the Roman Empire, industrial production gradually disappeared. The cities began to lose their economic importance and for the next five or six centuries the life of society was based again on the agricultural system. The tools and other products of craftsmanship which were still needed now came not so much from the cities as from workshops established on feudal domains. Because the free possession of land was burdened with many obligations which small farmers found too heavy to bear, many of them placed themselves under the patronage of more powerful lords. These lords exacted payment in kind, thereby constantly expanding their holdings; they often also oppressed independent farmers by calling them up for armed service or the administration of justice, which again led to an increase in their own holdings. All this resulted in the gradual establishment of the feudal system of lands possessed by the nobility and ecclesiastical institutions.

The eleventh century, however, witnessed the rebirth of towns as centers of crafts and industries. The industrial activity of such towns remained limited in size and aimed only at the local market. From the economic standpoint, these towns followed a protectionist policy: they wanted to provide solid goods and offer security to the craftsmen producing these goods. These goods were exchanged to take care of one another's needs and not to result in commercial profits. The economic advantage of living in such industrial centers was limited to a livelihood in keeping with one's position.

In addition to these centers of industry, there arose also centers of commerce. At first, the commercial towns were not much more than fortified localities, in which goods were stored until itinerant merchants could dispose of them. Gradually, however, these places acquired a secure market, the itinerant merchants established themselves in them and in due time became the patricians of the town population. In the twelfth century these towns gave rise to the flourishing condition of commercial capitalism.

In spite of the revival of commercial towns, medieval economy was still dominated by the local character of its social life. The market was not only the place for the exchange of goods but also the scene of social and political activities. A breach of the market peace meant also a religious misdeed. The technical knowledge embodied in the craftsman's industry did not exceed manual skill. The guilds in which craftsmen organized themselves gradually began to abuse their freedom and privileges, to pursue unduly their own particular interests, and even to practice a policy of restricting production. The merchants, who lived from their capitalistic foreign commerce, were at first also uninterested in technical progress.

Although work at that time did not yet demand any great psychical and intellectual talents, it began to be increasingly more esteemed. The craftsman represented a group which enjoyed the appreciation of society. The towns of the Middle Ages, in fact, owed their flourishing condition to the economic activities of craftsmen and merchants. In this respect the medieval town differed from the Greek *polis*, which owed its importance primarily to its political function. The Christian religion also tended to humanize the sphere of work. Feudal rights and duties had their basis in mutual trust, and the guilds called themselves not without reason "fraternities."

The medieval attitude toward economic activities was based primarily on the position of the craftsman. His income was restricted to what was traditionally required for his sustenance in accordance with his position. The era showed a kind of Christian aversion to commerce for the sake of profit. The first merchants were mainly strangers and itinerants, people who did not have any traditional social bonds with the local community. They were regarded as profiteers, living at the expense of those who produced the goods. The Middle Ages regarded the exchange of goods only as a means to supplement the needs of closed, self-sufficient family communities. They looked askance at commerce in money and goods for the sake of profit rather than the need of the consumer and viewed that kind of business as out of harmony with the Christian's obligation to be satisfied with his traditional sustenance according to his social status.

Medieval society continued to be a society composed of classes. According to Thomas Aquinas, work was a duty only for those who did not have other sources of income. Medieval man did not yet regard work as a necessary contribution which everyone should make to society. Those who did not have to work with their hands belonged to a higher class. Science and work had not yet met, and for this reason those who devoted themselves to intellectual pursuits were not considered to work. Because the occupations which required work did not demand any great talent, it stands to reason also that even Thomas Aquinas nowhere speaks about the inner value of work. He merely enumerates aims which are extrinsic to work itself. Thus he regarded work as a means to control man's unruly passions, to flee idleness, to earn a living, and to be able to give alms. Hardly any medieval writer spoke about the creative value of work itself. Only the monks tried to unite prayer, study and manual labor into a harmonious whole.

Work in the Sixteenth to the Nineteenth Centuries. A new mentality began to manifest itself around the sixteenth century. The world view of a cosmos which protected man as a sacred order of nature and offered him a conservative pattern of life gradually collapsed. Two main characteristics marked the new spirit of the time: a growing individualistic self-consciousness and a strong orientation of man's knowledge to the control of nature. These two characteristics were bound to go together. Because man began to place himself opposite nature and to regard nature as an object to be changed, he could see himself more profoundly as an "I" in contrast to nature as the "non-I." Man has, of course, always experienced nature as something to be used, but in the primitive stage of science and technology his manipulation of nature could not go beyond the utilization of possibilities which nature itself presented in a spontaneous way. Now, however, man's conforming to nature gradually changed into nature's conforming to man. Nature no longer spontaneously offered itself to man, but man began to place nature at his disposal and to change it into a source of limitless possibilities.

In this period the relatively stable economy, which permitted only the satisfaction of known and fixed needs, gave way to a dynamic system which aimed at unrestricted gains. All realms of life became the products of enterprise. The economy no longer aimed at the need for the product, but at the product as the expression of man's active personality. The organic society, intent on the preservation of established traditions, underwent a change and became a planned social organization, whose structure of government and power harmonized better with the new liberal world. Conscious of his individuality, man no longer was satisfied with traditional realities demanding a sacred dependence, but began to view the world as his own field of labor. Man's enterprising spirit turned its attention also to the sciences and endeavored to make everything the object of a rational approach.

All this led in these centuries to the collaboration of theoretical knowledge and practical experience and in this way gave rise to the bloom of the sciences of nature. Ancient and medieval science of nature had been too speculative for such a collaboration. It had been too strongly influenced by the philosophical sphere of thought. Its interest had not gone beyond a contemplative consideration of general laws applicable to nature, which were viewed as participations in an eternal order. On the other hand, the attention which ancient and medieval science paid to the sense-preceptible world had created the climate within which modern science of nature could develop. The Greek attitude of mind admitted the possibility of scientific knowledge based on the perception of the cosmos. However, sense experience did not yet go beyond a primitive stage and the value of experiments was not yet sufficiently realized; hence only those sciences could immediately flourish which did not require empirical investigations. In the Greek and medieval eras man's creative activity was orientated to cultural rather than technical possibilities. This situation began to change in the seventeenth century.

In this century the mathematico-empirical sciences, which based themselves not only on knowing but also on making, eliminated the barrier separating theory from praxis. On the one hand, the increase in empirical knowledge made a more scientific approach possible and, on the other, new technical discoveries offered the sciences the opportunity to perform new empirical experiments. The modern ways of scientific thinking put nature under man's control. Slowly man began to venture outside the narrow shell of the cosmos and to place himself opposite the world as a demiurge. He became acquainted with the infinite horizons of the macrocosm and the microcosm.

Nevertheless, technology developed only slowly. Although nature showed itself attainable through the approach of mathematical rationality, physical science at first remained purely theoretical and not yet sufficiently adapted in its thinking to experimental evidence. Not before the second half of the nineteenth century did the technological revolution take place. Before that time, technique remained on the level of skill and economic production stayed within the narrow framework of the craftsman's industry. The economic activity of that kind of home industry had, as it were, fallen asleep and become fixed in its routine. It made products on order, and the guilds, which had become closed groups, endeavored to prevent any competition.

Although the technico-economical organization of the craftsman's industry continued for centuries to be of a static nature, the economic category of commerce underwent a dynamic growth. The seventeenth century was the era of giant commercial enterprises *par excellence*. This commercial activity led to capitalism in its early form, which rejected as antiquated the medieval ideas about the illicit character of interest, just prices and corporate solidarity and let itself be led by principles of unlimited profit, interest-producing capital and individualism.

This commercial capitalism was not yet the modern type of capitalism and did not lead to any profound social changes. Industrial production remained a matter of manufacture by craftsmen and stayed outside the sphere of influence covered by this commercial capitalism. Moreover, commerce itself re-

mained a matter of market trade rather than exchange trans-
actions. Sometimes, however, it happened that wealthy commercial houses influenced the production process by undertaking to improve goods either under their own control or
through credits given to craftsmen. Because craftsmen in the
cities were organized in powerful guilds, the "industrial" efforts of these merchants had to rely on the home industry of
rural craftsmen, whose organization did not possess the same
powerful means to resist the encroachments of the merchants.

The French Revolution broke the power of the guilds, so
that in the nineteenth century industry and technique could
join hands. Their meeting gave rise to giant production
enterprises. Industrial production was born from the encounter of commercial capitalism and technical capitalism. In the
industrial production commercial and technical activities became interlocked. The new manufacturing enterprises constituted a new economic category, possessing both a technical
and a commercial character.

The individualistic spirit of the time, which had developed during the Renassiance and the Illumination, dominated
also the economic and technical realms. Capitalistic individualism's ideal was the liberal *homo economicus*. With unre-
mitting energy the latter devoted himself wholly to his economic task, making work his entire goal of life. Everyone had
to make his time productive to the utmost of his ability.
Those who did this walked on the road to salvation, while
the others, who indulged in idleness and pleasure, went to
perdition. Work saw itself raised to the level of being a kind
of spiritual exercise and endless laboriousness became the
principal virtue.

This cult of work, which was wholly orientated to man's
active control of nature, led people to think that human
nature and its passions should be controlled in the same way.
Man should keep aloof from personal enjoyment and personal
appreciation. The thriftiness of the *homo economicus* often
induced him to look upon ethics as a kind of moral book-
keeping. Yet it must be admitted that this asceticism of
work led to a general esteem for work and was a powerful
factor in the spread of general welfare. On the other hand, it
remains true that this convulsive ethics of work bore the

mark of the individualism of that era, which judged it more important to gather wealth than to make use of one's possessions.

The new "morality of work" exercised great influence upon Western civilization and this influence continues even in our days. At least partially born from Calvinistic thought, it placed life in the service of duty instead of duty in the service of life. Christian faith itself underwent its influence. For example, the mystery of the Holy Trinity, in which tranquil coexistence has priority over operative activity, was pushed into the background. Man in his restlessness regarded this mystery as an unintelligible theoretical dogma without practical appeal. He substituted for God the "Supreme Architect of the World," who was to be served by achievements and labor and who would recompense man according to his works. Nevertheless, in spite of these dark aspects, the duty of man to work became the positive and dynamic factor in the construction of the new society.

The Technological Era. In the new era the guilds and the feudal system, which were primarily based upon home industry and land holdings, made way for the industrial society, although at first this substitution often took place in a chaotic fashion. Man now appropriates the world in a new way by means of all-encompassing technical methods. A new world view arises, which no longer asks what nature is but what nature can become. While primitive technique replied, as it were, to nature's invitations, modern technology forces nature to reveal its secrets. Former ages viewed nature as formed and orderly, but the new technological age regards physical nature as unformed and disorderly and expects that man's interference will create order to it. Formerly man's work made use of nature by adapting him to nature's own finality, now the technological order adapts nature to man's own purposes. The natural world is replaced by an artifical world. Primitive techniques made use of the forces and materials which nature spontaneously offered, but modern technology is increasingly less dependent upon such spontaneous offerings of nature. Man now creates artificial raw materials, making them hard or soft, rigid or flexible, as he himself wants. He is constantly less limited by the forces which nature offers spontaneously and is in principle able to change any kind of material into useful energy. Man now succeeds in giving certain human abilities a kind of autonomous existence outside himself. The era in which he used tools and instruments as extensions of his own bodily organs is being succeeded by an era in which his abilities are objectified in machines. He no longer works with tools but operates machines which work for him. He has even managed to objectify certain psycho-motoric reactions in automation.

The old techniques aimed only at the products to be manufactured, but modern technology is concerned also with the manufacturer as such. The medieval rationalization of labor was based upon the development of man's natural and individual differentiation of abilities and talents. Modern rationalization, however, does not base itself upon this natural variety. The new rationalization is even planned according to a technical formula for the purpose of attaining maximum efficiency. Where formerly the rationalization of labor was developed around man and nature as given, now the situation is largely reversed. Nature and man are now adapted to the rational schema of production and assigned a function in that schema. Formerly man worked within the framework of the surroundings in which his life ran its course. Work, the soil, property and family constituted a natural unit. Now work no longer demands that man devote everything he is and has to it, but requires only a performance, the exercise of his function.

The old agrarian yards and craftsman's workshops produced only to satisfy existing demands. The need for goods determined their production. This production on order has given way to production for stock, so that in the new order of the industrial economy the center of gravity lies in the product's market possibilities. For this reason advertising, which tries to foster new needs, constitutes an essential part of the contemporary economic management of an industry. We may even say that today production determines demand rather than demand production. To survive, the technico-economic order needs constant growth. It has to remain orientated to new technical inventions, more rationalization, and greater markets. The realm of so-called "service industry" also expands enormously through the availability of technical means. The unlimited possibilities of development, however, are not solely concerned with the material world but also with man himself. All human activities lend themselves to a technico-scientific approach. Psychology, sociology and other sciences organize and cultivate man's expression and communication in every realm of life.

The artificial world with its unyielding purposiveness has become second nature to man. He uses the earth to support his structures, he exploits nature as a source of energy and as raw material for industrial production. The seas, the air and even the universe itself are regarded as roads of transportation or channels of communication. Man's roads no longer wind their way from dwelling to dwelling, inviting the traveller to linger. Anyone entering man's roads now has to adapt himself to a set speed and to hurry on to their terminus. His traffic arteries are as rigidly planned as the new cities to which they lead.

The modern world view is an artificial order which can maintain its equilibrium only through man's constant planning. According to H. Freyer, the modern industrial society may no longer be compared with an organism because that organic metaphor reminds man too much of a static natural world. Technological power now creates a new world, which it imposes like a steel structure on the old natural world and which is only here and there supported, as by pillars, by the old "given" world.

This description should not make one conclude that contemporary technology can proceed arbitrarily in its use of nature. We have sketched the technological era against the background of the old world view in order to make a comparison between the two. There is question of shifts in aspect which, as we have said in Chapter Seven, can be expressed only in conceptual opposites. The extent to which modern science imposes its forms on nature is still small in comparison with the extent to which nature has its own forms. Nevertheless, it remains true that the revolutionary development of science has made nature susceptible to change and modification. Man has managed to put nature within the grasp of the categories of mathematical reason and to open it to technical interference, even though we may still be only at the beginning of what can be done with nature in this fashion.

Social and Spiritual Consequences of Man's Technological Control of the World. The technological control over the world has produced profound changes in man's mentality. It forces contemporary man to revise his position with respect to the world and his fellow-men. We do not mean to say that the revolutionary change implied in the technological picture of the world is the direct cause of the changes introduced in man's life of the spirit and his social relations. Such a view would regard history in a materialistic fashion. Social and intellectual factors, on the other hand, have also contributed to the technological revolution. It is sufficient to think here of the fact that from the very beginning in the Greek era the philosophical tradition of Europe has endeavored to master the world and man himself by way of knowledge. This knowledge as power, however, at first led only to a purely intellectual and not to an effective mastership. Nevertheless, it remains true that the technico-scientific control of the world is an important factor in the contemporary view of man and offers a suitable starting point to obtain a total picture of the new society.

The technological revolution has thoroughly removed the last lingering remains of a conservative and closed world view. In the Middle Ages Christianity with its supernatural orientation had succeeded in breaking the stranglehold of the cosmos by opening a higher perspective on supraworldly reality. (A sign of this new-found openness may be seen in the bloom of lofty gothic architecture.) Nevertheless, the bonds of family and neighborhood still continued to separate men in closed groups. Science and technology have ruptured this narrow framework and at the same time caused the theonomy of the medieval world to give way for man's autonomy. They have changed the dimensions of time and place into a problem to be solved by man.

For this reason modern society is characterized by a great mobility in both the spatio-geographical and the social aspect. Formerly man worked within the narrow and closed area in which he lived. Together with his family and his land, he belonged to patriarchal farmsteads or workshops. Now work determines where man has to live. Modern man may no longer become unduly attached to local environment and location. The numerous possibilities of choosing a position and improving it require that he remains mobile. He no longer looks on his dwelling as something permanent. To represent ownership of one's house as a contributing factor in the formation of the person and the family now is an idol overtaken by history. That function of ownership corresponded to the cosmological limitations proper to a past period of human history. Today in most cases one's position and function in the world of work determines where he will live. Ownership of a house remains valuable as an investment and may become a suitable asset if one wants to exchange jobs with someone else.

Man's attitude toward his dwelling place is increasingly determined by rational purposiveness. The young couple begins with a small house, moves to a bigger place when the family increases, and changes to an apartment when the children are gone. Modern man looks upon his home in a functional way. In the pre-industrial era attachment to home and soil constituted an essential part and a real symbol of his cosmological security. This rural mentality, however, has given way for the attitude of the city dweller.

Urbanization takes over several tasks of family life. It divides life into functions. One part of the city contains the industrial center, another specializes in entertainment, a third in shopping and restaurants, others again are residential sections. In the latter there no longer exist any village-like ties. Contact in them is functional and anonymous. Formerly man was happy if he got along well with his neighbors, now he is satisfied if they do not trouble him. In our urbanized society man is in danger of becoming both internally and externally a nomad or rather a perpetual camper, at least if he does not succeed in finding a new anchor in small but close-knitted groups such as the family and a circle of intimate friends.

Man's social status in the modern industrial world also knows an increasing mobility. Former ages regarded the individual's social condition as something that he simply had to accept. They even looked upon the classes composing their society as willed by God. Any attempt to change from one class to another appeared to them as a revolt. Today, however, wealth and lineage have lost much of their social prestige. One's function in the world of work now is of more importance for one's social status in society. This change implies that there is now more vertical mobility. A change in an individual's position in the process of work can easily mean an ascent or descent on the social ladder. This social mobility affects not only the individual person but also the various social groups. A certain profession may rise or descend in social esteem in our modern society. We may even speak about a progressive levelling and equalization of all functions. Because men regard themselves more and more as equals in the world of work, they are less inclined to recognize privileged classes.

The technological evolution gives depth and breadth also to the social dimension of man. Because everyone becomes increasingly more dependent upon everyone else in the economic, industrial and technical realms, it is for the first time in history possible to say truthfully that the world is becoming unified. Foreign civilizations, which in former times were almost unknown to us, now penetrate into our own world of life by way of modern means of communication. Cultural sociologists point out that mankind stands at a decisive point in its history. All nations, even those which possess age-old civilizations, such as China and India, want to share in technological development and present themselves to Western culture. There is a growing urge to abolish all social inequality in the world. Technology and the art of organization make it possible in principle to let underdeveloped nations share in the results achieved by technological civilization. A kind of physical law appears to compel the world to collaborate. The functional unification of the world creates in this way the conditions for, and the possibility of, a genuine universal community of men.

The process of technification stimulates not only the growth and bloom of the human community as a totality, but also brings men in closer contact with one another. The specialization of work implies that people become more de-

pendent on one another in reworking the world. The technological rationalization of work with its far-reaching division
of tasks demands man's willingness to work together with his
fellow-men. Work, as creating products and rendering services, is orientated to society. Even the lowest forms of labor
demand esteem because they take care of a social necessity.
The order of work, which has replaced the privileges of
wealth and lineage, makes everyone more aware of his responsibility to society and of man's dignity. Because work
has become an indispensable necessity for every man and no
one wants to live in idleness as a parasite of society, all men
begin to feel themselves more and more equal.

Contemporary universal mobility affects also man's behavior. As long as he lived in a society of fixed classes, man
grew up, as it were, in a furnished dwelling and unconsciously
took over the traditional style of life. Now that the world is
characterized by mobility, human relations are no longer a
given fixed pattern but a task. In former ages the structure
of the family set the pattern for all social bodies. The family
extended into society, and vice versa. The feudal lord and
later, at the beginning of the industrial revolution, the factory
owner exercised a patriarchal authority. The guild relationship of master, mate and apprentice mirrored the family structure of father, older son and younger son. Like the family, all
these social groups aimed at the whole person. They had
economic, cultural and religious goals. The old traditional
society with its system of values common to all its members
offered a frame of life that could be understood and trusted.

Modern society, on the other hand, with its orientation to
large numbers of members, has a pluralistic character and
admits different types of social bodies, each with its own scale
of values and social roles. The separation of man's sphere of
labor from his sphere of life has become definitive. Work
relationships are no longer personal relationships of life, as
was the case in the feudal system and the guilds, but are
governed by a businesslike and free contract, which both
parties can always cancel. The family-like relation is no
longer extended into man's other social alliances.

It is not surprising that the contemporary way of life,
which makes it difficult for men to obtain a total picture of

the course their lives will run, causes feelings of insecurity and lack of freedom in many. We should not forget, however, that the former system of orientation in the closed society of classes provided much less freedom because it imposed itself on all as an inescapable system. The present uncertainty probably indicates an improvement in the sense that man can no longer find the orientation of his life in conditioned psychological and sociological reflexes. This orientation now has to be rooted in a certainty from within, a certainty based on creative freedom. His security is no longer primarily a question of conforming to an objective externally given norm, but rather of finding a hold in one's inner orientation to moral values and of letting this orientation bind the person in creative freedom. The dynamic group differentiation of the present time demands of man that he constantly renew his value judgments regarding his fellow-men and the world.

In the pre-technological era work had the character of making given nature more perfect. In this era man's self-development and self-loss through work were still of a partial nature because man felt a certain security derived from the fact that his work was accomplished against the background of the stabile world which encompassed him. Now that man himself begins to plan society through science and technology, he experiences both his self-development and self-loss through work as total. The atomic age makes him realize that a certain powerlessness grows in direct ratio with his increase in technological power. The vulnerability of the technological world has replaced man's powerlessness with respect to the natural world. This vulnerability cannot be overcome in its turn by new technological developments, but points to the necessity of a moral bond restraining man's technical powers.

Limitless optimism of faith in man's progress held fast for a long time to its belief that society would "make" man happy. The various systems, such as liberalism, socialism and solidarism, at first expected man's salvation to come from a particular social structure, but later these social trends of thought dropped many of their messianic aspirations. They are now less ideological and more inclined to defend their ideas on the basis of economic and social efficiency. The time is past in which the masses marched behind a band with flying pennants to dedicate themselves to build a better society. Work in social organizations is no longer a question of a vocation but of a profession. The building of society is not primarily a question of an ethico-religious doctrine but a matter of functional expertness. Society is now expected to create precisely the conditions and living space in which man can encounter his fellow-men in a genuinely loving way. Society itself does not make man happy, but is the preparatory stage in which man by way of functional contact and fellow-ship proceeds to genuine friendship and personal love. Society merely provides the functional basis of man's personal dimension.

Rationalism and positivism, which constitute the background of the social ideologies of "salvation," are losing ground. Since general prosperity has increased and the majority of men in the Western world no longer have to work to earn a bare sustenance of life, the view that man should not be a slave of labor is gaining rapid recognition. In contrast to the asceticism of work, whose major virtues were industriousness and diligence, contemporaries again regard as a virtue the genuine passivity which adds lustre to man's restful and happy togetherness with his fellow-men. Strange as it may sound to people with a pragmatic and utilitarian attitude of mind, the highest virtue lies in man's intimate and personal presence with his fellow-men, which is characterized by a minimum of activity. Until deep in the twentieth century mankind tended to seek freedom and happiness in control and power. Genuine wisdom, however, does not lie in the purely rational planning of aims to be attained through work but in the suprarational sphere of giving a personal meaning to the world, which requires a humble attitude of life.

The moments of self-development and self-loss, which remain essentially inherent in the functional world, cannot be reconciled as if they were a problem to be solved by "work." The "better world" desired by man is found primarily by means of man's respectful relationships with his fellow-men. Man's technical power reaches far, but it cannot master that which is properly human. To be genuinely human is something which man receives as a gift when he becomes humbly aware of his powerlessness and dependence. This joyful humility orientates him to unselfish giving and receiving, which greatly transcends the sphere of the calculating exchange of goods or services.

Modern industrial civilization has broken, both vertically and horizontally, the closed world view which for centuries offered security to mankind. Man must now rise above the old cosmic security, which was so strongly determined by local factors, and try to attain the personal security of the spiritual "we." He faces the task of finding a home with his fellow-man. The ultimate value of the technological control over the world lies in its orientation to man's intersubjective self-development in self-loss. This new spiritual orientation is growing, but in the transitional stage many feel lonely and lost because they do not yet regard themselves as persons whose unique value has been recognized by the other.

In modern civilization work has gained in value but, on the other hand, there exists also a greater danger of a negative self-loss. Thanks to man's technical power, this danger arises no longer from the blind forces of nature. It originates now in the fact that the technical order demands a "soul," something that can give meaning to it. Increasing prosperity alone does not make man happy, but offers him the possibility and the means to arrive at a fuller way of being man. The technological substructure invites and challenges mankind to build a more profound personal superstructure. General prosperity enlarges man's external freedom, but demands to be complemented by an increase in inner freedom.

5. *Philosophical Reflection and the Technological Control of the World*

Present-day philosophy mirrors the changed world view which we have described above. Philosophical reflection is always closely connected with the way man lives. There exists a dialectic relationship between non-philosophical experience and philosophy. Man's pragmatic busy-ness with the world is the basis and subject matter of his philosophical reflection, and on the other hand, his philosophical interpretation gives orientation to his busy concern with the world and makes him act with awareness of this orientation. A brief survey of this dialectic relationship may serve to illustrate this point.

Ancient and Medieval Naturalism. In the Greco-Roman time and in the Middle Ages, whose technical power did not go beyond the ability to adapt oneself to given nature, the question of what man is was raised against a cosmological background. Man's complete dependence on nature inspired thinkers to ask what place man occupied in the cosmological picture of the world. The sacred character especially and the mysterious nature of the cosmos, to which man also belonged, drew the attention of philosophers. Aristotle's philosophical wonder, for example, considered *inter alia* also man himself, but insofar as man was a part of the cosmos. Philosophers did not ask the question of what man is in an existential fashion, but were concerned with man as a species alongside the other species of living beings in the world.

The medieval view of nature agreed in many respects with that of the ancient world. When the upheavals following the collapse of the Roman Empire had subsided and a more peaceful condition began to reign, culture revived and with it interest in philosophy. Science, however, was not yet able to control nature; hence it was not surprising that medieval scholasticism reverted to the philosophy of the Greeks and their cosmological view of the world. Its attention centered on the universe as speaking of God. Man himself was the most important link in this order of creation. Medieval thinkers explained man's bond with his fellow-men on the basis of *natura humana*, conceived in a strongly specific fashion and only partially realized in the distinct individuals, so that the latter needed to complement one another.

Cartesian Rationalism. The birth of physical science in the sixteenth and seventeenth centuries caused man to assume a more active attitude toward nature. This change resulted in a modification of the question regarding man himself. Man's I-consciousness became more individualistic. While the medieval philosopher has started from the reality of the object, Descartes raised the philosophical question from the standpoint of the subject. His *cogito ergo sum*, however, exaggerated in a subjectivistic sense. The realism of the

Middle Ages, which placed man in an objectivistically conceived world of immutable essences, had to give way to the
philosophies of the Illumination, which echoed the subjectivation of man with respect to the world. Man regarded himself
no longer as a part of the world but placed himself in opposition to this world as the one who would create order in it.

Because of the successes obtained by the sciences, rationalism prevailed in the era of Illumination. Hobbes, Locke,
Bacon, Newton and others attached a one-sided value to the
measurability of reality. Enlightened thought regarded the
world no longer as a sacral and mysterious reality but viewed
it as a neatly laid-out garden, in which orderly reason felt at
home. Thirst for the infinite no longer inspired philosophical
thought, but petty concern tried to express all thinking and
doing in easily handled concepts. Most of the eighteenth
century philosophers disliked genuine metaphysics: mysteries
did not fit into their straight-lined world and its continuous
progress.

On the other hand, the Illumination made the anthropological phase of philosophy definitive and focussed attention
on man's autonomy. It preached the freedom and equality of
all men and liberated the individual from the bonds of tradition and conservative beliefs. As a reaction, however, against
a static religious world view, the thinking of the Illumination
remained too rationalistic. It gave too individualistic an
interpretation to freedom as a liberation from bonds. By way
of Kantian subjectivation, the humanistic and liberalistic tendencies of the Illumination reached their summit in the ideologies of progress formulated by Hegel and Marx.

Hegelian Idealism and Marxist Materialism. Both Hegel's
idealism and Marx's materialism ultimately placed man with
his desire to dominate the world in the center of attention.
Both systems attempted to explain the whole of history on
the basis of man and to give in this way control over history
to man. Idealism explained reality through the rational idea,
while materialism attempted to do the same through technology. Both these philosophies of progress, which in a certain
sense were at opposite poles, originated in the same fundamental tendency, viz., the absolutizing of the human person's

autonomy.   In the process man himself was ultimately degraded to being a *homo faber*, a worker.   Hegel's idealism was, strictly speaking, materialistic because in his view the spirit had to produce the world in order to become itself. Marx's materialism was, strictly speaking, idealistic because in his view matter would produce the ideal man.

Although the philosophical systems of Hegel and Marx radicalized the rationalism of the Illumination, nevertheless they endeavored to remodel its monotonous and colorless world into a home for man.   The cramped quarters of Cartesian self-being and man's "illuminated" homelessness in a mechanically analyzed world no longer satisfied these thinkers. The desire to secure a home for man's restless spirit constituted the driving force of their thinking.   Hegel sought man's salvation in the temple of reason, Marx in the classless society. Neither one nor the other, however, managed to overcome the rationalism of the Illumination.   They constructed ingenious systems, in which the person lost his unique and irreplaceable value and became a moment of a vague totality, known as "mankind" or "the people."   Within the framework of these systems the person could not feel secure and respected in his unique value.   Man remained uprooted; the problem of his loneliness and dread received no answer but was simply obscured.

Hegel's idealism tried to sublimate man's loneliness in an individualistic being-with-oneself in a divine humanity.   Conceived as a dialectic manifestation of the absolute *logos*, man withdrew from the real world and endeavored to live in an imaginary world of art, religion and philosophy.   The philosophers of materialism, on the other hand, attempted to escape from man's deterioration in his loneliness by assigning him a home in the technical collectivism of the all-encompassing mass.   While Hegel accepted a sublimation of loneliness, collectivistic thinking strangled this feeling.   Both these speculative systems, which had originated in technocratic scientism, appeared unable to provide man with a new anchorage now that he had drifted away from his former secure cosmic location.

Philosophy of Existence. The optimism of the Illumination could not be maintained very long. Man's nostalgic desire for security soon realized that the rational answers of "illuminated" thinking were merely pseudo-answers. All kinds of irrational movements arose in reaction against the thinkers of the Illumination. Especially contemporary existentialism protests against the rationalism and positivism of the eighteenth and nineteenth centuries. It is interested and concerned with existential man. The philosophy of existence views man's subjectivity from an entirely different viewpoint than the idealistic and materialistic systems. It endeavors to save man from being technified by anonymous powers. The philosophers of existence emphasize man's radical sociability and intersubjectivity, which, as personal solidarity, transcends the functional bonds of society and alliances based on selfish interests. The idea of intentionality discredits also definitively the solipsism based on the Cartesian idea of an isolated and separate consciousness.

Although all philosophers of existence emphasize man's social dimension, they greatly differ in the ways in which they develop this aspect of man. This difference indicates the insecurity feelings so characteristic of our time. Sartre, for example, describes the hopelessness of man's existence: in all his efforts to encounter the other subject he constantly suffers defeat. Although, according to Sartre, the other's presence is implied in everyone's self-consciousness, man is delivered without mercy to the other, and intrahuman relations are mostly characterized by strife. Heidegger, on the other hand, recognizes *Dasein-with*, but places it too much in care (*Sorge*) for the other. Jaspers devotes more attention to existential communication, which, however, is never definitive and therefore retains the character of a "warring 'we-ness'" (*kampfender Wirheit*). Others, like Binswanger, exaggerate human "communion." He personifies the "loving 'we-ness'" (*Liebender Wirheit*), in which the "you" and "I" are mystically at home (*beheimatet*), into a supra-individual but nonetheless human way of being. Such an absolutizing of the "we" as the primordial ground of everything does not do sufficient justice to the finiteness and imperfect condition of human communion.

Merleau-Ponty recognizes the finite character of human intersubjectivity, but is unable to transcend the limited horizon in his philosophy. In his view, absolute intersubjectivity will never be realized, there will never be a day without a night. Buber, Lavelle, Mounier, Marcel, Madinier, Nédoncelle and others believe in a transcendent God, who will take man's finite love into his own Infinity.

Existentialism mirrors the spirit of the time, which discards many inauthentic theories and practices and strives for a renewed authenticity. Despite the divergences in its development, existential thinking endeavors to give a new security to contemporary man, who suffers from homesickness in the changing world of technological achievements. Today's philosophy cares about man; despite its occasional pessimism, its regard is directed to the glowing horizon of man's togetherness with his fellow-men as person to person.

CHAPTER ELEVEN

THE VALUE OF OWNERSHIP

1. *Introduction*

Anyone who is familiar with the literature appearing in the realm of social philosophy knows that ownership has always been a much-discussed problem. The philosopher may not avoid that problem, for man's body belongs to the unity of the person and shares in the person's irreducible character; hence it is an inviolable principle of the natural law that man must have access to the goods of this world in order to take care of his life. The right of ownership is based upon man's spiritual-material existence in earthly conditions. This right expresses primarily that the goods of this world are destined for all men.

Private Ownership Versus Public Ownership. There exists, however, a great diversity of opinion about the way in which this general right to use these goods is to be realized. Some claim that the best way of promoting this general right lies in the institution of personal ownership, while others expect more from collective ownership. Surprisingly, both parties use the same arguments in favor of their positions. The proponents of the greatest possible private ownership defend their view by arguing that private property: 1. Safeguards social peace and security; 2. Leads to greater freedom and a more personal existence; 3. Is a powerful factor in raising the general economic welfare. The protagonists of the maximum of collective ownership use the same arguments claiming that private ownership: 1. Is the source of all social disorder and strife; 2. Leads to oppression and exploitation and consequently to the destruction of man's dignity and democratic freedom.

Today both liberalism and socialism have become less ideological and more interested in the pursuit of a realistic social policy. The contradictory opposition between their views concerning private ownership and collective ownership has become much less in consequence of that realism. Nevertheless, it is still possible to summarize the liberal preference regarding property in the slogan: private ownership when possible, socialization when necessary.   Conversely, the socialistic position can be described as: socialization when possible, private ownership when necessary.

The Philosophical Approach.   On the political level there may be a justification for such formulae, which start from the opposition between individual and collective ownership.   Politics has its own rules of rivalry and is bound to formulate its aims in terms of the existing political oppositions.   Social philosophy, however, should emphasize the unity of harmony rather than opposition.   Of course, we do not want to deny that there exist tensions of rivalry between the person and the society or even that these oppositions flow essentially from the spatio-temporal limitations of the conditions in which earthly life runs its course.   Yet an analogous ethical study tries to penetrate into the ideal situation.   It regards the contrasts between person and society, between the individual and the social aspects of man, as still-imperfect realizations of the ideal of the personal community.   On the level of the ideal, person and community, the personal and the social aspects, merge in identity.

In philosophical reflection the unity of these aspects should not be constructed from the standpoint of their presupposed opposition; rather the opposition should be viewed in the light of the given ideal of unity, of which ideal all those contrasting moments appear as still-imperfect participations. The imperfection of the identity remains the source of that duality, even though man's bond with his fellow-man is essentially an approximation of the ideal personal community and owes its concrete existence as a "human" bond precisely to this approximation.

The Danger of Dogmatism in the Solidaristic Theory of Society.   The solidaristic theory of society has always strongly defended private ownership and attributed to it the value of a principle.   The strong point of this traditional theory of ownership lies in the great value which it attributes to the person.   In its view, the irreplaceable uniqueness and freedom of the person have to be recognized also in the sphere of ownership.   Nevertheless, it cannot be denied that the Christian conceptions of ownership sometimes showed themselves somewhat dogmatic and did not sufficiently take into account the way in which ownership has historically developed. The principle of private ownership was not sufficiently studied with due regard for actual economic and social conditions. For this reason it implied certain historical backgrounds which had already long ago disappeared when social reality changed.

Christian tradition, while retaining essential values, will have to rid itself of the individualistic sphere which the Illumination and the French Revolution gave to the question of ownership. A theory of property must remain realistic and base its solutions on reality. If it assumes dogmatic positions, the result will be that certain historical situations are declared to be a supratemporal natural law. Since the institute of private property is primarily a social and not a personal principle, great care must be taken not to neglect the changeable and situational aspect of that institute.

A principle which expresses essential human values in a given historical constellation of factors and is absolutized in too rational and too univocal a fashion may fail to do justice to these same values when the situation becomes different. The perspective to which the principle refers has to be kept in mind. One and the same abstract formulation can refer to different states of reality. As a matter of fact, this has happened with the principle of private ownership. Formerly it was meant primarily to defend individual property as an "inviolable and sacred right," while today it is rather intended to express that everyone in human society has a right to property. The accent now falls on fostering the possession of property by everyone rather than safeguarding established rights.

State, Individual, and Private Ownership. The social situation prevailing in the nineteenth century has contributed to place the question of ownership in the polar contrast between individualism and collectivism. Because the French Revolution had abolished many antiquated social structures without replacing them by new bonds, individual and state came to occupy opposite positions. As a consequence of this, the phenomenon of group property was virtually unknown in the nineteenth century. Because there were no intermediary social organs between individual and state authority, the terms "private" and "social" came to be identified at once with "individual" and "collective." Yet the terms "private" and "social" have a broader sense. The term "private" is used in matters of ownership to refer to the sphere which should defend itself against the all-pervading influence of the state. This sphere encompasses not only the individual but also private social groups. "Social" property was likewise immediately understood as collective state property because of the prevailing opposition of individualism to collectivism. However, in addition to the state's collective ownership, many other social forms of group ownership are possible. These forms can restrict the individualism of the owners without making the possession a collective state property.

If the opposition between individual and state is made a central issue, the synthesis of the individual and social dimensions of man will inevitably bear the stamp of compromise. The principle of private property has then constantly to be corrected by other social principles. A social mortgage, so it is said, rests on private property. Such a way of expression places too much emphasis on the opposition between individual and social.

Co-existence with Our Fellow-Men and Private Property. Care must be taken to pay sufficient attention to the fact that the right of the private owner is essentially a right possessed *in* society. It would be wrong to represent matters as if the owner with his properties precedes social life in such a way that the social order must in principle abstain from touching the persons and his properties. If such a position is taken, it is not surprising that our era with its growing social consciousness considers that kind of private property an inferior type of institution.

A social-ethical study, on the other hand, endeavors to consider the phenomenon of property against the background of man's co-existence with his fellow-men in the world. It raises the question of the correct technical and juridical forms to be given to human ownership in the light of this perspective. If private property is to have a claim to ethical esteem, it too must be regarded from the standpoint of the ideal of man's co-existence with his fellow-men in the world.

To prevent confusion, we should add that, contrary to what happens in civil law, the present philosophical study regards possession and property as synonymous. In the juridical sense property is the right of dominion, while possession is that dominion itself. Juridically speaking, therefore, a thief may be a possessor. Moreover, we understand property or possession in a broad sense, so that the term covers also titles to debts, stocks and bonds, royalties and similar claims.

2. *The Essential Structure of Property*

The Analogous Character of the Term "to Possess." A brief reflection suffices to show that the term "to possess" has an analogous character. It is used in reference to objects as well as subjective features, such as "to possess one's soul in patience" and "to possess friendship." In a very general way we may say that the term "to possess" indicates the relationship of man to an object, taking both "object" and "relationship" in the broadest possible sense. Like work, possession refers to a typically human *existentiale*, which is based upon the person's corporeal-spiritual structure. Neither an animal nor a pure spirit possess in the proper, i.e., univocal, sense of the term. An animal does not possess an object as something belonging to itself, it does not have free control over it. We may even say that the animal is possessed by the object. A pure spirit is above the situation of possession, for he does not need to enrich himself by means of the material world.

Like the term "work," the relationship of possessing gives expression also to the bodily structure of man and consequently can be more easily approached in a univocal way than love, which refers solely to something spiritual. In the matter of possessing there is question also of a logical analogy, in which the concept is transferred from lower forms of possession to higher forms. The primary analogate lies here in the possession of material goods, and from this starting point the concept is broadened in its applications. For instance, the possession of friendship is described as a higher and richer form of possessing. If emphasis is placed on the univocity of possessing, i.e., on its bodily character, one cannot say that God possesses anything. God is perfect poverty in supreme detachment. Possession, however, is a typically human dimension and therefore implies also a spiritual aspect. In this sense the concept has also an analogous ideal value. If, then, we consider especially the analogous and spiritual aspect of possessing, we should say that God possesses everything. He is perfect poverty through the fullness of wealth; He is supreme detachment because of the fullness of His possessing.

Ownership in Relation to "Being" and "Having." With respect to the ownership of spiritual objects or rather subjects, we should not speak of problems but of mysteries. Problems of ownership occur only in the material world, which is characterized by contrasts of individuality. The problem of ownership therefore refers to the possession of material goods, of spiritual goods embodied in matter, and rights to such goods. Ultimately, however, possession is not solely concerned with "having," but contributes to the "being" of man.

Possessing is an ambiguous reality: by the ownership of material goods man can enrich himself, but he can also impoverish himself through them in estrangement. For this reason it is possible for a man to possess much and nonetheless little, or to possess little and nonetheless much. The decadent form of possessing submerges man's "being" in his "having." Men who possess in such a wrong fashion manifest a perverted bourgeois mentality and live the life of a capitalist in the evil sense of the term. Their sole interest lies in displaying their possessions. Such a man speaks all the time about "my" money, "my" car, "my" mansion, "my" wife. He appears more interested in having everyone know about his possessions than in making use of them.

To have ethical value, ownership must give reality to man's social dimension in the sphere of having. The possession should serve the person as an intersubjective being. If Christian morality teaches that man should possess as if he does not have anything, it demands nothing other than that he live his co-existence with his fellow-men on the level of owning also. This demand is not yet immediately concerned with the problem of individual, social, or collective ownership and the technical-juridical forms which this ownership can assume, although it is true that this problem is intimately connected with that demand. The emphasis still lies here on the fundamental moral attitude, which experiences the universal orientation of ownership, so that the opposition between personal and social does not directly arise. On the other hand, it is possible to remark even at this stage that morality imposes the obligation of making the juridical organization and institutions of ownership and property serve to promote as much as possible human solidarity in the material world.

Although love has a universal orientation because of its spiritual character, we should not forget that the human spirit is an embodied spirit. For this reason his love will assume a particularized form. Because of the limitations of material reality and the exclusive character of individuality resulting from these limitations, man's universal solidarity will be embodied in particular persons and groups of persons. A consequence of this embodiment is that the mystery of person-and-community manifests itself as a problem in the spatio-temporal world.

Property and Mutual Rivalry. Thus it follows that ownership, which regulates the person's relation to the material world, has to face the question of the rivalry resulting from the fact that material reality places the one person "opposite" the other and "opposite" society. The more, however, the goods in question are spiritual, the less there will be a problem of exclusiveness and rivalry. For the spiritual is by its very nature capable of being shared and transcends the limitations of space and time. If, for example, two people share the friendship of a third, their mutual friendship is bound to increase. Likewise, the beauty of a landscape is enjoyed more intensely if one can admire it in the company of a fellow-man. As soon, however, as there is question of appropriating material goods, the problem of ownership manifests itself in all its sharpness.

The goods of the earth are destined for all men. However, this universal destiny, which may be called "negative communism," is only potentially realized. The ideal of the universal right to use the goods of the earth is given actuality when human beings in their individual distinctness concretely face the world and appropriate it. No matter how common such an appropriation is conceived to be, it will always split into private groups and persons because matter implies essentially an element of dispersion. The spirit unites but matter divides. For this reason man's appropriation of the world is accompanied by a certain exclusiveness and rivalry with respect to others.

Considered in itself, that rivalry in the acquisition of property is good. Man's condition requires that this moment of rivalry be maintained even if society reaches the highest possible form of development. However, if rivalry is to remain a healthy force and not become a source of undesirable effects, then its influence should from the very beginning be exercised within the restraining bonds of a co-ordinating principle of order. In other worlds, although rivalry remains an important structural moment, it does not determine the whole property relationship between men.

The individualizing appropriation of earthly goods exhibits an ambivalent character, as happens in everything material in which man's spirit is at work; it brings together while keeping separate. The property laws, which co-ordinate the rivalry and solidarity between human beings, on the one hand, demarcate a person's rights with respect to others and, on the other, endeavor to attune these private rights to man's universal right of use.

Exclusiveness of Property and Man's Personal Being. Ownership rights include a certain particularization and exclusiveness because of the fact that the material world is limited and therefore implies an element of scarcity. There is, however, also another reason for that exclusive character. This additional reason lies in the corporeal-spiritual unity of man, for "having" is a specifically human activity and therefore shares in the unique value of the person. The person's uniqueness and originality express themselves in the property relationship, especially when there is question of possessions which touch man's life more immediately. Man becomes himself by appropriating the world; hence possessions are not wholly extrinsic to man. The human personality expresses itself in the material world and is, as it were, present in the objects touched by it. For this reason these material objects lose their "thing-like" character and become permeated with the spiritual uniqueness of the person. They are no longer immediately exchangeable and transferable. Goods, such as savings, wages and furniture, in that way become real symbols of human existence and embody that existence in an inalienable way.

The full meaning of property is not exhausted by paying attention to the scarcity of mere utilitarian objects. Even if industrial production were to reach the utopian stage of eliminating entirely the problem of scarcity, the intimate relationship between man and his property would still demand a certain exclusive right of possession. For this reason, apart from the factor of scarcity, the uniqueness of the person is an additional foundation on which property right is based.

3. *Property as Private Appropriation*

In the preceding section we have seen that the universal right to use earthly goods demands an individualizing or private appropriation because matter is characterized by an exclusive individuality. The expression "private appropriation" in that context was understood in a very broad and analogous sense both with respect to "private" and "appropriation."

Meaning of "Private." The term "private" refers not only to an individual's personal property but also to any form of group property, including even the state's collective ownership. For, by definition, property implies a certain exclusiveness, by virtue of which something belongs to a person or a group and not to another person or another group. In other words, a universal property without any form of being someone's "own," of being "private," would be a contradiction in terms. Any type of common property is *de facto* always a form of private possession.

There are several reasons why even the state's collective ownership implies a certain exclusive and private character. The first of them is that the state itself is a particular concrete form of man's universal community and as such divided from other states. Secondly, if collective property is opposed to private property, that distinction, strictly speaking, wants to oppose the common property of a particular society to the personal property of a particular individual. Finally, if the state wants to exercise its ownership's right as a social body, it has to act by means of individual persons. Although these persons represent the state, they act to a certain extent as private individuals. All this indicates that a certain particularization or private character is essentially inherent in the institution of property.

As we have said, the term "private" can be realized in various ways in the property relationship. There may be question of the private character of the person, the group, the state, and even a federation of states. In the problem of property we may not assign the primary place to any particular institution of property, such as personal property or collective property, and consider all other property relationships as inevitable concessions and secondary forms of property with respect to that allegedly primary system of property.

All forms of property are equally primary because the person, free social groups and the state, each, have their own irreplaceable function in the life of man. The important point is to establish correct harmony between the various forms of possession, which, because of their historical character, are constantly subject to change. It would be wrong to regard these forms in an either—or fashion. The nineteenth century doctrinal opposition between liberalism and socialism should not be allowed to dominate the problem of how to regulate property.

Meaning of "Appropriation." This term also should be conceived in a very broad sense. Social philosophy is not concerned with finding a univocal and uniform property formula. Otherwise it would ethically absolutize historical property relations, embodied in certain juridical institutions, and try to squeeze all new relations of dominion or use into this strait jacket. The result would be that the ethical dimension would be made subservient to the juridical dimension, while rather the latter should serve to do justice to the former. When we speak here of "appropriation," therefore, we do not simply mean the property formula which, by way of the French *Code Civil*, has become part of many legal systems. In that *Code* personal property is always the most complete right, and all other relations of appropriation, such as short or long term leases and loans, are derived from this right.

From the standpoint of social ethics, the term "property" indicates man's relationship to earthly goods in a very general way. This analogous property relationship leaves room for many different ways of owning these goods in a juridical system; moreover, a multitude of other rights, such as that to social security, fall within its compass.

The juridical development of the property relationship needs to be the subject of constant reflection in the light of the historical situation. In that reflection the juridical order should be adapted to the evolution of social reality rather than adapting reality to the established juridical order. Property laws are in a constant process of development.

Although the contemporary legal order is still based on a formal and uniform principle of property, the content of property laws no longer shares in that uniformity. All kinds of new relationships have developed under the same formal system. Moreover, property rights have been made more relative through all kinds of restrictions, and the growing labor laws have taken over part of the former domain of property laws, for example, by giving employees a certain influence in the management of industries, as is done in some parts of Europe.

If we want to formulate a principle in the realm of property, we would have to say that man's corporeal-spiritual essence demands a certain individualizing kind of appropriation in which, on the one hand, property rights create a certain distance between the subjects of these rights, but on the other, by creating this distance, lead to mutual solidarity and a just division of earthly goods. By speaking here about a "certain" individualizing property system, we do not want to minimize the principle of property but rather to emphasize the

complexity and manifold possibilities contained in the analogous expression "private appropriation." The property principle is analogous, i.e., it refers to a plurality of forms in which
earthly good can be appropriated and made private.

4. *The Various Forms of Property*

Insufficiency of the System of Personal Property. The
dynamic development in the realms of economics and technology has consequences also for the problem of property. The
pre-capitalistic economy of covering existing demands com-
prised only an economic order of farmers and craftsmen,
each of whom earned his living by his work and provided for
the other's needs through individual exchanges of services
and goods. The economic order was directly geared to the
consumers' interests and took place wholly within the framework of individual persons. For this reason it was fully
adapted to the system of personal ownership. Whenever in
this period there was any problem of property, it was always a question of personal ownership or no ownership at all.

However, subsequently, industrial production led to the
creation of larger economic units, which were preserved
through the common labor of many and whose structure gave
them a far-reaching social significance. The modern economic
order with its national and international ramifications has
outgrown the domain of the individual person. The personal
property system becomes less and less suitable to function all
by itself as a norm of social relationships.

The pre-capitalistic period rightly based itself upon this
system of personal property, for there existed a close individual connection between the person and the product of his
work. Moreover, it was quite normal that the farmer or the
craftsman possessed his own tool kit and workshop. Tools
still had the character of being mere extensions of the person's
limbs. Contemporary economic activity, however, is essentially a social event. Its industrial production is based upon a
radical specialization of labor and results from a common
effort. Even the mere establishment of a manufacturing enterprise presupposes that society has been made mature
enough for industrial undertakings. The labor force, for ex-

ample, which it uses has been trained by society. The apparatus of production represents a social capital and is by its structure orientated to the economic interest of many.

Distinction between Property of Natural Person and of Juristic Person. In the early stage of capitalism the system of personal property gave impulse to the new development of the economy. The high capitalistic period, however, showed that unlimited personal property rights undermined precisely those values which they had fostered in the previous era of familial economic relationship. For this reason contemporary society has developed a pluralistic system of property. This system manifests especially a clear separation between property of natural persons and that of juristic persons. While formerly the rights of dominion and of use were regulated by way of the personal property system, at present personal property is gradually shifting to the right of use. Personal property becomes more and more something man acquires for his enjoyment rather than his work. If any impersonal aim places the element of control and management of property in the foreground, man now prefers to create a juristic person for this purpose. The property of that juristic person is not destined to strictly personal use but to serve a wider purpose. Because the purpose for which a juristic person is created is generally of a wider scope than the personal interest of a particular individual, the juristic person has a more or less social orientation.

In our contemporary society properties are increasingly managed in a "social" fashion. The holdings of juristic persons constantly increase in variety and size. In the realm of production corporations own most industries. Pension funds, insurance companies and real estate corporations own a large part of our modern homes. Co-operatives and foundations no longer even have owners in the strict sense but are wholly devoted to social purposes. Even if the property of a natural person remains equal to that of a juristic person from a formally legal standpoint, the two forms of property are socially quite different. This difference exists not only if the juristic person is a "public" person, such as the state or the city, but also if he is a "private" person, such as a corporation, a foundation, or an organization. Properties belonging to a juristic person are not for the benefit of a single individual but more or less attuned to social purposes. The changing situation of modern society demands more differentiated forms of property than former ages, both with respect to the object possessed and the subject most appropriate to possess property.

5. *Personal Property*

Continued Importance of Personal Property. Personal property continues to play an important social role. Although it is no longer the central form of ownership, it remains one of the most significant forms. We see no reason to agree with those who claim that personal property is an individualistic and asocial institution. This form of ownership is important, first of all, because it embodies family property, and the family is precisely the highest form of social bond. Personal property is used primarily for the sustenance of the individual and his family. It therefore serves to support this most profoundly human of all bonds. The ideal of the personal community is most strongly realized in the bond uniting the family.

Secondly, the ideal of the personal "we" makes an appeal to each one's own initiative and responsibility. This creative freedom is possible only if the person, because of the situational aspect of his existence, has a certain amount of leeway and material independence. Since the person's freedom is an embodied freedom, he needs to be free *from* to be free *for*. For this reason the individual should be made the focal point of rights, including property rights, designed, on the one hand, to protect his personal existence and, on the other, to be the starting point of his social development. However, these rights should not be overemphasized, for otherwise the multilateral reality of the person would fail to receive due regards especially in its social aspects.

Because of man's multilateral social dimension, the personal property right is not sacred and inviolable. It would be wrong to think that personal ownership and its inherent rights have priority over one's fellow-men and society and that the social order simply has to respect the consequences flowing from personal ownership. Like any right of a subject, personal property rights are rights within the human society. The owner can make his claims prevail only insofar as they harmonize with the common interest of the society. His subjective right is codetermined and limited by the objective right of the society in which he makes his claims. However, this limitation does not mean that society's legislative power can unrestrictedly undermine personal property rights. By doing so, it would harm the individual's personal rights and consequently also the common good, for the common good is nothing else but the good of the persons constituting the society.

Those who argue in favor of increasing collective property as much as possible on the ground that only in this way justice will be done to man's social dimension fail to take into consideration that this dimension represents an analogous ideal value. The tendency to collectivation is a misunderstanding of social personalism. As we have repeatedly pointed out, the social dimension may not be identified with the state. The bond uniting men in the state represents only a particular form of social union. All kinds of interpersonal relations and ties to groups also embody man's social dimension and they do it even in a higher way than the state. The ideal of a personalistic community demands precisely that that kind of relation be made more profound. For this reason collectivistic tendencies should not be allowed to throttle man's inclination to enter into such interpersonal relationships. Persons experience collective ownership too little and too remotely as their common property. They are not sufficiently involved in it because its control and use are too much regulated without them.

The Changing Function of Personal Property. Although the institution of personal property continues to exercise an important function in our social order, its role has undergone significant changes. Aims which in former ages were pursued in this form of property can now be attained in other and more effective ways, while other aspects of personal property now reveal themselves much more clearly than formerly.

For example, in former times personal property was the only safeguard against the vicissitudes of life. This function of personal property is now much less important. By contributing to certain funds and forms of social security, modern man gives up an important part of his earnings in exchange for the right to receive income when he or his family are struck by misfortune or loss of earning power. It stands to reason that this right safeguards man's security more effectively than his attempts to acquire and retain sufficient personal property.

Personal property used to be also an important status symbol. He who had many possessions was highly regarded by society. Today, however, society bases its regard on man's work rather than on his possessions. A typical manifestation of this changed mentality is the fact that today's woman wants to make her contribution to the world of work. In the nineteenth century it was different. According to the mentality of that era, it was a sign of social standing if the financial position of a girl's parents freed her from having to work. That bourgeois mentality has largely disappeared. Modern man considers himself a success if he recognizes himself as the bearer of achievements of value for society rather than the possessor of many properties.

Formerly also personal property offered the only real possibility to acquire a broader personal development and to achieve thereby a higher social position. Modern society, however, has opened new perspectives in this matter by offering all kinds of loans, grants and scholarship funds to those whose personal property would not give them the opportunity to develop their personal aspirations.

Since the industrial revolution also the value which individual property possesses for the formation of man's personality has undergone a change. Personal property now consists mostly of abstract titles of ownership and is a question of owning money. Formerly private property consisted more of goods, such as grounds, workshops, tools and products of work. Because their owner saw his own creativity reflected in these concrete goods and personally took care of their management, that personal property possessed a binding and formative value. Modern private owners with their capital

rights are the legal but not the real owners of the capital
goods which they finance.   The share-holders, for example, of
a factory may legally own a part of the enterprise, but its
managers, who perhaps have no personal investment in it,
exercise control over it.   Even if someone owns and manages a
factory he no longer remains fully in control over it.   His chief
financial officer, for example, may rise in defense of the industry against him.   Control and management of a large
industry now require so many abilities and skills that the
individual owner, as such, is no longer directly concerned with
them.   The private capitalist is now connected with "his"
factory by way of a bank.

These industrial developments have changed the family
from a productive unit into a pure consumer unit.   A consequence of this change is a modification in the value attached
to personal property.   It has now primarily a consumer function.   This is a fortunate development.   The nineteenth century mentality of ownership often tended to the preservation
and increase of possessions at no matter what cost.   People
lived soberly and sometimes even in poverty to preserve their
capital.   Today, however, it is realized that possessions should
serve man and not vice versa.   People still save, but they do
it now in order to spend opportunely and to acquire durable
goods.   Just as nature has become more useful and serviceable to man, so now we realize that property also ultimately
should be made to serve man.   Parents will now prefer to
provide for their children's education rather than give them
money when they marry and start their own family.

The tendency of our time to promote ownership and have
more people share in the benefit of possessions is a healthy
social sign because it makes it possible for everyone to share
in the rising general prosperity.   Often, however, this tendency
is promoted also on grounds of political economy, as a way to
spread economic power over many and make it more stable.
Those who base themselves on this reason seem to forget
that personal property is no longer able to exercise such a
stabilizing influence.   Even if employees acquire shares in an
industry and thereby furnish its capital, this does not mean
that economic power has been spread and subjected to greater
control.   In our modern society ownership and power are

gradually being separated. It is possible now to be an owner
without power and to have power without ownership. In
other words, a different approach has to be used to give a
more social orientation to the economic control over the
means of production, which constitute the source of a nation's
prosperity. This point will be considered more in detail in the
remainder of this chapter.

6. Social Property

Personal Property and Group Property. As long as man
lived mainly within the narrow confines of the family community, personal property safeguarded peace and order in society.
Moreover, ownership referred mostly to physical goods, so
that the character of these goods placed a limit on the
usefulness of property rights. Technology, however, has
broadened man's horizon and given a more radical social
dimension to all sectors of life. In addition, property has
assumed the form of capital, which in principle is unlimited in
its possible uses. Today man no longer lives mainly in the
community of his family but increasingly spends more time in
various social groups. All this means that today the figure of
the personal owner no longer suffices when there is question of
the control and management of immovable goods. Moreover,
modern industrial production requires huge capital investments. These investments demand a rational social management, which is difficult to reconcile with the free and arbitrary control of a private owner.

It is sometimes claimed that the social function of ownership is sufficiently fulfilled if the properties belong as much as
possible to physical persons and the latter use and manage
them as if they belonged to society. Such a claim, however, is
too simplistic and unrealistic. Justice has as its task to
develop juridical institutions which legally support the
broadened social role of property. This is the reason why we
see increasingly more differentiated forms of group property.
They have already become so diverse that it is difficult to
classify them all under a common name. There even exist
different forms of "autonomous" property, property of which
no one can be called the owner in the traditional sense of the

term, but whose responsible manager is a group of men in the form of a juristic person. Such property is wholly tied to a certain purpose. Its managers can use its goods only for the purpose of their institution.

This type of group property now exists in various forms, such as foundations and trust funds. The fact that the production apparatus has become preponderantly the property of juristic persons indicates that even that apparatus has been socialized to a certain extent. For the juristic person orientates property more to its own purpose than to private interests. Even personal property itself which enters into the realm of an enterprise as its financial support undergoes a certain modification and becomes also to some extent a social property. For, in determining dividends, the management of the enterprise will be concerned above all with the interest of their undertaking and not with that of its financial backers.

Structure of Production Enterprises. In the Western world the structure of production enterprises remains a crucial problem. Legally speaking, the enterprise is owned by the shareholders, each of whom shares in the property with a limited extent of responsibility only. The supreme power in the enterprise lies formally in the hands of the combined shareholders. The juridical form of the limited corporation is still based upon traditional property relations and one-sidedly emphasizes the capital factor. Social democracy demands that the labor factor be given an increasing role alongside the capital factor in the structure of the enterprise. The emancipation of the laborer, which is promoted by society's increasing prosperity, leads to a feeling of dissatisfaction with the fact that his work contract relegates him to a position which is exclusively one of subordination. The question is asked whether it is correct to retain the standpoint that capital takes labor into its service. Should not modern development rather go in the direction of having labor attract capital? Should not the structure of industry be a labor order rather than a capital order? At any rate, the labor unions want to strengthen the position of the laborers in the enterprise.

These new trends of development should not be viewed primarily as a reaction against a bad situation. That is definitely not the case, for the share of the laborer in the general prosperity is growing. The core of the problem does not lie in the desire for a more social-minded management and better labor contracts. The crucial point is an increasing democratic consciousness, which wants to give the labor factor a voice in the enterprise on the basis of responsibility for the interests of the laborers.

Before we can reflect on the solution of this problem, we must devote closer attention to the present-day situation of the industrial enterprise. This consideration will show that, on the one hand, the contemporary structure of industry has outgrown its juridical form and that, on the other hand, it does not yet fully correspond to the image of social democracy.

The Antiquated Juridical Structure of the Enterprise. The juridical form of the limited liability company is solely capital structure. The modern enterprise, especially in the case of an open company, does not correspond to this juridical structure. The management of the enterprise has been separated from the capital by which it is financed. The owner-industrialist increasingly gives way to the non-owning industrialist, and even the situation in which large shareholders are directors of an enterprise becomes less frequent. Financial backers now often remain wholly foreign to the management of the enterprise whose formal owners they are. The shareholders' right to elect the members of the board and the chief executive officers is often reduced to a mere formality. The annual meeting of the shareholders is practically without any influence on these elections if only because the corporation's bylaws contain all kinds of restrictive conditions.

Parallel with the separation of management and ownership there is a shift in the aim pursued by the enterprise. While originally the profit motive of the owners occupied the center, today the main emphasis falls on keeping the enterprise in a sound condition and expanding its activities. From being a material object of wealth the enterprise has developed into an autonomous institution in the service of which its manager performs his function. He regards the expansion of his enterprise as an indication of the success of his business activities. This new aim shows a more explicit social orientation than the old profit motive which worked solely for the benefit of the capital element. The new aim includes also the interest of the employees and the growth of jobs. Profit remains important, of course, but it is now pursued also for the sake of internally financing the growth of the enterprise. Partly as a result of the new autonomy enjoyed by the enterprise, private property itself now thinks along the lines of a social function. However, this line of development has not yet affected the juridical structure of the enterprise. This structure still continues to correspond to the original aim which was solely based on the profit motive.

Oligarchic Tendencies. The present transition from control by financial backers to an independent management which aims at more than just making a profit may be considered progress in comparison with the antiquated juridical form based on traditional ownership titles. Nevertheless, even the present form does not sufficiently correspond to man's growing social consciousness. Undoubtedly it is true that the business world takes the social aspect of the enterprise more into consideration than was the case in former times. Nevertheless, this social aspect is not sufficiently embodied in the very structure of the enterprise. The labor factor has not yet obtained the place which belongs to it in that structure.

Society, which must constantly be on guard lest a small group acquire too much power, no longer faces so much the power of capitalistic ownership as the growing influence of the manager and director group. The separation of management and ownership has not resulted in a different stratification of power. The industrial growth, which is connected with the development of man's technical apparatus, fosters the concentration of economic power in the hands of a limited group of managers.

There exists now a group of managers and specialists who have too much power at their disposal because they control property which does not belong to them. Some sociologists do not hesitate to speak in this connection about the danger of neo-feudalism. At any rate, the business world sometimes reveals oligarchic tendencies and has practically no vertical mobility. Although the law tries to place the supreme power over the limited liability company in the general meeting of shareholders, in practice the company's management has used its function to acquire an almost untouchable position. It usually determines the choice of new members of the board, and sometimes this choice is dictated by family relations and interest rather than greater competence. The position of the president is occasionally so independent that he can become guilty of gross neglect without running the risk of being fired. The power of board members and directors is not sufficiently regulated. Few rules bind them in determining profits and assigning their destination. The board itself fixes its salary and percentage of the profit, and this often goes beyond reasonable bonds. This position of power is often even accentuated by the fact that one and the same person functions as both president of one company and member of the board of many others.

Insufficient Sense of Social Responsibility. One who is impartial should admit that there remains a certain lack of a sense of responsibility both within the enterprise and with respect to its external relations. Although labor laws, taxation and other legal obligations actually regulate industry and limit the power of its directors, nevertheless it remains true that in our Western world a greater sense of responsibility needs to become part of industrial control. That control should be broadened to include also representatives of labor and of society at large.

In spite of all social improvements, there remains a separation of capital and labor. The laborer's distrust of capital, among whose representatives he counts especially management and board of directors, continues to exist. Social democracy has not yet managed to overcome this impasse. There remain hidden tensions and desires, which have to meet in the correct way if they are not to develop in too revolutionary a direction. The deeper penetration of social democracy in industry and the elimination of conflicts arising from a capitalistic mentality remains the most urgent problems of Western civilization. The desire to find a solution exists, but it is not yet clear in what direction the answer should be sought.

Dangers of Nationalization. Several proposals have been made to solve the question. We will consider them here. First of all, society could nationalize the means of production, as is suggested by the followers of Marx. Undoubtedly, Marx deserves credit for having exposed the capitalistic structure of enterprises which are owned by a small group. Something which through its structure has become of interest to many or even to society at large may not be left to the arbitrary decisions of individuals. The socialization of production means is a healthy step if it places responsibility for them in the hands of those who have interest in them. Nationalization of the production means, however, is not in itself a solution. It actually is a new form of private property, that of the state, which is made the greatest capitalist of all. Society at large can manage nationalized goods only by delegating this function to individual persons or particular groups. The big question then remains whether these persons or groups which institutionalize the totalitarian state will not place their own special interests above that of all the members of society.

A national-collectivistic structure offers no safeguards at all that the common interest will not be made subservient to personal interest. Many of the objectionable features inherent in the capitalistic system are found also in the state's totalitarian system. The Western nations, which under the influence of socialistic tendencies have sometimes resorted to large-scale nationalization, now see less and less advantage in the substitution of government officials for company officers. The East-European countries living under Marxist regimes likewise experience that nationalization and state control are only a partial solution. They try to decentralize the governmental system of control and bring the level of decision making closer to those who are involved in the industry. Marx himself wanted to limit rigid economic concentration to the period of transition and to have self-government in the final stadium.

Co-Ownership of Laborers. Others seek to achieve social democracy in industry too one-sidedly in making the laborers share in the ownership of the factory in which they work. They hope that this co-ownership will, on the one hand, distribute the power of capital over many and, on the other, help the workers to obtain a greater share in the general prosperity. Ownership and control used to be so tightly connected in the past that many continue to regard ownership as the only possible ground on which someone can share in control. This connection, however, is no longer necessary: today it is possible to have control without ownership, just as one can be an owner without having control over the use of one's property. Nevertheless, the past historical bond between ownership and control continues to invest ownership with a symbolic kind of power, which because of its symbolism is still real to some extent although it falls short of its former full reality. For this reason our present economic constellation presents us with two problems which are intimately connected but which nonetheless should be distinguished. They are the problem of fostering a wider distribution of possessions and the problem of distributing the power of economic control.

The ultimate aim behind the idea of making the employees co-owners of industry is to give them a voice in the control of the enterprise. However, only a certain aspect of that aim is touched by the question of co-ownership. Participation in an industry's management cannot be primarily reached by distributing shares but only by a structural change of the enterprise. To put shares into the hands of the laborers is merely a symbolic gesture in the right direction. As such it undoubtedly has some value. However, of itself it does not mean that the relationship between the elite of economic leaders and the mass of laborers becomes more democratic.

The important point in this matter is that the question of giving the laborers shares in the company and in its profits should be faced realistically. Industrial production requires the company to reserve capital for operation, modernization and expansion. For this reason the capital needed for the internal financing of these aims is reserved and separated from the company's capital stock. Hence the shareholder does not really possess a pro rata part of the company's capital with the right to a pro rata part of the profits.

Sometimes, however, laborers who receive shares are led to think that they can now dispose of a pro rata part of the company's funds just as they dispose of their own private income. Even if laborers or employees would hold a large percentage of the company's shares, the necessity to reserve capital for internal financing would impose all kinds of restrictions on the dividends which their shares could earn. We must ask ourselves therefore whether the tendency to modify the anonymous company capital into a larger capital stock is not a step backwards.

That tendency would seem to show that in the West we still cling too much to an antiquated way of thinking, which wants to reduce all capital somehow to a form of personal property. Are we not here in a process of development in a different direction? Formerly any territory had to belong to someone. Today, however, the question of to whom belongs, for instance, the territory of the United States is no longer meaningful. It would seem that something similar is happening with respect to large industrial corporations. Is it not becoming less and less relevant to whom such corporations really belong? They are becoming autonomous forms of property, with respect to which the most important point is that they are managed by competent authorities. Because of this development, it would be wrong to place too much emphasis on the question of the personal possession of shares. A wider distribution of possessions among the laboring classes should be promoted by fostering more personal income for them and by making them share in the industry's dividends rather than by expanding its stock at the expense of the working capital which is needed for the internal financing of its operations. No matter how important the question of promoting the workmen's pride of ownership may be in itself, it is of little relevance to the problem of modifying the structure of industry in the direction of greater regulation of its managerial powers.

Laborers' Representation on the Board of Trustees. Occasionally efforts are made to strengthen the employees' position by having their representative become a member of the corporation's board of trustees. Understandably the success of this move is regarded with much skepticism. It looks too much like "pouring new wine in old skins." As long as the employees think that that board represents the capital inter-

ests of the enterprise and is mainly interested in financial
profits, the laborers' representative is out of his place on such
a board.   Neither the other trustees nor the employees will
consider him as "one of theirs."

Nevertheless, that move can be a significant step in the
right direction if the board admits trustees to represent the
element of *work* rather than the *workers*.   These representatives should be sought among people who are socially independent and who have great merits in the realm of work rather
than labor union leaders.   Their function would be to safeguard that the enterprise pay attention not only to making
profits but also to the other aims involved in modern industrial
undertakings.   In this way it would be possible to make a
beginning by giving the work factor an institutional embodiment in the management of the enterprise.

Complexity of the Problem.   The desire to give the workers a direct voice in a company's management is difficult to
execute.   One could refer, of course, to the possibility of
production cooperatives, whose members both work and furnish the necessary capital.   However, the experiments in this
direction, which began in the nineteenth century, have not
been successful.   Either they failed or they changed their
character and became private capitalistic enterprises.   They
were still too much based on the idea that ownership and
control should go together and be shared equally.

The experience with these production cooperatives shows
that the complexity of the problem requires great prudence in
the structural modification of industrial enterprises.   Changes
should not be radical but proceed step by step.   The proper
character of the enterprise should not be disregarded.   An
industrial company is a functional society, in which democracy
may not do violence to the relationship between those who
direct and those who are directed.   It is impossible to obtain
here a direct democracy in which everyone shares to a greater
or lesser extent in the function of directing the society.   The
ideas explained in a preceding chapter about formal and material democracy apply here also in an analogous way.   Because the industrial company has become a rational organization of interests, it requires more than ever before a strong
management position.   However, management must rule the

company in the spirit of material democracy. In a company, social democracy should aim most of all at improving the social-psychological climate, so that employers and employees can better understand each other's interests.

For this reason it remains a fundamental characteristic of democracy that a controlling position is not assigned on the basis of extraction, wealth or relations but solely on that of ability. It should be possible to be promoted from the ranks to the executive level if someone shows the required talents. Vertical mobility should become a characteristic of social democracy in an enterprise.

In the present stage of development it is not yet possible to indicate what the correct formal democratic structure of industry will be. Moreover, the task of determining that structure belongs to the specialists in the field and not to the philosopher. His function is simply to draw attention to this growing and justified desire.

The Need for a New Structure of Society. The main reason why it will be difficult to find the correct solution lies in the fact that probably only a new structure of society can solve the problem. The same difficulty has occurred in other economic problems. For instance, former ages saw the problem of wages and working conditions as a question pertaining to commutative justice. They limited the role of social justice to making, if needed, the necessary corrections in individual agreements. In the long run, however, it became apparent that the problem could be solved only by reversing the distribution of functions assigned to commutative and social justice.

Social justice creates the social conditions and agreements, which commutative justice in its realm must observe and endeavor to bring about as much as possible. In this way wages have become an external social datum for the enterprise, which it is permitted to determine only within the margin left by social justice.

It would seem that the Western world must abandon the interplay of individual forces in the realm of private industrial production, while retaining the valuable elements that are embodied in this form of production. Here too social justice

ought to attune itself not to individual commutative justice,
but the individual rights should be attuned to social justice.
It is possible that an entirely new structure may have to be
built, a structure which is not yet clear in the present phase
of transition. The reality of modern economics with its complete social dependence demands embodiment in the form of
society. All this, however, as we have repeatedly emphasized,
does not mean state collectivism, but should be in harmony
with the demands of a healthy subsidiarity.

In the long run the employees will not be satisfied with a
situation in which their material existence depends on a
management whose control lies entirely outside their influence.
By trial and error a satisfactory solution of this problem has
to be found. If the Western world remains blind to the ideal
demands of social democracy, it may suddenly find itself faced
with a new social revolution. The argument that the laborers
are not mature enough to acquire some kind of influence on
the control of industry is not entirely to the point. That
argument forgets that man acquires a sense of responsbility
only when he is given a chance to have responsibility. We
cannot dispense with experimenting in this matter. Prudence,
of course, should guide such experiments, for the structural
modifications should not damage the economy.

Modern society must try to find the correct economic and
social structure for its large industrial enterprises. That is a
problem facing not only the "personal capitalism" of the West
but also the "collective capitalism" of Russia and East Europe. Man cannot eliminate the possibility that individuals or
small groups will appropriate productive goods to their own
advantage. This individualizing appropriation centers no longer on the question of ownership but on that of having the
power to dispose of these goods.

In Marxist countries the group of capitalist owners has
been replaced by the state as the sole capitalist. All the
disadvantages of capitalism are thereby retained. Here also a
small group—a bureaucratic elite—can make the general good
subservient to their personal interest. Even if that bureaucratic elite is animated by excellent intentions, the combination
of political power and economic control is bound to be disadvantageous. For this reason Marxism also struggles with the

problem of spreading the control of its powerful institutionalized ownership of industrial enterprises over many and of making it the responsibility of those who are directly involved in them. The emancipation of the laborers is a fact which has to be taken into account in Marxist countries also.

The West with its system of private industrial production and the corresponding mechanism of price and marketing faces the desire for a greater social democracy. The concentration of economic power in the hand of company executives demands that their duty to account for the way in which they fulfill their function be broadened. However, the disadvantage attached to the identification of economic and political structures in Marxist countries should put the West on guard against making political power subservient to economic interests. Both the communist East and the Western countries should show an objective scientific interest, without ideological prejudices, in each other's economic systems and the results attained by them. It is quite possible that an understanding of each other's functional efficiency will purify the air of ideological presuppositions—just as in the history of Europe man's increasing rational knowledge of the world has led to a more striking revelation of his proper suprarational dimensions. The critical study of each other's economic development offers itself as an important topic in an East-West dialogue.

7. Public Property

For a long time the term "socialization of property" was understood to mean that property became the public or collective property of the state. From the preceding pages it should be evident that there are other ways of socializing which do not directly involve state ownership. If there is question of socialization in the form of state ownership, we now speak of "nationalization." Nationalization may be desirable in the case of industries or services which cannot remain in the hands of private persons or groups without endangering the common good.

The enterprises in question are those which are monopolies by virtue of their production or the character of their services rather than those which try to monopolize the market by means of cartel agreements. After World War II many West European nations went through a period in which especially the socialist parties tried to enforce large scale nationalization. From the economic standpoint, however, nationalized enterprises often compare unfavorably with private enterprises. For this reason the socialist parties themselves now realize that nationalization itself is not the solution for the problem of efficient social control.

Nevertheless, certain sectors of production and service industry are so intimately connected with common welfare that they should not be in the control of private companies. With respect to them nationalization can be an advantage. The typical characteristic of those kind of enterprises is that they are based not so much on being economically rewarding as on serving the common good. They will sometimes have to render services which from the standpoint of economics are not justifiable but which have to be performed for the sake of the common good; for example, certain forms of transportation in thinly populated areas. These services often are not paid for at market prices but at set legal prices.

8. *Property According to the View of Marxism-Leninism*

Unselfish Orientation to One's Fellow-Men. The principal characteristic of Marxism is often said to lie in the abolition of private property and its transfer to state property. That description, however, is only partially true. In the transition period to the communist ideal Marxism attaches the highest importance to the introduction of collective property, but in the final stage the institution of property in any form whatsoever will have no longer any meaning. Following Marx, Lenin and Stalin stressed that the realization of the communist ideal does not demand the equal distribution of material goods. As long as the members of society still attach importance to such an equal distribution, society has not yet eliminated the spirit of private property, the desire to have and possess, even though it may have abolished the institution of private property. In the stage of genuine communism, however, the exaggerated tendency to have, the desire to distinguish mine and thine, will be wholly overcome by man's unselfish social orientation. By insisting on collective property, Marx wanted not only to eliminate private property but also to rise above the whole mentality of selfish interest.

In the final stage everyone will work according to his capacities because he is unselfishly orientated to the universal community of mankind. Man will find his happiness in making his contribution to this goal and he will no longer seek it one-sidedly in the greatest possible material reward. In the perfect society the person will no longer be motivated by selfish interest in the process of production. The slogan "Everything in the name of man and for man's welfare" will then be a reality. Everyone will share in the general material prosperity according to his needs.

Subordination of "Having" to "Being." In Marxist ideology the individual's remuneration implies an equality that is proportional but not levelling. If people continued to attach importance to a levelling equality, it would be a sign that they had not yet completely abandoned the mentality of capitalistic ownership. Hence by equality Marxism does not mean uniformity in the realm of needs and their satisfaction, but the liquidation of all privileges resulting from extraction, class and wealth. It refuses to accept any difference based exclusively on "having," but accepts a certain inequality in "having" arising from a person's "being."

In mankind's capitalistic period "being" was wholly subservient to "having." Man's aim in that period was solely to *have* more and not to *be* more. The proletarian was alienated from himself because he was possessed by the capitalistic class. The capitalist himself also suffered from self-estrangement because he was willing to sell his "being" to "have" more. He "had" much but "was" little. In order to overcome that mentality of capitalistic "having," which estranges the person from his own dignity, the transitional period from capitalism to communism must have recourse to the institution of socialistic property.

Provisional Phase of Equality. In this transitional stage a certain levelling equality is necessary to arrive at the elimination of property privileges. In this period all persons are considered according to a common levelling denominator, that is, they are considered as workers and rewarded according to the work which they perform. However, this period has merely a provisional character and is necessary only to pass from a society based on property privileges to a social structure in which each one works according to his capacities.

Lenin calls this phase the socialistic stage. In it, each one has an equal obligation to work according to his capacities and an equal right to be rewarded according to his work. Because this equality is still too much based on "having," it is not yet ideal. For this reason the socialistic stage will be followed by the final communist stage. In that final stage everyone will still have the obligation to work according to his capacities, but he will have the right to be rewarded according to his needs.

The idea of Marxism is precisely to respect the unique and proper character of the person. Marx rejects as an insult to communism the thought that every person should be reduced to the same uniform level, which is still too much based on materialistic desires of having. He does not want to level all needs, tastes, desires and personal life, but recognizes that persons are unequal and that everyone should be done justice according to his own unique way of being. The final stage will know inequality in the realm of "having," but this inequality will be adapted to the person's "being" rather than that his "being" is adapted to his "having" as happened in the capitalistic period.

As we have pointed out in speaking about work, Marxism is too high an ideal for this world. Material reward remains always a stimulus urging man to work, whether there is question of individuals or of society as a whole. This motive, however, should be counterbalanced by other higher motives and be in harmony with them. Despite all its exaggerations, Marxism has contributed greatly to reveal the one-sided and unbalanced character of the capitalistic profit motive.

9. *The Situation of Property in Contemporary U.S.S.R*

The Constitution of the U.S.S.R. makes a distinction between socialistic property and personal property. Practically speaking, personal property is possible only in the realm of consumer goods and arises from income derived from work. Income without work is not permitted in the U.S.S.R. Article Twelve of the Constitution expresses the principle that "one who does not work should not eat." Property belonging to society, also called "socialistic property," exists in two forms: the property of the state or the people and cooperative-collective-domestic property. This distinction is based on the question whether the production unit aims more at society at large or a relatively small group.

Whenever production is geared primarily to society at large, the means of production and, of course, also the goods produced are property of the state or the people. According to Article Six of the Constitution, the following goods are state properties: land, minerals, water, industries, mines, railroads, ships and planes, banks, means of communication, state farms, city dwellings, and production centers. If, however, production aims primarily at the benefit of a certain group, then the goods in question assume the form of cooperative-collective-domestic property. According to Article Seven, No. One, of the Constitution, this form of property belongs to collective farms and cooperative societies with movable and immovable goods and live stock as well as to the products of these small groups. This cooperative type of property is fully regulated by government rules, so that it differs only in degree but not in kind from state property. It is really only an intermediary phase. According to Marxism, every form of property depends on the level of productive forces. In the present stage of development agrarian enterprises still demand a cooperative-collective-domestic type of property. They tend, however, to develop toward progressive mechanization and will then terminate in the form of general people's property.

Articles Seven and Nine of the Soviet Constitution deal with personal property. As such are considered the two acres of land which Kolkhoz farmers may possess and the possessions of independent farmers and craftsmen insofar as in their trades they do not employ any other workers than members of their family. However, the category of independent farmers and craftsmen has practically disappeared from the Soviet

Union. Private property in the U.S.S.R. therefore, is almost unknown now. Socialistic ownership now encompasses 100 per cent of gross industrial production and 99.9 per cent of gross agricultural production.

The other countries of Eastern Europe ideologically approach property in the same way as the U.S.S.R. However, the difference in their historical development leads to differences also in the proportion between socialistic property and personal property in these countries. At any rate, socialistic ownership prevails in the realm of industry and in most countries also in agriculture. The following table shows the existing proportion.[1]

Country	Percentage of gross production, 1959-60, under socialistic control	
	Industry	Agriculture
Czechoslovakia	100	85.2
North-Korea	100	99.9
Communist China	100	99.1
Mongolia	100	99.7
Poland	99.1	13.2
Bulgaria	98.9	97.4
Albania	98.3	86
Hungary	93.6	71.3
Rumania	98	81.3
East Germany	88.9	96
North Vietnam	80.5	96

10. *Historical Sketch of the Development of Ownership in Connection with the Relationship Between Individual and Society*

Necessity of a Historical Approach. The historical relativity proper to ownership forms came indirectly to our attention when we analyzed the contemporary forms of ownership. We must now consider that historical evolution more in detail. Our interest will center on the question how man and society have experienced their relationship to material goods

---

[1]Cf. S. Zjoerba, *Bratske Spirvrobitnytstwo,* 1961, pp. 11-12.

in dealing with each other during the various periods of history. In that historical study we must be on our guard lest ideological presuppositions tend to falsify the resulting picture. Machiavelli cynically remarked that people are more inclined to forget the murder of their relatives than the confiscation of their possessions. In other words, property is something that touches man to the quick.

Moreover, the whole question easily becomes supercharged with emotional factors, so that it is quickly drawn into the sphere of political ideology. These ideologists usually appeal to history to prove that their view is historically the only correct position. The historical hypothesis of materialism, for example, is that mankind originally knew only collective property and that only subsequently it entered the road of estrangement by introducing first familial property and then personal property. For this reason mankind will have to return to the first stage of community property, while retaining the good achieved in the intermediary stages. The individualistic view of man and society, on the other hand, holds that it has been demonstrated that personal property is as old as mankind's history and therefore expresses a demand of man's unchangeable nature.

However, it is illicit simply to project our contemporary property structures back into preceding phases of culture. The phenomenon of property must always be understood in the light of the cultural picture of its own time. Claims that the Romans knew an absolute and exclusive system of private property and that the Germanic tribes from the very beginning attributed to property an intrinsically social character fail to take into consideration the old structures of society in the Roman and Germanic lands. Such views are too much based on twentieth century politico-ideological contrasts. Both the modern concept of personal private property and that of property of the state as a juristic person did not exist in times when the individual had hardly emerged from primitive communal bonds and when the idea of the state as a society with a political aim of its own still belonged to the future.

Primitive Man and Property. To understand the background of the Roman and Germanic conceptions of property, it is necessary first to pay attention to the way property was experienced in the life pattern of primitive man. For many aspects of the primitive idea of property were still present in the early Roman and early Germanic times. The primitive man, who did not isolate his awareness of his own individual autonomy within the context of family or tribe, did not place distinct concepts of "individual" and "collective" in contrast to each other. It would be useless to look among them for property either in its private form in contrast to the group or in its collective form in contrast to the individual. The individual and the collective were still a single datum. Moreover, there was no question at all yet of strict ownership in the sense of having the power to dispose of an object. The entire primitive world was permeated with the sacred as a mysterious power. Neither individual nor tribe exercised dominion over nature as a thing, but rather both man and world were the "property" of higher divine powers. For this reason the primitive felt obliged to offer to the gods firstlings of agricultural produce, animals, and sometimes even of man himself.

The primitive mind with its undifferentiated compenetration of the various categories of life did not draw any sharp dividing line between persons and things. Relations between individuals were not purely personal because the world was not purely impersonal. For example, the grounds on which people lived and the soil which they cultivated were integrated in the diffuse unity of the tribal bond. Man and nature constituted a mythical organic whole. The question of dominion over nature, which is implied in the right of ownership, did not yet arise in this condition.

The intimate bond between primitive man and the utensils and ornaments which he used in daily life likewise did not point to any form of individual property right. What in the primitive world belonged to a person *was* that person himself. For this reason primitives buried with their dead his ornaments, clothes, weapons, personal utensils, and sometimes even his wife and slaves. In its primitive stage mankind exercised neither individually nor collectively any right over nature.

Rather the opposite was the case. Mythical nature imposed its right on man in the form of reverence and cultic ritual. The right of property developed only according as man began to distinguish himself from nature's non-human reality and wanted to exercise control over it.

Roman Law and Property. Roman law has exercised a major influence upon the development of the European system of property. The Roman laws of property, however, should be understood in the light of their origin, no matter how obscure this origin may remain. Because of their formal abstract character, laws readily lend themselves to be interpreted in changed conditions quite differently from the way they were understood in their original phase. As a matter of fact, this is what has happened with the revival of Roman law in the modern period. For a long time it was generally accepted that the Romans had a concept of exclusive and absolute private property. No attention was paid to the fact that this exclusive and absolute character of property had to be understood with much greater differentiation against the background of the original mythical life of the Roman community.

From the foundation of Rome to the time of Justinian the Roman Empire went through centuries of development; hence the law of the period of decline may not simply be identified with that which governed the original Roman *civitas*. Nevertheless, throughout the entire period of Rome the familial community was recognized as the most important unit alongside that of the state. Till deep in the classical period the family remained, as it were, a state within the state. In the primitive stage the family exercised the same functions as the sib or tribal bond among other peoples. In addition to its strictly familial functions, the family community of the Romans had also a political task. As a political unit, the structure of the family possessed an all-encompassing and closed character.

The authority of the *pater familias*, as head of this closed world, was absolute and total, as in any political society. This absolute paternalistic authority, however, did not have an individualistic and subjective character, but was im-

posed by the sacral tradition of the familial community. The
pater familias was the person representing the mythical mandate and radiated his magical authority over the members of
the family. His dominion was not a question of strict ownership but a sacral authority over the persons and things of the
family. It was an "office" (*officium*) and not a property
right, although the exercise of this "office" contained aspects
of property rights because of the goods belonging to the
family.[2]

In the law of the Twelve Tables, dating from about 450
B.C., everything belonging to the family community is called
the "patrimony." This patrimony contained not only persons
and objects but also the cult of the ancestors and the ances-
tral grounds. A man's dwelling, it should be recalled, was at
the same time the temple of the familial gods. For this
reason the paternal dominium, to which the sacred patrimony
was entrusted, was absolute and inviolable with respect to the
public authority of the *civitas*.

Originally especially the ground and its superstructures
were considered subject to this patrimonial dominium. The
ground shared in the sacral sphere of the family community.
This sacred ground was not the object of mere ownership but
represented the ritually consecrated "domain" within which
familial authority applied without limits. The transfer of
dominium over familial ground was more than a simple transfer of ownership. It was regarded as a new demarcation of
each other's domain of authority and took place according to
a carefully prescribed religious ritual.

Accordingly, the unlimited power of the father over everything on, above or below the ground should not be explained
on the basis of an absolute and exclusive power over real
property but on that of the mythical familial structure which
included the ground as its territory. The dominium was not
a personal property right. A sign of this is the fact that the
pater familias could not disinherit his children, for his "domain" represented familial property entrusted to his responsibility. His children were of necessity his heirs and, if their
father died, they founded a *consortium* of brothers, the eldest

---

[2]Several data mentioned in this matter have been borrowed from J.
Mekkes, *Ontwikkeling der humanistische rechtstheorieën*, 1940.

of whom exercised the patrimonial authority in the name of all. He was even entitled to exercise this authority without consulting his brothers. Only if all heirs together demanded their share was it permissible to divide the patrimony among them. The individual's right to demand his share arose only in the classical period of Roman civilization when the familial structure began to crumble.

The original structure of Roman contract law also shows that, like all other peoples, the Romans at first did not grant much individual freedom to individuals. Among them also the concept of civil freedom resulted only from a long process of development. For this reason we see the old Roman contract law regulate the relationships between sovereign families. There was no question of contracts between individual persons or of obligations resulting from property rights. These old laws resembled the modern *jus gentium* rather than laws governing personal claims. Their violation was held to be a *delictum*, a crime, which had to be punished. Guilt in these matters was more than an obligation to pay damages. There was no question of bilateral agreements or relative rights; hence each of the contracting parties remained bound by its obligation even if the other did not fulfill his. For the obligation was not derived from the contract itself. The sacral sovereignty of the familial community had to be respected and for this reason in the primitive stage of Roman civilization the *pater familias* had the power to impose punishment on the guilty.

Accordingly, the Romans at first did not know any absolute and exclusive right of private property. Such an exclusive ownership neither fitted the framework of the familial community nor that of the Roman economic system. Even after the Constitution of the Gracchi, Roman economic activity was based not so much on familial lands as on public lands, over which individual families could not obtain any absolute power but only a dependent right of *"possessio."* Familial lands were only of limited size and had to be regarded as closely connected with the family as a community of life.

Only at the time of the republic the primitive and undifferentiated family structure began to crumble, giving rise to a sphere of individual rights. The old dominium developed into an individual right of ownership having a real character. Contractual obligations also developed into agreements made between subjects of rights on the basis of their property. These new forms of real property, however, did not entail the exclusive and absolute powers of the original dominium. Roman law imposed several restrictions on individual owners. In an indirect way, however, the right of real property still profited from the political immunity of the family community, even though this immunity had begun to diminish. The latter still prevented the state from interfering too arbitrarily in matters of civil property. For instance, legally it was not possible to expropriate property in the common interest. That power of eminent domain, however, was hardly needed at the time, because the Emperor and magistrates had enough power at their disposal, for instance, by their domain over public lands, to force the individual owners to sell their lands.

The rights of *possessio* over public lands, which constituted the state's dominium, also developed only in the second century after Christ into a real property dominium. Ownership rights over these domains remained limited by all kinds of third party rights and also by public law. In addition, many other property institutions arose in the form of hereditary fiefs and hereditary tenure.

Regarding civic freedom, even in its classical period the Romans never fully knew a genuine sphere of such freedom. Analogously to the family, the Roman state remained a mythical undifferentiated community, which, as a religious and cultic bond, exercised a totalitarian power. As long as the family also enjoyed absolute sovereignty within its domain, it managed to keep this power of the state under control. In the classical period there could be question of a measure of freedom for the individual only within the shadows of the closed family community.

With the decline of the family structure, however, the individual became a victim of the state's religious absolutism. This happened during the Byzantine Empire. The power of private ownership declined and the old dominium was reintroduced, but with this difference that now the Byzantine Emperor with his functionaries seized exclusive and absolute power over their subjects and the latters' possessions. In the

Western Empire, however, the state's authority in the long run proved unable to resist the pressure of the Germanic tribes. Here we find a revival of the old dominium structure among private primitive groups, especially in Gaul. Instead of the old *patres familias*, powerful landed lords exercised an exclusive power over their domain and its inhabitants.

Comparing the Roman property rights with the absolute and inviolable individual property right of the French Revolution, we note a number of essential differences. First of all, at the end of its development with the death of Justinian the Great in 565, Roman law knew a varied system of property institutions. The *Code Civil* could have made a choice between many other elements of Roman law to incorporate them into its system as the basis of different systems of property, rather than giving the central position to the dominium figure. Moreover, in Roman law the right of dominium did not have the far-reaching importance which the individualism of the new era assigned to it. True, the original undifferentiated dominium which was attached to the old family structure, had developed into an individual real property right in the classical and post-classical periods. However, this right was given only to Roman citizens. In addition, only a limited part of the Roman land was available for this kind of dominium and the individual's right of disposal remained restricted by all kinds of governmental regulations and by familial tradition. There did not yet exist any genuine civic freedom. Finally, attention should be paid to the fact that among the Romans the main object of this dominium was land, which by its very nature has only a limited use. In the nascent industrial period, on the other hand, capital became the main object of ownership and, because of its abstract character, ownership of capital gave a much more unrestricted power.

Property Among the Germanic People Till the Middle Ages. Like the Romans, the old Germanic peoples in their first stage of development did not yet have any theory of property in the strict sense. Their primitive way of life likewise preceded the stage in which there are sharp dividing lines between the individual and the collective, between the personal and the real. On the one hand, there existed a strong bond between the person and his movable goods, on the other, immovable goods belonged to the primitive group considered as a unit. As long as the tribes were nomadic and did not have any territory of their own, they collectively used different grounds in turn. When the Germanic tribes invaded the Roman provinces, the two ways of life met. The tribal bond disappeared, but the individual did not profit from its disappearance. The place of the old tribal bond was taken by seignioral and corporate bonds, which exercised an undifferentiated dominium over the ground and its inhabitants. As among the Romans, so here also personal relationships merged with real relationships.

The great migrations caused commerce and industry to disappear, so that agriculture remained the only important economic activity. This factor greatly fostered the development of the seignioral system. Moreover, the Merovingian and Carolingian rulers established the Frankish kingdom on the basis of their seigniorage. They considered the kingdom as their patrimony and divided this royal domain into counties. When subsequently the royal power began to diminish, the king's officials usurped his authority; they became powerful lords exercising a sovereign and exclusive dominium over persons and things within their territory. We find a similar development in the feudal system. The benefice which the vassal received from his lord in exchange for certain services was a dominion which did not imply a strictly real right of property but an undifferentiated authority over the feudal estate and its inhabitants.

In the early Middle Ages the grounds and their inhabitants went together. This did not mean that the inhabitants of a feudal property were considered to be real objects. Partly under the influence of Christianity, fealty knew a personal relationship of authority, which was based on the oath of loyalty. The possession of grounds merely accentuated the authority over the serfs. Monasteries often likewise possessed estates with numerous serfs and exercised dominium over their grounds and inhabitants. Later, however, the personal character of vassalage became more and more a realty relationship.

All this shows that the Germanic Middle Ages no more knew a socialistic property right than the Romans knew an individualistic form of that right. Individual and group constituted an organic unit. The group had not yet developed into a strict superstructure or organization with functional autonomy with respect to its members. There was no question of a differentiated real property right. Property relations were still fully encompassed by the primitive, undifferentiated authority relations of the feudal system. The question of who exercised an exclusive property right cannot even be raised. The feudal system knew an ascending hierarchy, in which the feudal lord in his turn had a vassal relationship to a higher lord; hence the opposition between independent and dependent right of possession did not yet arise.

The Germanic property relationship did not differ essentially from that of the Romans. In both cases property rights were exercised within the framework of autonomous and undifferentiated group alliances. The only difference was that the Roman figure of the dominium was mainly attached to the structure of the *familia* while the Germans knew more vertical relationships going beyond the family.

The bloom of commerce and industry which began in the twelfth century added all kinds of horizontal corporate bonds to the existing vertical feudal bonds. These "communal" movements of towns, guilds, class confederacies and market associations undoubtedly meant a forward step in development toward individual freedom. Generally speaking, however, even they did not rise above the level of undifferentiated group alliances within which the individual enjoyed only a relative independence. The guilds, for example, with their compulsory membership, their monopolistic rules, and their executive and juridical powers exercised authority over their members and their families in every realm of life. Only with the beginning of the Renaissance in the sixteenth century did the individual start to conquer his freedom in the modern sense of the term.

In the medieval situation no one was wholly free or not free, but everyone was more or less free. The various autonomous social groups, on the one hand, protected freedom against the centralizing tendencies of kings and emperors, but on the other, they restricted the individual's freedom. To be free at that time meant to be free from certain obligations toward the king or other rulers, but he who possessed this freedom was at the same time wholly dependent on the privileged group or class to which he belonged. A free citizen was still an impossible concept at that time; such a free man would have been unfree in the medieval situation. As among the Romans in their more developed period, in the Middle Ages the bonds with the group came first. By virtue of a privilege a person or a group could be dispensed from certain obligations of dependence. He then possessed certain freedoms. In our time freedom comes first and he who makes a claim against this freedom has to show cause. Medieval man regarded the situation from the opposite angle: the bond came first and freedom was determined in reference to the obligations from which privilege liberated the person or group.

For this reason in the Middle Ages no one had a strictly free and individual right of property. The hierarchical structure of medieval society entailed insoluble confusion in the realm of property with rights and restrictions crisscrossing one another. The feudal system allotted unwritten property rights and restrictions over one and the same domain to feudal lord, vassal and serf; the craftsman, who as owner had power to dispose of his workshop and the product of his labor, saw this power restricted by all kinds of regulations imposed by town and guild. In the Middle Ages every individual freedom, even that of property, remained limited within the boundaries of the autonomous undifferentiated social group. The idea of free property was unknown, as was that of the free person. Only after the sixteenth century man became acquainted with the idea of freedom of property and of person.

For this reason it is wrong to defend the modern right of free personal property by simply appealing to arguments proposed by medieval scholasticism. St. Thomas' texts apply to the property of his time, which was greatly limited by the social framework of the medieval world. A sign of this is that he rightly considered lending against interest an infraction of the medieval economic situation.

The modern idea of right which wants to derive all real rights somehow from a strict property right was foreign to the Middle Ages. Medieval man did not ask who, strictly speaking, owned a particular property. He felt no need to ask such a question. Anyone who made use of certain goods, no matter in what relation of dependence, automatically possessed certain rights. For this reason the vassal's rights of possession can be described neither as ownership rights nor as rights on goods owned by someone else (*iura in re aliena*) but only as *sui generis* rights of possession.

Property from the Renaissance to the French Revolution. The Renaissance and the Reformation inaugurated the triumph of individualism, which would reach its political apex in the French Revolution. In the Middle Ages individual and society had formed a diffuse organic unit, protected by sacred traditions. In the new era the individual and the state broke these established bonds and faced each other as rivals in their individualistic tendencies to power. Through its centralistic endeavors the state developed into a governmental organization, which absolutistic monarchs tried to use to seize control over society. The functional element of government took the place of the normative tradition of the Middle Ages. The individual, on the other hand, also liberated himself from the controlling autonomy of feudal and corporate bonds and wanted to strike out on his own.

Hitherto farming and crafts had prevailed in society; they had prevented a sharp distinction between real and personal relationships. Economic relationships encompassed life also. Economic activity was not characterized by a calculating business mentality; and the bonds of life were feudal and corporative rather than personal.

In the fifteenth century commercial capitalism became the main factor in the birth of a new kind of economy based on progress and expansion. Predictability and efficiency, based on the dynamism of individual forces, replaced the elements of the natural and the socio-organic. The work relationship, which formerly constituted a life-long bond, assumed the form of a free contract. Production was no longer geared to the satisfaction of existing needs, but to self-interest motivated by the desire for profit. Commercial capitalism offered new and unrestricted possibilities. The development of trading in goods and money was at first mostly in the hands of itinerant strangers, for these people were less restricted in their activities by feudal and corporate traditions.

The individualistic ethos, which developed irresistibly in the economic and political realms, demanded, of course, also the right to dispose freely of the results obtained by a person's own activity. In this way this epoch gave rise to the idea of individual and absolute ownership of goods and capital. It even led to the idea of "intellectual ownership." Rights to immaterial goods, such as copyright, were entirely unknown in the Middle Ages, but fully adapted to the modern epoch, in which man wanted to be himself as an individual, even with respect to the creation of his ideas. The Middle Ages envisaged only the idea of passing on to posterity a stable possession of truth. Scholasticism gave preference to the tradition of the group. Even if an author had ideas of his own, he did not emphasize their originality, but, driven by respect for tradition, attributed them to scholars of the past.

Both among the Romans and in the Middle Ages property rights were always limited by the various autonomous social bonds in which man lived. The merchant was the first—as early as the thirteenth century—to acquire the right of free disposal over his property. The property in question consisted primarily of money capital. Gradually, however, the commercial capitalists began to use this capital to buy all kinds of immovable goods, such as land. The effect of those purchases was that in the feudal agricultural society there arose a tendency to describe feudal relations in terms of real property relations.

At first this tendency faced an insoluble problem. The juridical theorists, who during the Renaissance revived Roman law, tried to solve the situation by means of the legal dominium figure. This figure, however, which had a uniform and indivisible character, hardly fitted the feudal situation of property with its many forms and divided character. True, as early as the thirteenth century, writers of Romanizing glossaries had introduced the distinction between "direct dominium" and "dominium of use." The former was described as "superior ownership" in the sense of the undifferentiated right of authority, and the latter as "inferior ownership" in the sense of a dependent right of possession owned by the user of lands. In the sixteenth century, however, the problem centered on the question to whom belonged the free and absolute real right of property: to the superior owner or to the inferior owner.

Both views found supporters during the centuries of struggle between state absolutism and the idea of civil freedom. Jurists who favored the absolutism of the state ascribed an individual and absolute ownership to the monarch. In this way the ruler's superior ownership became a real property title, to which personal obligations were subordinated. The opposite relationship had prevailed in the preceding centuries, in which the real element had been subordinated to the personal element. The dominium was now no longer primarily a domain over which the prince or lord exercised his paternal authority, but became a real property title.

Burghers and bourgeois, however, tried to liberate themselves from feudal burdens and obligations, for they regarded these no longer as matters of common interest but as the private interests of princes and lords. Most jurists supported the burghers' standpoint and demanded the absolute property title for the inferior owners. The liberal theory of state led the French Revolution to include the inviolable character of civil ownership in the Declaration of the Rights of man and citizen. It abolished the remaining feudal rights and the monopolies of the guilds.

The French Revolution abolished all forms of superior and inferior ownership and recognized only civil private property. The power of the state over this property was no longer a dominium but based solely on the public authority of the state over private freedom. Superior ownership as a mixed form of ownership and authority was abolished. In this way the process by which individual capital rights arose through differentiation from the old dominium figure came to an end. Dominium itself ceased to exist.

The expropriation of feudal and ecclesiastical properties took place without indemnity payment. Contrary to what some claimed, the refusal to pay indemnities did not go against Article Seventeen of the Declaration, which permitted expropriation in the common interest only against payment of a just indemnity. For superior ownership itself was abolished and no longer of any legal validity. Only civil ownership now possessed a sacred and inviolable right.

Property in the Post-Revolutionary Period. Since the French Revolution civil freedom has become an essential feature of the modern constitutional state. The individual's freedom now enjoyed priority, in contrast to the Middle Ages, which let undifferentiated group alliances prevail and thus were able to guarantee a relative autonomy for the individual. After the Revolution, however, the lack of public and private legal regulations allowed this freedom to degenerate into extreme individualism in the economic realm. This individualistic mentality regarded private property as a sacred and inviolable dogma and made it serve to maintain vested interests.

It is true, of course, that individual freedom, liberated from the strait jacket of outlived group patterns, gave the main impetus to industrial development. In the long run, however, economic individualism again deprived the working man of his freedom. While formerly personal dependence obliged to material services, now material dependence threatened to lead to personal servitude.

A reaction against this situation was bound to occur. It gave rise to all kinds of absolutistic theories of state, which aimed to oppose individualism by restoring the social solidarity of former ages. These theories, however, did not manage to transcend the level of the view which they endeavored to combat. As a result, the state, which in the preceding centuries had developed from an organic community (*Gemeinschaft*) into a functional society (*Gesellschaft*), now in its turn threatened to use its functional authority to make man as a person subservient to itself. It proved impossible to restore the medieval situation, in which the individual had a relative autonomy by virtue of the undifferentiated bond uniting his group, and to bring it to life again in a state which had become differentiated into a functional organization.

The Contemporary Situation. In our time the medieval solidarity of individual and society has become differentiated into a private sphere and a public sphere. A similar differentiation has led to the distinction of personal and functional spheres of life.

This differentiation between person and function, between personal bonds and functional bonds, must be respected also in the realm of property. As a person, man demands the right to share in our growing prosperity. Every man has a right to have a real possibility of owning property, because the property in question is something man needs for his own private personal purposes; he needs it as the material basis for the development of his personal bonds.

As a private person, however, man should not have control over productive or social capital, which serves the need of many. This functional capital should be organized in such a way that its functional aim is reached to the fullest possible extent. A greater functionalization, in the good sense of the term, needs to be pursued in this matter, for the mixture of personal and functional bonds leads here to undesirable contrasts between personal and social interests.

In the political realm the development advocated here has already taken place. The distinction made between formal and material democracy in political matters shows the way. We experience as meaningful the relationship of authority between those who govern and those who are governed in a formal democracy because that relationship is required by the functional and formal structure of a political democracy. If the government were too much a matter of the governors' individual interests, those who are governed would be disinclined to accept their subordinate position. As organization, the formal democracy, however, is subservient to the material democracy, in which the interest of the governors and the governed are equal. Since the governors derive their authority from their functions and these functions are subservient to the interest of all, modern man is willing to accept the democratic relationship of authority.

The economic sector needs to be organized in an analogous way. In the functional productive sector man experiences his functional dependence still too much as a personal dependence. The industrial enterprise still manifests a structure placing it at the disposal of the director for his personal interests. It is still too much the personal property of someone or some group and for this reason continues to experience difficulties in the relationship between those who manage and those who are managed. The enterprise will have to develop toward a structure making it subservient to the interest of all who are concerned with it. In enterprises in which the management derives its authority from its function and exercises it in the interest of the enterprise, the ideal of formal democracy in the service of material democracy has become a reality.

As long, however, as the enterprise is still too much the personal property of a certain group and the management disposes of the organization in view of these individual interests rather than being at the service of the organization, modern man will experience the contract between management and employee as undemocratic. As in other realms of life, so also in the economic realm the one who holds authority must be the servant of all. This will be the case if his authority is derived from a function in the service of the organization and if the organization in question serves the interest of all. Management and employees will then show greater understanding of each other because on their own level both will be concerned with the interest of all.

BIBLIOGRAPHY

This bibliography lists only the books and articles consulted in the preparation of this study.

Angelinus, *Wijsgerige gemeenschapsleer*, 4th. ed., 1946.
P. Archambault, *La famille, oeuvre de l'amour*, 1950.
A. Arntz, "Het aanvaarden der lichamelijkheid," *Lichamelijkheid*, 1951, pp. 121-156.
F. Aron, *Dimensions de la conscience historique*, 1961.
H. Arvou, *La philosophie du travail*, 1961.
A. Ayfre and others, *La présence d'autrui*, 1957.
W. Banning, *Karl Marx*, 1960.
Chr. Barendse, "Over de graden van het zijn," *Tijdschrift voor Philosophie*, vol. 11 (1949), pp. 155-202.
    "Op de grens tussen ontologie en metaphysica," *op. cit.*, vol. 19 (1957), pp. 687-694.
    "Intersubjectief verkeer en lichamelijkheid," *Lichamelijkheid*, pp. 85-119.
G. Barrow, *The Romans*, 1963.
J. Bartstra, *Handboek tot de staatkundige geschiedenis*, 4 vols., 1948-54.
F. Baud, *Les relations humaines*, 1955.
N. Berdiaeff, *Das Ich und die Welt der Objekte*, n.d.
L. Binswanger, *Grundformen und Erkenntnis menschlichen Daseins*, 2nd ed., 1953.
M. Bochenski, *Der sowietrussische dialektische Materialismus*, 1950.
O. Bollnow, *Neue Geborgenheit*, 1955.
    Vom Wesen der Stimmungen, 3rd ed., 1956.
    Die Ehrfurcht, 2nd ed., 1958.
D. Brinkmann, *Mensch und Technik*, 1946.
C. Bronkhorst, "Recht en wereld," *Tijdschrift voor Philosophie*, vol. 17 (1955), pp. 591-622.
A. Brunner, *La connaissance humaine*, 1943.
    La personne incarnée, 1947.
    Der Stufenbau der Welt, 1950.
    Glaube und Erkenntnis, 1951.
E. Brunner, *Gerechtigkeit*, 1943.
M. Buber, "Das Problem des Menschen," *Dialogisches Leben*, 1947.
    Ich und Du, 1923.
A. Burghardt, *Eigentumsethik und Eigentumsrevisionismus*, 1955.
F. Buytendijk, *De zin van de vrijheid in het menselijk bestaan*, 1958.
J.Y. Calvez, *La pensée de Karl Marx*, 1956.
M. Chastaing, *L'existence d'autrui*, 1951.
M. Chenu, *Pour une théologie du travail*, 1955.
G. Clark, *The Seventeenth Century*, 1929.
C.N.V. "De structuur en de rechtsvorm van de onderneming," *Evangelie en Maatschappij*, vol. 15 (1962), pp. 67-132.
D. Cohen and others, *De pelgrimstocht der mensheid*, 5 vols., 1960.
L. Cottrell, *The Anvil of Civilization*, 1958.
S. Couwenberg, *De vereenzaming van de moderne mens*, n.d.
P. de Bruin, *Het sociaal probleem*, 1956.
J. de Finance, *Existence et liberté*, 1955.
S. de Lestapis, *Amour et institution familiale*, 1947.
B. Delfgaauw, *Wat is existentialisme?*, 1952.
    Waarom philosophie?, 1953.
    "Perspectief op de geschiedenis," *Wijsgerig Perspectief*, vol. 11 (1960), pp. 12-18.
    Geschiedenis en vooruitgang, 2 vols., 1961-62.
P. Delhaye, *Permanence du droit naturel*, 1960.
J. de Meyer, *Crisis der europeesche staatsphilosophie*, 1949.

336

D. de Petter, "Impliciete intuitie," *Tijdschrift voor Philosophie*, vol. 1 (1939), pp. 84-105.
"Intentionaliteit en identiteit," *op. cit.*, vol. 2 (1940) pp. 515-550.
"Zin en grond van het oordeel," *op. cit.*, vol. 11 (1949), pp. 3-26.
"De oorsprong van de zijnskennis," *op. cit.*, vol. 17 (1955), pp. 199-254.
"Het persoon-zijn onder thomistische-metaphysische belichting," *Verslag der 13e alg. verg. v.d. Vereniging v. Thom. Wijsbegeerte*, 1948.

A. de Ruiter, *De grenzen van de overheidstaak in de antirevolutionaire staatsleer*, 1961.

J. de Valk, *De evolutie van het wetsbegrip in de sociologie*, 1960.

A. de Waelhens, *Une philosophie de l'ambiguité. L'existentialisme de Maurice Merleau-Ponty*, 1951.
Phénoménologie et vérité, 1953.
La philosophie et les expériences naturelles, 1961.

A. de Wilde, *De persoon. Over de grondslagen van het personalistisch denken*, 1950.

J. Donnedieu de Vabres, *L'état*, 1954.

H. Dooyeweerd, *De verhouding tussen individu en gemeenschap in de romeinse en germaanse eigendomsopvatting*.

A. Dordett, *Die Ordnung zwischen Kirche und Staat*, 1958.

W. Duynstee, *Over recht en rechtvaardigheid*, 1956.

J. Elders, *Staatsbegrip en institutionalisme*, 1951.

M. Eliade, *The Sacred and the Profane*, 1959.

J. Evans, *Life in Medieval France*, 2nd ed., 1958.

E. Fechner, *Rechtsphilosophie*, 1956.

J. Fellermeier, *Abrisz der katholischen Gesellschaftslehre*, 1956.

R. Firth, *Human Types. An Introduction to Social Anthropology*, rev. ed., 1958.

J. Folliet and others, *Civilisation du travail? Civilisation du loisir?*, 1956.

G. Friedmann, *Ou và le travail humain?*, 13th ed., 1950.
Problèmes humains du machinisme industriel, 20th ed., 1946.

H. Freyer, *Theorie des gegenwärtigen Zeitalters*, 1956.

J. Galbraith, *The Affluent Society*, 1958.

Th. Geppert, *Teleologie der menschlichen Gemeinschaft*, 1955.

C. Gits, *Recht, persoon en gemeenschap*, 1948.

E. Girardeau, *Le progrès technique et la personnalité humaine*, 1955.
Les aventures de la science, 1957.

M. Grant, *The World of Rome*, 1960.

P. Grimal, *La vie à Rome dans l'antiquité*, 1959.

R. Guardini, *Vom Sinn der Gemeinschaft*, 1952.

J. Guitton, *Essai sur l'amour humain*, 1948.

G. Gusdorf, *La parole*, 1953.
Traité de métaphysique, 1956.
Introduction aux sciences humaines, 1960.

E. Hamilton, *The Roman Way to Civilization*, 1958.

M. Hättich, *Wirtschaftsordnung und katholische Soziallehre*, 1957.

H. Hays, *From Ape to Angel*, 1958.

F. Heer, *Das Mittelalter; 1100-1350*, 1961.

M. Heidegger, *Sein und Zeit*, 6th ed., 1949.

F. Heidsieck, *La vertue de justice*, 1959.

H. Hommes, *Een nieuwe herleving van het natuurrecht*, 1961.

J. Hommes, *Der technische Mensch*, Eros, 1955.

B. in den Bosch, "Medezeggenschap in de onderneming," *Economie*, vol. 27 (1963), pp. 615 ff.

L. Janssens, *Personalisme en democratisering*, 1957.

K. Jaspers, *Einführung in die Philosophie*, 1957.

F. Jeanson, *La phénoménologie*, n.d.

F. Jonas, *Sozialphilosophie der industriellen Arbeitswelt*, 1960.

W. Jonkers, *Het subjective recht in het licht der rechtvaardigheid*, 1962.

H. Kitto, *The Greeks*, 1963.

F. Klüber, *Grundlagen der katholischen Gesellschaftslehre*, 1960.

O. Klug, *Volkskapitalismus durch Eigentumsstreuung*, 1962.

J. A. Kockelmans, "Eenheid en verscheidenheid in de wetenschap volgens het standpoint der phaenomenologie," *Tijdschrift voor Philosophie*, vol. 22 (1960), pp. 331-361.
   "Over de methode der wijsbegeerte," *Alg. Ned. Tijdschr. v. Wijsb. en Psychol.*, vol. 54 (1962), pp. 201-218.

M. Krinkels, "De staat in sociaal-wijsgerig perspectief," *Sociale Wetenschappen*, vol. 3 (1960), pp. 202-233.
   "Ethiek en cultuur," *Annalen van het Thijmgenootschap*, vol. 50 (1962), pp. 269-286.

R. C. Kwant, *Philosophy of Labor*, 1960.
   Het arbeidsbestel, 1956.
   "Arbeid en leven," *Annalen v.h. Thijmgenootschap*, vol. 45 (1957), pp. 247-263.
   The Phenomenological Philosophy of Merleau-Ponty, 1963.
   Encounter, 1960.

J. Lacroix, *Personne et amour*, 1955.
   Force et faiblesse de la famille, 1948.

L. Landgrebe, *Philosophie der Gegenwart*, 1957.

L. Lavelle, *Conduite à l'égard d'autrui*, 1957.

H. Lefebre, *Problèmes actuels du marxisme*, 1958.

F. Leist, *Liebe und Geschlecht*, 1953.

W. Leonhard, *Sowjetideologie heute*, 1962.

I. Lepp, *L'existence authentique*, 1951.
   La communication des existences, 1952.

E. Link, *Das Subsidiaritätsprinzip*, 1955.

J. Loeff, *Taak en onderlinge verhouding van kerk, particulier initiatief en overheid t.a.v. de maatschappelyke zorg*, 1948.
   Sociale grondrechten van de mens, 1953.
   Varhounding staats- en rechtsgemeenschap, 1955.
   "Het natuurrecht en de ontwikkeling in het ethisch denken," *Sociale Wetenschappen*, vol. 3 (1959), pp. 1-50.
   "Over het wezen der democratie," *op. cit.*, vol. 4 (1961), pp. 332-347.

D. Loenen, *Mens en cultuur van Hellas*, 2nd ed., 1960.

J. Lotz, *Von der Einsamkeit des Menschen*, 1957.

K. Löwith, *Weltgeschichte und Heilsgeschehen*, 1954.

J. Lucas-Dubreton, *L'age d'or de la renaissance italienne*, 1959.

W. Luijpen, "Phaenomenologie van het recht," *Annalen v.h. Thijmgenootschap*, vol. 46 (1958), pp. 281-317.
   Existential Phenomenology, 3rd impr., 1963.

N. Luyten, *La condition corporelle de l'homme*, 1957.

G. Madinier, *Conscience et amour*, 2nd ed., 1947.
   Conscience et signification, 1953.
   "Nature et mystère de la famille," *Famille d'aujourd'hui*, 1958.

A. Marc, "Personne, société, communauté," *Revue philosophique de Louvain*, vol. 52 (1954), pp. 447-461.

G. Marcel, *Etre et avoir*, 1935.
   "Esquisse d'une phénoménologie et d'une métaphysique de l'espérance," *Homo Viator*, 1944, pp. 39-91.
   "Lettre introductive," *Recherche de la famille*, 1949.
   L'homme problématique, 1955.
   Les hommes contre l'humain, 1951.

J. Maritain, *L'homme et l'état*, 1953.

K. Marx, *Das Kapital*, 5th ed., 1922.

R. Mayntz, *Die moderne Familie*, 1955.

R. Mehl, *La rencontre d'autrui*, 1955

J. Mekkes, *Ontwikkeling der humanistische rechtsstaatstheoriën*, 1940.

338

M. Merleau-Ponty, *Phénoménologie de la perception,* 14th ed., 1945.
  La structure du comportement, 3rd ed., 1953.
J. Messner, *Das Naturrecht,* 1950.
  Der Funktionär, 1961.
A. Mirgeler, *Geschichte Europas,* 1958.
H. Mitteis, *Der Staat des hohen Mittelalters,* 5th ed., 1955.
J. Mouroux, *Je crois en toi,* 1949.
  Sens chrétien de l'homme, 1953.
Th. Mulder, "Economie en christendom," *Economie,* vol. 51 (1963), pp. 33-50.
Ned. Gesprek Centrum, *Centralisatie en decentralisatie,* no. 5, n.d.
Ned. Kath. Werkgevers Verbond, *Medezeggenschap in de onderneming.* 1961.
M. Nédoncelle, *La réciprocité des consciences,* 1942.
  De la fidelité, 1953.
  Vers une philosophie de l'amour et de la personne, 1957.
J. Newman, *Foundations of Justice,* 1954.
N.V.V., *Medezeggenschap van de werknemers in de onderneming,* n.d.
A. Oldendorff, *De vreemdeling,* 1956.
  "Arbeid, sociologisch beschouwd," *Annalen v.h. Thijmgenootschap,* vol. 45 (1957), pp. 217-277.
G. Oltheten, "De liefde als grondslag van de gemeenschap," *op. cit.,* vol. 42 (1954), pp. 287-303.
R. Palmer, *A History of the Modern World,* 1960.
A. Peperzak, "Kan de verlichting ons verlichten?" *Tijdschrift voor Filosofie,* vol. 24 (1962), pp. 243-278.
J. Peters, *Metaphysics,* 1963.
  "De plaats van de persoon in de hedendaagse philosophie," *Verslag v.d. 13e Alg. Verg. der Vereniging voor Thom. Wijsb.,* 1948.
  "Over de oorsprong van het woord," *Tijdschrift voor Philosophie,* vol. 13 (1951), pp. 163-248.
  and others, *Hedendaagse visie op den mens,* n.d.
J. Pieper, *Ueber die Gerechtigkeit,* 1954.
  Was heisst Philosophieren?, 1956.
H. Pirenne, *Histoire de l'Europe des invasions au XVIe siècle,* 7th ed., 1936.
  "La civilization occidentale au moyen âge, le mouvement économique et sociale," *Histoire générale,* ed. by G. Glotz, vol. 8, 1959.
M. Plattel, *De ambiguiteit van de gemeenschapsorganisatie,* 1954.
  La sociologie moderne et la crise morale, 1952.
  Sozialphilosophie: Der Mensch und das Mitmenschliche, 1962.
  Situatie ethiek en natuurwet, 1961.
  "Wijsgerige beschouwingen rond het arbeidsbegrip," *Sociale Wetenschappen,* vol. 1 (1958), pp. 149-161.
  "Des mens in de hedendaagse samenleving," *op. cit.,* vol. 2 (1959), pp. 213-230.
  "Personal Response and the Natural Law," *Natural Law Forum,* vol. 7 (1962), pp. 16-36.
  "Het gezin als levensgemeenschap, speciaal in zijn verhouding tot de staat," *Economie,* vol. 21 (1956), pp. 124-140.
  "De onontkoombare ervaring van het persoon-zijn als een samenzijn-met-anderen," *Sociale Wetenschappen,* vol. 1 (1958), pp. 149-159.
J. Ponsioen, *De menselijke samenleving. Wijsgerige grondslagen,* 1953.
  and G. Veldkamp, *Vraagstukken der hedendaagse samenleving,* 1956.
R. Prigent and others, *Renouveau des idées sur la famille,* 1954.
J. Pucelle, *Le temps,* 1955.
  La source des valeurs. Les relations intersubjectives, 1957.
K. Rahner, *Geist in Welt,* 1939.

A. Rauscher, *Subsidiaritätsprinzip und berufständische Ordnung in "Quadragesimo Anno,"* 1958.
A. Reinach, *Zur Phänomenologie des Rechts,* 1953.
G. Renard, *La philosophie de l'institution,* 1939.
A. Rich, *Christliche Existenz in der industriellen Welt,* 1957.
P. Ricoeur, *Philosophie de la volonté,* 1949.
C. Roldanus, *Zeventiende-eeuwse geestesbloei,* 2nd ed., 1961.
C. Romme, *De onderneming als gemeenschap in het recht,* 1946.
    "Sociale democratie," *Sociale Wetenschappen,* vol. 5 (1962), pp. 262-277.
F. Rutten and others, *Menselijke verhoudingen,* 1955.
H. Ruygers, *De beide geslachten,* 1952.
G. Sabine, *A History of Political Theory,* 1959.
B. Saris, "Aantekeningen betreffende de dialoog tussen natuurwetenschappen en theologie," *Annalen v.h. Thijmgenootschap,* vol. 51 (1963), pp. 1-16.
J. Sartre, *L'être et le Néant,* 29th ed., 1950.
W. Sauerbaum, *Vom Antiken zum Frühmittelalterichen Staatsbegriff,* 1961.
B. Schaper, *Tussen machtsstaat en welvaartsstaat,* 1963.
J. Schasching, *Kirche und industrielle Gesellschaft,* 1960.
M. Scheler, *Wesen und Formen der Sympathie,* 5th ed., 1948.
    Liebe und Erkenntnis, 1955.
H. Schillebeeckx, "Het niet-begrippelijk kenmoment in onze Godskennis," *Tijdschrift v. Philosophie,* vol. 14 (1952), pp. 411-454.
E. Schleth, *Der profane Weltchrist,* 1957.
J. Simon, *Trois leçons sur le travail,* 2nd ed., n.d.
G. Simondon, *Du mode d'existence des objets techniques,* 1958.
V. Soloviev, *Le sens de l'amour,* 1946.
E. Spranger and others, *Wo stehen wir heute?,* 1961.
P. Steenkamp, *De zeggenschap in de onderneming,* 1962.
S. Strasser, "Het wezen van de mens," *Annalen v.h. Thijmgenootschap,* vol. 46 (1958), pp. 1-31.
F. Tannenbaum, *Eine Philosophie der Arbeit,* 1954.
F. Tellegen, "Gelovig denken over de techniek," *Ned Katholieke Stemmen,* vol. 52 (1956), pp. 166-197.
    Samenleven in een technische tijd, 1957.
    "Wat is arbeid?" *Annalen v.h. Thijmgenootschap,* vol. 45 (1957), pp. 228-246.
    Zelfwording en zelfverlies in de arbeid, 1958.
H. Teuben, *Recht op arbeid,* 1955.
W. Theimer, *Geschichte der politischen Ideen,* 2nd ed., 1959.
R. Troisfontaines, *De l'existence à l'être,* 1953.
A. Utz, *Das Subsidiaritätsprinzip,* 1953.
    Sozialethiek, vol. 1, 1958.
J. van Boxtel, "Democratie en menselijke verhoudingen," *Menselijke Verhoudingen,* 1955, pp. 89-109.
    "Metaphysiek van het wezen of metaphysiek van het zijn?" *Annalen v.h. Thijmgenootschap,* vol. 39 (1951), pp. 129-144.
    Herstel der liefde in de sociale wijsbegeerte, 1953.
J. van Campen, *Onderneming en rechtsvorm,* 1945.
R. Vancourt, *La philosophie et sa structure,* n.d.
J. van den Berg and J. Linschoten, *Persoon en wereld,* 2nd ed., 1956.
F. van de Ven, *Bedrijfsleven en democratie,* 1955.
    Sociale grondrechten, 1957.
    "Het veranderend wereldbeeld," *Economie,* vol. 21 (1957), pp. 193-212.
    "Waardering van hoofd-en handenarbeid in het veranderend cultuurbeeld," *Sociale Wetenschappen,* vol. 2 (1959), pp. 73-92.
    Theorie der sociale politiek, 1961.

340

"Directie en aandeelhouders in de open vennootschap," *Economie,* vol. 26 (1961), pp. 1-15.
L. van der Kerken, "Menselijke liefde en vriendschap," *Bijdragen,* vol. 7 (1946), pp. 161-199.
R. van Dijk, *Mens en medemens,* n.d.
C. van Gestel, *Kerk en sociale orde,* 1956.
I. van Haren, *Personeelbeleid en ondernemingsstructuur,* 1961.
H. van Hengstenberg, *Grundlegung zu einer Metaphysik der Gesellschaft,* 1949.
A. van Leeuwen, "Persoon-Gemeenschap," *Bijdragen,* vol. 14 (1953), pp. 29-53.
    "De staat en zijn taak," *Annalen v.h. Thijmgenootschap,* vol. 42 (1954), pp. 273-287.
    "Over wilsvrijheid en zedelijkheid," *Verslag v.d. 11e Alg. Verg. v.d. Vereniging v. Thom. Wijsbegeerte,* 1946.
A. van Melsen, *Science and Technology,* 1961.
C. van Peursen, *Lichaam-ziel-geest,* 1956.
    Riskante filosofie, 2nd ed., 1955.
    Filosofische orientatie, 1958.
H. van Riessen, *De maatschappij der toekomst,* 4th ed., 1957.
H. van Zuthem, *De integratie van de onderneming als sociologisch vraagstuk,* 1961.
J. Vernant, "Travail et nature dans la Grèce archaique," *Le travail, les métiers, l'emploi,* 1955.
J. Vialatoux, *L'intention philosophique,* 1952.
A. Vierkandt, *Staat und Gesellschaft in der Gegenwart,* 1916.
D. von Hildebrand, *Metaphysik und Gemeinschaft,* 1955.
E. von Hippel, *Geschichte der Staatsphilosophie,* 2 vols., 1955-57.
A. von Martin, *Soziologie. Der Hauptgebiete im Ueberblick,* 1956.
    Soziologie der Renaissance, 2nd ed., 1949.
O. von Nell-Breuning, *Beiträge zu einem Wörterbuch der Politik,* 1947-51.
    Wirtschaft und Gesellschaft heute, 3 vols., 1956-60.
    "Ist Eigentum eine Ordnungsmacht?" *Sociale Wetenschappen,* vol. 2 (1958), pp. 1-31.
    Kapitalismus und gerechter Lohn, 1960.
    Vom Geld und Kapital, 1962.
J. vom Schmid, *Groote denkers over staat en recht,* 1934.
C. von Weisäcker, *The World View of Physics,* 1952.
J. Vuillemin, *L'être et le travail,* 1949.
W. Walter, *Die sozialethische Definition der Democratie,* 1962.
A. Weber, *Kulturgeschichte als Kultursoziologie,* 2nd ed., 1960.
M. Weber, *Wirtschaft und Gesellschaft,* 2 vols., 4th ed., 1956.
E. Welty, *Herders Sozialkatechismus,* 3 vols., 1952-58.
G. Wetter, *Der dialektische Materialismus,* 1953.
F. Weve, *Sociaal-wijsgerige opstellen,* 1948.
    "Staat en algemeen welzijn," *Annalen v.h. Thijmgenootschap,* vol. 42 (1954), pp. 250-272.
H. Witteveen and others, "Open ondernemerschap," *Geschriften v.d. Prof. Mr. B. M. Felderstichting,* 1962.
E. Zalm, *Soziologie der Prosperität,* 1960.
H. Zbinden, *Der bedrohte Mensch; zur sozialen und seelischen Situation unser Zeit,* 1959.

INDEX OF NAMES

341

INDEX OF SUBJECT MATTER